Yasuhiro Kotera · Julie Beaumont · Rory Colman ·
Annabel Rushforth · Kenichi Asano
Editors

Compassion-Focused Therapy for Mental Health: International Perspectives

Exploring Cultural Variations in Compassion and Wellbeing

Springer

Editors
Yasuhiro Kotera
Institute of Mental Health
University of Nottingham
Nottingham, UK

Rory Colman
University of Derby
Derby, UK

Kenichi Asano
University of Tsukuba
Tsukuba, Japan

Julie Beaumont
Queen's University Belfast
Belfast, UK

Annabel Rushforth
Annabel Rushforth Therapies
Sheffield, UK

ISSN 2570-3390 ISSN 2570-3404 (electronic)
Advances in Mental Health and Addiction
ISBN 978-3-032-12437-1 ISBN 978-3-032-12438-8 (eBook)
https://doi.org/10.1007/978-3-032-12438-8

This Springer imprint is published by the registered company Springer Nature Switzerland AG
The registered company address is: Gewerbestrasse 11, 6330 Cham, Switzerland

Advances in Mental Health and Addiction

Series Editor

Masood Zangeneh, Richmond Hill, Canada

Over the past several decades we have witnessed dramatic shifts in prevailing approaches to mental health and addiction. Significant scientific achievements have led to novel treatment options that impacted the experiences of individuals with mental disorders. In recent years, new perspectives have begun to influence the way we address mental health and substance dependencies, resulting in a greater emphasis on mental health promotion and prevention strategies. Despite these progressions, mental health care systems too often remain stagnant, fragmented, and peripheral.

Preface

Compassion-Focused Therapy (CFT) has found its way into the hearts and practices of mental health professionals across the world. Developed by Professor Paul Gilbert in the United Kingdom, CFT offers a unique blend of evolutionary psychology, cognitive behavioural therapy, attachment theory, and mindfulness practices to help individuals cultivate compassion and regulate difficult emotions. As CFT continues to spread internationally, it has become increasingly clear that compassion—while a universal potential—takes different forms depending on cultural contexts, social norms, and lived experiences.

This book was born from the recognition that, although CFT is now practiced globally, we still lack a comprehensive resource that speaks directly to its international applications. How is compassion understood in different cultures? What does it mean to foster self-compassion in societies that prioritise collective identity or emotional restraint? And how are CFT interventions adapted in practice to meet the unique needs of diverse communities? These are the questions that shaped the vision for this volume.

Bringing this book to life has been a deeply collaborative and meaningful process. I have been privileged to work with an inspiring team of co-editors—Julie, Rory, Annabel, and Kenichi—who bring distinct cultural, clinical, and scholarly perspectives to the project. Together, we invited contributions from around the world, aiming to capture not only the diversity of how CFT is used, but also the shared values that unite us in our commitment to compassionate care.

We hope this book serves as a bridge between cultures, disciplines, and practice settings. It is our belief that CFT has the potential to support mental health and wellbeing in ways that are sensitive, inclusive, and responsive to the realities of people across the globe. As the demand for culturally attuned interventions grows, so too must our willingness to listen, adapt, and evolve.

I am deeply grateful to all the chapter authors, reviewers, and collaborators who made this project possible. And I am especially thankful to Paul—not only for writing the foreword to this volume, but for his pioneering work and his generosity in supporting the growth of CFT across communities and continents.

May this book inspire ongoing dialogue, curiosity, and compassion.

Yasuhiro Kotera
Lead Co-Editor
University of Nottingham
Nottingham, UK

University of Osaka
Osaka, Japan

Azerbaijan University
Baku, Azerbaijan

Contents

1 Introduction to Compassion Focused Therapy 1
Yasuhiro Kotera, Julie Beaumont, Rory Colman, Annabel Rushforth, and Kenichi Asano

2 The Impact of Compassion in Multicultural, Multifaith Communities, and Workplace Environments 15
Carlo Lazzari and Yasuhiro Kotera

3 Culturally Sensitive Compassion-Focused Therapy for Adult ADHD in Latin America: Integrating Familismo and Attachment Perspectives 55
Carolina Eugenia Cáceres Videla and Rosemary Sibley

4 West Meets East in Compassion: Exploring CFT for Individuals with Dyslexia Across Cultures 75
Dana Abu Omar

5 Culturally Sensitive Applications of Compassion-Focused Therapy for Perfectionism: Conceptual and Clinical Perspectives 97
Naoki Kawasaki

6 Cultural Adaptation of Compassion Focused Therapy to East Asian Culture 121
Kenichi Asano

7 Compassion-Focused Therapy in European Latin Cultures 139
Noelia Lucía Martínez-Rives and Julie Beaumont

8 Culturally Adapted CFT Group Psychotherapy: A US Perspective 155
Derek Griner, David M. Erekson, Kristina Hansen, Mark E. Beecher, and Hiu Wai Yoko Caldwell

9 Compassion-Focused Therapy in Ireland: Cultural, Clinical, and Systemic Perspectives Across the Island of Ireland 177
Julie Beaumont

10 Future Directions and Recommendations 193
Yasuhiro Kotera, Julie Beaumont, Rory Colman, Annabel Rushforth, and Kenichi Asano

Index 207

Chapter 1
Introduction to Compassion Focused Therapy

Yasuhiro Kotera, Julie Beaumont, Rory Colman, Annabel Rushforth, and Kenichi Asano

Introduction

Compassion Focused Therapy (CFT) is a psychological approach developed by Paul Gilbert (2010b) to help individuals manage distress by cultivating compassionate motivation, emotion regulation, and self-soothing strategies. Recognising that shame and self-criticism are major barriers to mental health, CFT integrates principles from evolutionary psychology, attachment theory, affective neuroscience, and cognitive-behavioural therapy (CBT). By fostering compassionate engagement with oneself and others, CFT aims to counteract negative affective loops that sustain psychological distress (Gilbert, 2017).

Author Contribution Conceptualisation: YK; Investigation: YK, JB, RC, AR, KA; Resources: YK; Writing–original draft: YK; Writing–review & editing: YK, JB, RC, AR, KA; Project administration: YK.

Y. Kotera (✉)
Faculty of Medicine and Health Sciences, University of Nottingham, Nottingham, UK
e-mail: yasuhiro.kotera@nottingham.ac.uk

Center for Infectious Disease Education and Research, University of Osaka, Osaka, Japan

Department of Social Sciences, Azerbaijan University, Baku, Azerbaijan

J. Beaumont
School of Psychology, Queen's University Belfast, Belfast, UK

R. Colman
College of Health, Psychology and Social Care, University of Derby, Derby, UK

A. Rushforth
Clinical and Applied Psychology Department, University of Sheffield, Sheffield, UK

K. Asano
Institute of Human Sciences, University of Tsukuba, Tsukuba, Japan

Y. Kotera et al. (eds.), *Compassion-Focused Therapy for Mental Health: International Perspectives*, Advances in Mental Health and Addiction,
https://doi.org/10.1007/978-3-032-12438-8_1

Theoretical Underpinnings and Mechanisms

CFT is rooted in the three-system model of emotion regulation, which posits that human emotions are governed by three interacting systems:

1. The Threat System (focused on detecting danger, linked to anxiety, fear, disgust, and anger),
2. The Drive System (associated with achievement, motivation, and reward-seeking, related to joy and excitement), and.
3. The Soothing System (associated with calmness, social connection, and safeness).

Individuals prone to high levels of shame and self-criticism often exhibit an overactive Threat System and an underdeveloped Soothing System (Kirby et al., 2019). CFT explicitly strengthens the Soothing System through compassion-focused practices, such as compassionate imagery, mindfulness, and self-kindness exercises (Kotera, Beaumont, et al., 2024). Recent meta-analyses (Craig et al., 2020a; Leaviss & Uttley, 2015) support the effectiveness of CFT in enhancing self-compassion, reducing distress, and improving emotional regulation across clinical and non-clinical populations.

Clinical Applications of CFT

Compassion Focused Therapy (CFT) has been increasingly recognised as an effective intervention across a range of clinical conditions. Its emphasis on cultivating self-compassion, reducing self-criticism, and promoting emotion regulation makes it particularly beneficial for individuals experiencing chronic psychological distress and complex mental health difficulties.

One of the key areas where CFT has demonstrated efficacy is in the treatment of personality disorders, particularly borderline personality disorder (BPD) (Pol et al., 2023). Individuals with BPD often experience intense emotional dysregulation, unstable relationships, and a heightened tendency towards self-criticism and shame. Traditional therapeutic approaches can be challenging due to these individuals' hypersensitivity to rejection and self-perception of inadequacy. CFT, by activating the soothing system and encouraging self-kindness, has shown promise in reducing emotional instability and promoting self-acceptance (Kolts et al., 2016).

CFT has also been effectively applied in the treatment of post-traumatic stress disorder (PTSD), a condition characterised by intrusive memories, emotional numbness, and heightened threat sensitivity (Ressler et al., 2022). Many individuals with PTSD struggle with self-blame and feelings of unworthiness, which exacerbate their symptoms (Rushforth et al., 2024). By integrating mindfulness and compassion-based imagery techniques, CFT helps individuals reprocess traumatic experiences in a way that fosters self-compassion rather than self-condemnation (Karatzias et al.,

2019). This approach has been particularly useful for survivors of childhood abuse, military combat, and interpersonal violence.

Another area where CFT has gained traction is in the treatment of eating disorders, including anorexia nervosa, bulimia nervosa, and binge-eating disorder (Steindl et al., 2017). People with eating disorders often engage in severe self-criticism, body shame, and rigid self-punishment behaviours. CFT interventions help these individuals develop a more compassionate relationship with their bodies, reduce self-judgement, and adopt healthier coping mechanisms (Kelly & Carter, 2015).

Beyond psychological disorders, CFT has also been applied to chronic pain and physical health conditions (Gooding et al., 2020). Chronic illness often leads to feelings of helplessness, frustration, and self-directed anger, which can intensify physical pain and distress (Boulazreg & Rokach, 2020). By enhancing self-compassion and acceptance, CFT interventions have been shown to reduce perceived pain severity, improve emotional resilience, and enhance overall well-being in individuals with conditions such as fibromyalgia, rheumatoid arthritis, and chronic fatigue syndrome (Austin et al., 2021; Malpus et al., 2023).

A recent meta-analysis (Vidal & Soldevilla, 2022) further confirmed that CFT interventions are particularly effective for individuals with high levels of self-criticism, a transdiagnostic factor implicated in multiple mental health conditions. Given its broad applicability and effectiveness in reducing shame, self-attack, and distress (Kotera et al., 2023) (Kishimoto et al., 2024), CFT continues to be a promising approach across diverse clinical populations.

CFT's International Adaptation and Cultural Relevance

Compassion-Focused Therapy (CFT) has emerged as an effective approach for addressing self-criticism, shame, and emotional regulation difficulties, particularly in individuals who struggle with harsh self-judgement and perfectionism. Originally developed in Western psychological frameworks, particularly within cognitive-behavioural and evolutionary psychology, CFT emphasises the development of self-compassion (or described as self-reassurance) as a counterbalance to self-criticism, which is often linked to early attachment experiences, social comparisons, and fear-based conditioning (Kotera, Dosedlova, et al., 2021).

As mental health awareness grows globally, the need for culturally sensitive approaches to therapy has become increasingly evident. Mental health is deeply intertwined with cultural norms, social structures, and historical contexts, meaning that a universal therapeutic approach may not always be effective in every society (Kotera, Taylor, et al., 2023). The adaptability of CFT has allowed it to be successfully implemented in various cultural settings, where modifications ensure greater relevance and accessibility. Studies suggest that aligning CFT with the core cultural values, collective beliefs, and societal expectations of different populations enhances its effectiveness (Kariyawasam et al., 2022) (Bennett-Levy et al., 2020; Kariyawasam et al., 2023).

CFT in Japan: Integrating Compassion with Collectivist Values

In Japanese culture, self-compassion can be perceived as self-indulgence, weakness, or selfishness (Kotera et al., 2022b), which can make the implementation of CFT approaches challenging. Japanese society places a strong emphasis on humility, self-discipline, and collective harmony, which can create resistance to the idea of prioritising self-kindness (Kotera, Miyamoto, et al., 2024). Many individuals fear that being compassionate towards oneself may lead to complacency or a failure to meet social expectations, reinforcing high levels of self-criticism and perfectionism (Kotera, Mayer, et al., 2023).

Asano et al. (2022) conducted a pilot randomised controlled trial to assess the feasibility and effectiveness of group-based CFT for treatment-resistant depression (TRD) in Japan. Participants who underwent group CFT showed significant reductions in depressive symptoms and fears of self-compassion compared to the control group. The study demonstrated that CFT, when adapted to emphasise collectivist values, social harmony, and group support, could be successfully integrated into Japanese clinical settings. Patients who initially resisted self-compassion due to cultural expectations became more receptive when it was framed as a socially beneficial practice rather than an individualistic pursuit. While the study did not explicitly focus on cultural adaptation, the successful implementation of CFT in a Japanese clinical setting implies critical modifications to make the therapy more culturally congruent.

Three key cultural adaptations can be noted.

Reducing Fear of Compassion

A significant challenge in Japanese mental health care is the fear that self-compassion may be perceived as self-indulgence or weakness. This belief is deeply rooted in cultural values that prioritise perseverance (gaman, 我慢) and endurance. To address this, the intervention reframed self-compassion as a means to enhance resilience rather than diminish it. Patients were encouraged to view self-kindness as a way to sustain their ability to contribute to their families and society, thereby aligning the concept with collectivist values rather than individual self-care.

Integrating a Group Therapy Approach

In Japan, individual therapy is often associated with stigma, whereas group-based approaches align more with collectivist cultural norms. To facilitate greater social acceptance of CFT, the therapy was delivered in a group format rather than an individual setting. This structure reinforced shared experiences and allowed participants to support each other, which helped reduce feelings of isolation and further destigmatised seeking psychological help. The mutual encouragement model within the group dynamic also made the therapy feel more like a community-building experience rather than an isolated self-improvement effort.

Emphasising Social Harmony (Wa, 和)

Japan's cultural emphasis on social harmony often leads individuals to suppress personal emotions to avoid disrupting group dynamics. Traditional Western therapeutic models that emphasise self-expression may not align well with this value system (Asano et al., 2017). The adaptation of CFT in this study acknowledged the importance of maintaining interpersonal balance by demonstrating how self-compassion could enhance, rather than disrupt, relationships. Patients were taught that reducing self-criticism could lead to better communication, improved empathy, and healthier interpersonal relationships, making the therapy more acceptable within a culturally interdependent framework.

The above study from Japan illustrates the needs for cultural adaptation when CFT is used in different contexts, especially in non-Western contexts. This is an under-researched area, and this book aims to provide studies, cases and insights to fill this knowledge gap.

Theoretical Foundations of CFT

Evolutionary Psychology

CFT is rooted in evolutionary psychology, which posits that human emotions evolved to enhance survival. Gilbert identified three affect regulation systems (Gilbert, 2010b): Threat, drive, and soothing systems.

The threat system focuses on noticing danger, associated with fear and anxiety. This system is activated to protect people from harm but can become hyperactive, leading to chronic stress and anxiety symptoms. The drive system pursues rewards and achievements, linked to excitement. While motivating goal-directed behaviour, an over-reliance on this system can lead to burnout and dissatisfaction when rewards are unattainable. In life, you don't always get what you want, so over-reliance on the drive system entails high risk of burnout. The soothing system facilitates calmness and safety, based on affiliative emotions. This system is critical for mental health recovery and emotional balance, but is often underdeveloped or under-used in those with mental health challenges.

Psychopathology often arises from an imbalance between these systems, particularly an overactive threat system (Gilbert, 2014). CFT aims to cultivate the soothing system, counteracting excessive threat responses. By enhancing the soothing system, clients develop resilience and greater emotional flexibility, enabling them to manage distress more effectively (Beaumont et al., 2021) (Kotera, Cockerill, et al., 2021).

Attachment Theory

Attachment theory (Bowlby, 1983) highlights the importance of secure relationships for psychological wellbeing. Secure attachments provide a foundation for trust, emotional regulation, and interpersonal connection. CFT leverages attachment principles to foster self-compassion, treating the self as a caregiver might treat a child (Gilbert, 2014). In therapy, clients often exhibit attachment-based insecurities that fuel self-criticism and shame. Through CFT interventions, such as compassionate imagery and letter writing, clients can internalise nurturing and supportive inner voices, mitigating attachment-related distress. Rushforth et al. (2024) highlight that these approaches are particularly effective for clients with histories of trauma and neglect.

Neuroscience and Compassion

Neuroscientific research concludes that compassion training activates brain regions associated with positive affect and social bonding, such as the medial orbitofrontal cortex, ventral striatum, and anterior cingulate cortex, while also enhancing parasympathetic activity and promoting prosocial behaviour (Klimecki et al., 2013) (Engen & Singer, 2015) (Kim et al., 2019). Compassion-focused practices stimulate oxytocin release, enhancing feelings of safety and trust (Rockliff et al., 2011).

Core Principles of CFT

Compassion-Focused Therapy (CFT) is built on the understanding that compassion plays a crucial role in emotional regulation, healing from trauma, and reducing self-criticism and shame. CFT centres around developing the three flows of compassion.

Compassion for Others

This involves developing empathetic concern and the ability to support and care for others in times of suffering. Individuals learn to recognise distress in others and respond with kindness, understanding, and support, rather than avoidance or judgement. Cultivating compassionate behaviours towards others fosters stronger social connections and emotional resilience.

Compassion from Others

Many individuals struggle to receive care and kindness from others, often due to past trauma, feelings of unworthiness, or distrust. CFT helps individuals break down barriers that prevent them from accepting compassion and support. This principle emphasises feeling safe and valued within relationships, which is essential for emotional healing.

Self-Compassion

A core element of CFT, self-compassion involves treating oneself with the same kindness and understanding that one would offer a close friend. Individuals learn to replace self-criticism with self-reassurance, especially during moments of failure or distress. Self-compassion fosters greater emotional balance, resilience, and motivation, helping individuals move forward instead of getting stuck in self-judgement.

Compassion as Motivation

CFT defines compassion as a sensitivity to suffering coupled with a commitment to alleviate it (Gilbert, 2010b). This dual focus on awareness and action distinguishes compassion from empathy, which involves understanding emotions but not necessarily acting upon them. Compassion is framed as a strength rather than a weakness. By normalising the need for care and support, CFT helps clients dismantle societal stigmas around vulnerability and dependency (Craig et al., 2020b; McManus et al., 2018). This shift in perspective empowers clients to embrace compassion as a transformative force in their lives.

Addressing Shame and Self-Criticism

Shame and self-criticism perpetuate mental health difficulties, particularly depression and anxiety (Kotera et al., 2022a) (Kotera & Maughan, 2020). These emotional states often stem from unmet attachment needs and internalised negative evaluations.

CFT employs compassionate mind training to disrupt these patterns, fostering self-acceptance (Gilbert, 2010b). Techniques such as compassionate breathing, imagery, and letter writing create a psychological space where clients can process painful emotions safely (Gilbert, 2010a). These techniques can reduce shame and increase emotional resilience.

Practical Applications of CFT

CFT incorporates a range of cognitive, behavioural, and mindfulness-based techniques to develop self-compassion, regulate emotions, and foster psychological resilience. These techniques are particularly effective in reducing self-criticism, alleviating distress, and promoting a sense of inner safety. The following therapeutic methods are central to CFT.

Compassionate Imagery

Compassionate imagery involves visualising a caring and supportive figure that embodies wisdom, warmth, and kindness. This figure can be based on a real person, a spiritual guide, an idealised compassionate presence, or even an animal. By engaging in this visualisation, individuals evoke feelings of reassurance and security, helping to regulate distressing emotions. The process activates the soothing system within the brain, counterbalancing threat-based responses associated with anxiety and self-criticism. Over time, this practice enables individuals to internalise compassion, allowing them to develop a more nurturing self-relationship.

Compassionate Letter Writing

This technique encourages individuals to write a letter to themselves from the perspective of a compassionate and understanding figure. The letter may address difficult experiences, acknowledge struggles, and offer encouragement in a non-judgemental and supportive manner. Writing such letters helps reframe distressing thoughts and emotions, allowing individuals to develop a kinder, more balanced perspective on their challenges. Research indicates that this practice reduces shame and fears for compassion, and fosters greater self-compassion (Kelly & Waring, 2018).

Breathing and Physiological Regulation Techniques

Breathing techniques play a fundamental role in CFT by helping individuals regulate their autonomic nervous system. Soothing rhythm breathing is a core practice that involves deep, slow breaths designed to stimulate the parasympathetic nervous system, inducing a state of calmness and relaxation. This technique is particularly useful for individuals who experience heightened anxiety or emotional dysregulation. By focusing on their breath, individuals can develop a greater sense of stability and presence, allowing them to engage with difficult emotions in a more grounded and compassionate way.

Compassionate Self-Talk

Many individuals who struggle with self-criticism engage in harsh and punitive inner dialogue. Compassionate self-talk involves consciously shifting this internal narrative to one that is kinder, more encouraging, and understanding. Instead of criticising themselves for perceived failures, individuals are encouraged to adopt a compassionate perspective, recognising that struggles and mistakes are a universal part of the human experience. This shift in self-perception allows for a reduction in self-judgement and promotes emotional resilience.

Chair Work for Compassionate Dialogue

Chair work is a technique used to externalise different aspects of the self, particularly the self-critic and the compassionate self. In this exercise, individuals switch between chairs to express different perspectives. One chair represents the self-critic, articulating harsh judgements and negative beliefs. The second chair embodies the compassionate self, responding with understanding, reassurance, and encouragement. This method enables individuals to gain distance from their inner critic and cultivate a stronger sense of self-compassion.

Mindfulness and Self-Awareness Training

Mindfulness practices in CFT focus on developing non-judgemental awareness of thoughts, emotions, and bodily sensations. Individuals are guided to observe their experiences with openness and curiosity rather than avoidance or suppression. This practice helps individuals become less reactive to distressing emotions and cultivates a more accepting and compassionate relationship with themselves. Regular mindfulness practice has been shown to improve emotional regulation, reduce rumination, and enhance overall psychological well-being.

Safe Place Imagery

Safe place imagery involves visualising a comforting and secure environment that evokes feelings of peace and safety. This could be a natural setting, such as a beach or forest, or a familiar and comforting space from childhood. By engaging in this imagery, individuals create a mental retreat that can be accessed during moments of distress. This technique is particularly beneficial for those who have experienced trauma, as it provides a sense of stability and emotional grounding.

Integration of CFT into Therapy and Daily Life

The techniques within CFT can be tailored for individual therapy, group therapy, or self-practice. Therapists work with clients to identify patterns of self-criticism and distress, gradually replacing them with compassionate coping strategies. Clients are encouraged to integrate self-compassion techniques into their daily lives through structured exercises such as mindful breathing, compassionate self-talk, and letter writing. Over time, these practices lead to a fundamental shift in self-perception, fostering greater emotional resilience and a more nurturing internal environment.

Through consistent engagement with these techniques, individuals develop the capacity to cultivate self-kindness, reduce psychological distress, and enhance their overall well-being.

Conclusion

CFT has emerged as a transformative approach to addressing psychological distress by targeting self-criticism, shame, and emotional dysregulation. By harnessing insights from evolutionary psychology, attachment theory, and affective neuroscience, CFT offers a structured yet flexible framework that fosters emotional resilience, self-reassurance, and psychological healing. Research consistently supports its effectiveness across a range of clinical and non-clinical populations, including individuals with personality disorders, post-traumatic stress, eating disorders, and chronic health conditions.

As mental health care increasingly recognises the role of self-compassion in fostering psychological well-being, CFT stands as a promising approach that empowers individuals to develop healthier relationships with themselves and others. By normalising compassion as a fundamental aspect of mental resilience, CFT provides a pathway for individuals to break cycles of self-criticism and cultivate a life marked by emotional balance and self-kindness.

References

Asano, K., Tsuchiya, M., Ishimura, I., Lin, S., Matsumoto, Y., Miyata, H., Kotera, Y., Shimizu, E., & Gilbert, P. (2017). The development of fears of compassion scale Japanese version. *PLoS One, 12*(10). https://doi.org/10.1371/journal.pone.0185574

Asano, K., Tsuchiya, M., Okamoto, Y., Ohtani, T., Sensui, T., Masuyama, A., Isato, A., Shoji, M., Shiraishi, T., Shimizu, E., Irons, C., & Gilbert, P. (2022, 2022-08-12). Benefits of group compassion-focused therapy for treatment-resistant depression: A pilot randomized controlled trial. Frontiers in Psychology, 13. https://doi.org/10.3389/fpsyg.2022.903842.

Austin, J., Drossaert, C. H. C., Schroevers, M. J., Sanderman, R., Kirby, J. N., & Bohlmeijer, E. T. (2021, 2021/01/02). Compassion-based interventions for people with long-term physical conditions: A mixed methods systematic review. Psychology & Health, 36(1), 16–42. https://doi.org/10.1080/08870446.2019.1699090.

Beaumont, E., Bell, T., McAndrew, S., & Fairhurst, H. (2021, 2021/12/01). The impact of compassionate mind training on qualified health professionals undertaking a compassion-focused therapy module. Counselling and Psychotherapy Research, 21(4), 910–922. https://doi.org/10.1002/capr.12396.

Bennett-Levy, J., Roxburgh, N., Hibner, L., Bala, S., Edwards, S., Lucre, K., Cohen, G., O'Connor, D., Keogh, S., & Gilbert, P. (2020, 2020-12-16). Arts-Based Compassion Skills Training (ABCST): Channelling Compassion Focused Therapy Through Visual Arts for Australia's Indigenous Peoples. *Frontiers in psychology, 11*. https://doi.org/10.3389/fpsyg.2020.568561

Boulazreg, S., & Rokach, A. (2020, Oct 20). The lonely, isolating, and alienating implications of Myalgic encephalomyelitis/chronic fatigue syndrome. *Healthcare (Basel), 8*(4). https://doi.org/10.3390/healthcare8040413

Bowlby, J. (1983). *Attachment*. Basic Books.

Craig, C., Hiskey, S., & Spector, A. (2020a, Apr). Compassion focused therapy: A systematic review of its effectiveness and acceptability in clinical populations. *Expert Review of Neurotherapeutics, 20*(4), 385–400. https://doi.org/10.1080/14737175.2020.1746184

Craig, C., Hiskey, S., & Spector, A. (2020b, 2020-03-20). Compassion focused therapy: A systematic review of its effectiveness and acceptability in clinical populations. Expert Review of Neurotherapeutics, 20, 385–400. https://doi.org/10.1080/14737175.2020.1746184

Engen, H., & Singer, T. (2015, 2015-09-01). Compassion-based emotion regulation up-regulates experienced positive affect and associated neural networks. Social Cognitive and Affective Neuroscience, 10(9), 1291–1301. https://doi.org/10.1093/scan/nsv008.

Gilbert, P. (2010a). *Compassion focused therapy*. Routledge.

Gilbert, P. (2010b). *The compassionate mind: A new approach to lifes challenges*. Constable.

Gilbert, P. (2014). The origins and nature of compassion focused therapy. *British Journal of Clinical Psychology, 53*(1), 6–41. https://doi.org/10.1111/bjc.12043

Gilbert, P. (2017). *Compassion: Concepts, Research and Applications* (P. Gilbert, Ed.). Routledge.

Gooding, H., Stedmon, J., & Crix, D. (2020, Feb). All these things dont take the pain away but they do help you to accept it': Making the case for compassion-focused therapy in the management of persistent pain. *British Journal of Pain, 14*(1), 31–41. https://doi.org/10.1177/204946371985 7099

Karatzias, T., Hyland, P., Bradley, A., Fyvie, C., Logan, K., Easton, P., Thomas, J., Philips, S., Bisson, J. I., Roberts, N. P., Cloitre, M., & Shevlin, M. (2019, May). Is self-compassion a worthwhile therapeutic target for ICD-11 complex PTSD (CPTSD)? *Behavioural and Cognitive Psychotherapy, 47*(3), 257–269. https://doi.org/10.1017/s1352465818000577

Kariyawasam, L., Ononaiye, M., Irons, C., & Kirby, S. E. (2022). A cross-cultural exploration of compassion, and facilitators and inhibitors of compassion in UK and Sri Lankan people. *Glob Ment Health (Camb), 9*, 99–110. https://doi.org/10.1017/gmh.2022.10

Kariyawasam, L., Ononaiye, M., Irons, C., & Kirby, S. E. (2023, 2023/03/01). Compassion-based interventions in Asian communities: A meta-analysis of randomised controlled trials. Psychology and Psychotherapy: Theory, Research and Practice, 96(1), 148–171. https://doi.org/ 10.1111/papt.12431

Kelly, A. C., & Carter, J. C. (2015, Sep). Self-compassion training for binge eating disorder: A pilot randomized controlled trial. *Psychology and Psychotherapy, 88*(3), 285–303. https://doi.org/10. 1111/papt.12044

Kelly, A., & Waring, S. (2018, 2018-08-01). A feasibility study of a 2-week self-compassionate letter-writing intervention for nontreatment seeking individuals with typical and atypical anorexia nervosa. International Journal of Eating Disorders, 51, 1005. https://doi.org/10.1002/ eat.22930

Kim, J., Cunnington, R., & Kirby, J. (2019, 2019-11-04). The neurophysiological basis of compassion: An fMRI meta-analysis of compassion and its related neural processes. Neuroscience & Biobehavioral Reviews, 108, 112–123. https://doi.org/10.1016/j.neubiorev.2019.10.023

Kirby, J. N., Day, J., & Sagar, V. (2019, Jun). The flow of compassion: A meta-analysis of the fears of compassion scales and psychological functioning. *Clinical Psychology Review, 70*, 26–39. https://doi.org/10.1016/j.cpr.2019.03.001

Kishimoto, K., Asano, K., Colman, R., Kameo, Y., Aledeh, M., Barnes, K., & Kotera, Y. (2024). The development of the japanese version of the forms of self-criticising/attacking & self-reassuring scale (j-fscrs): Implications for cross-cultural research on self-criticism and self-reassurance. *Mental Health, Religion & Culture, No Pagination Specified-No Pagination Specified*. https:// doi.org/10.1080/13674676.2024.2313462

Klimecki, O., Leiberg, S., Lamm, C., & Singer, T. (2013, 2013-07-01). Functional neural plasticity and associated changes in positive affect after compassion training. Cerebral Cortex, 23(7), 1552–1561. https://doi.org/10.1093/cercor/bhs142

Kolts, R. L., Hayes, S. C., & Gilbert, P. (2016). *CFT made simple: a clinicians guide to practicing compassion-focused therapy*. New Harbinger Publications. https://search.ebscohost.com/login. aspx?direct=true&scope=site&db=nlebk&db=nlabk&AN=1245562

Kotera, Y., & Maughan, G. (2020, 2020/4/24). Mental health of Irish students: Self-criticism as a complete mediator in mental health attitudes and caregiver identity. Journal of Concurrent Disorders, 2(1), 14–26. https://doi.org/10.54127/bhnm9453

Kotera, Y., Asano, K., Jones, J., Colman, R., Taylor, E., Aledeh, M., Barnes, K., Golbourn, L.-M., & Kishimoto, K. (2023). The development of the Japanese version of the full and short form of attitudes towards mental health problems scale (J-(S) ATMHPS). *Mental Health, Religion & Culture, 1–13*. https://doi.org/10.1080/13674676.2023.2230908

Kotera, Y., Beaumont, J., Edwards, A.-M., Cotterill, M., Kirkman, A., Tofani, A. C., McPhilbin, M., Takhi, S., Barnes, K., Todowede, O., Ingall, B.-R., Asano, K., & Arimitsu, K. (2024). A narrative review of compassion focused therapy on positive mental health outcomes. *Behavioral Sciences, 14*(8), 643. https://www.mdpi.com/2076-328X/14/8/643

Kotera, Y., Cockerill, V., Chircop, J. G. E., & Forman, D. (2021, May). Mental health shame, self-compassion and sleep in UK nursing students: Complete mediation of self-compassion in sleep and mental health. *Nurs Open, 8*(3), 1325–1335. https://doi.org/10.1002/nop2.749. Epub 2020 Dec 23.

Kotera, Y., Dosedlova, J., & Andrzejewski, D. (2021). From stress to psychopathology: Relationship with self-reassurance and self-criticism in Czech university students. *International Journal of Mental Health and Addiction.* https://doi.org/10.1007/s11469-021-00516-z

Kotera, Y., Mayer, C. H., & Vanderheiden, E. (2023, Feb). Self-compassion, mental health shame and work motivation in German and Japanese employees. *International Review of Psychiatry, 35*(1), 113–124. https://doi.org/10.1080/09540261.2022.2148829

Kotera, Y., Miyamoto, Y., Vilar-Lluch, S., Aizawa, I., Reilly, O., Miwa, A., Murakami, M., Stergiopoulos, V., Kroon, H., Giles, K., Garner, K., Ronaldson, A., McPhilbin, M., Jebara, T., Takhi, S., Repper, J., Meddings, S., Jepps, J., Simpson, A. J., Kellermann, V., Arakawa, N., Henderson, C., Slade, M., & Eguchi, S. (2024, 2024/07/05). Cross-cultural comparison of recovery college implementation between Japan and England: Corpus-based discourse analysis. International Journal of Mental Health and Addiction. https://doi.org/10.1007/s11469-024-01356-3

Kotera, Y., Maybury, S., Liu, G., Colman, R., Lieu, J., & Dosedlová, J. (2022a). Mental Well-being of Czech university students: Academic motivation, self-compassion, and self-criticism. *Healthcare, 10*(11), 2135. https://www.mdpi.com/2227-9032/10/11/2135

Kotera, Y., Ozaki, A., Miyatake, H., Tsunetoshi, C., Nishikawa, Y., Kosaka, M., & Tanimoto, T. (2022b). Qualitative investigation into the mental health of healthcare Workers in Japan during the COVID-19 pandemic. *International Journal of Environmental Research and Public Health, 19*(1). https://doi.org/10.3390/ijerph19010568

Kotera, Y., Taylor, E., Brooks-Ucheaga, M., & Edwards, A. M. (2023). Need for a tool to inform cultural adaptation in mental health interventions. *ISSBD Bulletin, 1*(83), 2–5. https://issbd.org/wp-content/uploads/2023/06/JBD_47_3S_Combined-pdf.pdf

Leaviss, J., & Uttley, L. (2015, Apr). Psychotherapeutic benefits of compassion-focused therapy: An early systematic review. *Psychological Medicine, 45*(5), 927–945. https://doi.org/10.1017/s0033291714002141

Malpus, Z., Nazar, Z., Smith, C., & Armitage, L. (2023, Feb). Compassion focused therapy for pain management: 3 systems approach to understanding why striving and self-criticism are key psychological barriers to regulating activity and improving self-care for people living with persistent pain. *British Journal of Pain, 17*(1), 87–102. https://doi.org/10.1177/20494637221133630

McManus, J., Tsivos, Z.-L., Woodward, S., Fraser, J., & Hartwell, R. (2018, 2018-07-02). Compassion focused therapy groups: Evidence from routine clinical practice. Behaviour Change, 35, 167–173. https://doi.org/10.1017/bec.2018.16

Pol, S., De Jong, A., Trompetter, H., Bohlmeijer, E., & Chakhssi, F. (2023, 2023-11-09). Effectiveness of compassion-focused therapy for self-criticism in patients with personality disorders: A multiple baseline case series study. Personality and Mental Health. https://doi.org/10.1002/pmh.1597.

Ressler, K. J., Berretta, S., Bolshakov, V. Y., Rosso, I. M., Meloni, E. G., Rauch, S. L., & Carlezon, W. A., Jr. (2022, May). Post-traumatic stress disorder: Clinical and translational neuroscience from cells to circuits. *Nature Reviews Neurology, 18*(5), 273–288. https://doi.org/10.1038/s41582-022-00635-8

Rockliff, H., Karl, A., McEwan, K., Gilbert, J., Matos, M., & Gilbert, P. (2011, 2011-12-01). Effects of intranasal oxytocin on compassion focused imagery. Emotion, 11(6), 1388–1396. https://doi.org/10.1037/a0023861.

Rushforth, A., Kotera, Y., & Kaluzeviciute, G. (2024, 2024/02/01). Theory paper: Suggesting compassion-based approaches for treating complex post-traumatic stress disorder. International Journal of Mental Health and Addiction, 22(1), 12–23. https://doi.org/10.1007/s11469-022-00856-4.

Steindl, S. R., Buchanan, K., Goss, K., & Allan, S. (2017, 2017/07/01). Compassion focused therapy for eating disorders: A qualitative review and recommendations for further applications. Clinical Psychologist, 21(2), 62–73. https://doi.org/10.1111/cp.12126.

Vidal, J., & Soldevilla, J. (2022, 2022-09-29). Effect of compassion-focused therapy on self-criticism and self-soothing: A meta-analysis. The British Journal of Clinical Psychology, 62, 70–81. https://doi.org/10.1111/bjc.12394.

Chapter 2
The Impact of Compassion in Multicultural, Multifaith Communities, and Workplace Environments

Carlo Lazzari and Yasuhiro Kotera

Introduction

Compassion plays a pivotal role in promoting mental well-being and overall health within the adult population (Gilbert, 2010a, 2010b). Etymologically, compassion signifies a feeling of sorrow or profound tenderness for an individual who is suffering or experiencing misfortune, dating back to the mid-fourteenth century. Compassion, which translates to 'suffering with another,' is derived from Old French compassion, meaning 'sympathy' or 'pity' (12c.), and from Late Latin compassionem, denoting 'sympathy,' a noun form derived from the past-participle stem of compati, meaning 'to feel pity,' which is composed of *com*, meaning 'with' or 'together,' and *pati*, meaning 'to suffer' (Online Etymology Dictionary, 2025). The Cambridge Dictionary (2025) defines compassion as a profound feeling of sympathy and sorrow for the suffering or misfortunes of others, accompanied by a desire to assist. Furthermore, the Merriam-Webster Dictionary (2025) defines compassion as a sympathetic awareness of the distress of others, accompanied by a desire to alleviate that distress.

Research indicates that the perception of compassion can relieve stress and anxiety by activating the parasympathetic nervous system, thereby reducing cortisol levels and promoting relaxation (Kirby et al., 2017). This physiological response

C. Lazzari (✉)
International Centre for Healthcare and Medical Education, London, UK
e-mail: Carlo.Lazzari@nottingham.ac.uk

C. Lazzari · Y. Kotera
Faculty of Medicine and Health Sciences, University of Nottingham, Nottingham, UK

Y. Kotera
Center for Infectious Disease Education and Research, University of Osaka, Osaka, Japan

Department of Social Sciences, Azerbaijan University, Baku, Azerbaijan

Y. Kotera et al. (eds.), *Compassion-Focused Therapy for Mental Health: International Perspectives*, Advances in Mental Health and Addiction,
https://doi.org/10.1007/978-3-032-12438-8_2

not only provides immediate stress relief but also strengthens long-term resilience, thereby enabling individuals to navigate future challenges with enhanced confidence (Neff, 2003a, 2003b). For instance, research has demonstrated that adults who perceive elevated levels of compassion within their social networks report significantly reduced levels of depression and anxiety (Kirby et al., 2017). In addition to mental health benefits, perceived compassion enhances personal well-being by fostering improved self-perception and facilitating emotional regulation (Neff, 2003a, 2003b). When individuals experience support and understanding, they are more likely to develop self-compassion, which is strongly correlated with increased life satisfaction and reduced self-criticism (Gilbert, 2010a, 2010b). The dynamic interplay between receiving compassion and cultivating self-compassion stresses the transformative potential of compassionate interactions (Sinclair et al., 2015). Similarly, self-compassion is a foundation for self-acceptance, built upon three key aspects: (a) treating oneself with kindness during moments of perceived inadequacy, (b) acknowledging that discomfort is a natural part of life, and (c) maintaining awareness of distressing thoughts (Neff, 2003a, 2003b).

In healthcare settings, the perception of compassion from caregivers has a profound impact on patient outcomes (Kotera et al., 2022a). Compassionate care has been associated with faster recovery rates, improved adherence to treatment protocols, and higher levels of patient satisfaction (Sinclair et al., 2015). For individuals managing chronic illnesses, the perception of compassion from healthcare providers can help alleviate feelings of isolation and hopelessness while promoting a sense of agency and optimism (Sinclair et al., 2015).

The influence of compassion extends beyond individual well-being to shape social dynamics. Compassionate communities cultivate trust, cooperation, and social cohesion, which are essential for collective mental health (Cacioppo & Patrick, 2008). Adults who perceive compassion within their social environments are more likely to engage in prosocial behaviours, establishing a positive cycle that reinforces community well-being (Gilbert, 2010a, 2010b). Conversely, the lack of perceived compassion can lead to detrimental consequences. Social rejection or indifference heightens the risk of mental health issues, including anxiety and depression, emphasising the significance of nurturing compassionate interactions within settings such as workplaces, families, and communities (Kirby et al., 2017; Neff, 2003a, 2003b). Nonetheless, obstacles to compassion remain. Cultural norms, personal biases, and systemic constraints can hinder the expression and perception of compassion, complicating the maintenance of compassionate interactions across various contexts (Babaei & Taleghani, 2019; Gilbert, 2010a, 2010b).

Addressing these barriers requires deliberate efforts to cultivate empathy and foster understanding at both individual and institutional levels (Sinclair et al., 2015). Research findings suggest that patients perceive compassion as both context-dependent and inherent, necessitating that healthcare providers blend their personal qualities with their professional skills to effectively alleviate patient suffering (Sinclair et al., 2015). While compassion might seem instinctive, a disconnect persists between patients' expectations of this crucial aspect of care and healthcare providers' ability to deliver it in a structured, evidence-based manner (Sinclair et al., 2015).

Theoretical frameworks of compassion outline its essential components, serving as a guide for clinical practice and research (Gilbert, 2009a, 2009b). However, the expression and interpretation of compassion will always differ based on the individuals involved in the clinical interaction (Sinclair et al., 2015). As reported in this chapter, we link compassion to the concept of altruism, as described by Preston (in Gilbert, 2020), where altruistic responding refers to intentional helping behaviour driven by perceiving another person's distress or need. Altruism and compassion are fundamental to societal interactions, promoting mutual support, empathy, and ethical responsibility. Research highlights their interconnected role in enhancing social cohesion and well-being (Batson, 2011; Neff, 2003a, 2003b). However, compassion can be understood through several theoretical frameworks, which are discussed in this chapter, along with our research that has explored compassion and these frameworks in greater depth.

By emphasising a culture rooted in compassion, society can unlock its transformative potential to enhance individual and collective well-being. While self-compassion—extending kindness and forgiveness towards oneself—has garnered substantial attention in psychological research (Neff, 2003a, 2003b), gaps remain in the research on how perceived compassion from others is experienced in multicultural contexts. The perception of compassion from external sources significantly contributes to overall well-being. Acts of compassion, whether from family, friends, or even strangers, foster a sense of connection and emotional support, which are essential for maintaining mental and physical health. Research indicates that receiving compassion can reduce stress, enhance resilience, and promote positive emotions (Mascaro et al., 2020a, 2020b). There is a significant opportunity to improve clarity regarding the methodologies used to assess compassion within organisations and communities, ensuring a more precise and effective evaluation (Seppälä et al., 2017; Kotera & Van Gordon, 2021). Furthermore, the consistency of the three fundamental components of compassion—recognising suffering, experiencing an emotional response, and feeling motivated to assist—at these levels and within a multifaith society remains ambiguous (Mascaro et al., 2020a, 2020b). If this is the case, inquiries arise concerning the manifestations of 'recognition' and 'emotional response' within organisational or community realms and how they can be accurately measured (Mascaro et al., 2020a, 2020b).

Compassionate interactions significantly strengthen social bonds, creating an environment that fosters support and nurtures personal growth and psychological stability (Seppälä et al., 2017). Furthermore, external expressions of compassion can effectively mitigate feelings of isolation and loneliness, fostering a profound sense of belonging (Vieten et al., 2024a, 2024b). These benefits highlight the significant impact of compassion on both individual and collective well-being. When individuals perceive themselves as supported, valued, and nurtured, they develop enhanced emotional resilience, stronger interpersonal relationships, and increased trust within social contexts (Gilbert, 2014). Consequently, the perception of compassion from others constitutes a fundamental cornerstone of mental and personal well-being among the adult population (Sinclair et al., 2015). The implications of compassion extend broadly, influencing individual and collective well-being by fostering emotional resilience, enhancing self-perception, and promoting social cohesion (Cacioppo & Patrick, 2008). Furthermore, prioritising compassionate interactions within personal relationships, healthcare settings, and community environments can contribute to the establishment of a more supportive and healthier society (Gilbert, 2010a, 2010b). In summary, compassion functions as a personal virtue and as a foundational force driving the development of resilient, connected, and thriving communities.

In an attempt to organise an operational definition, kindness, support, and caring during challenging circumstances are reported as examples of others' compassion. (Gilbert et al., 2017). For instance, Gilbert (2009a, 2009b) argues compassion builds resilience. Hermanto et al. (2016) suggest compassion is a calming, listening, and accepting approach in supportive social contexts. In stressful conditions, compassion from others may enhance the calming mechanism in emotion regulation through strong attachment links (Gilbert, 2011) while promoting both mental and physical health (Stellar et al., 2015; Di Bello et al., 2020). Research by Singer and Klimecki (2014) found that compassion training activated the ventral striatum, pregenual anterior cingulate cortex, and medial orbitofrontal cortex in the brain. We will discuss the neurophysiological aspects of compassion later in the chapter.

Compassion is communicated in multiple ways—verbal, nonverbal, emotional, and supportive actions—all of which significantly shape an individual's mental health, interpersonal connections, and overall well-being (Davidson & Harrington, 2002). More than a fleeting emotion, compassion is a foundational element of human interaction, fostering social cohesion, emotional resilience, and ethical responsibility. It is closely intertwined with individual well-being, as health is not merely the absence of disease but is also influenced by favourable socioeconomic conditions, strong social networks, and a psychologically safe environment (World Health Organization, 2025a, 2025b).

Despite the growing body of literature on compassion, a standardised, practical framework for analysing its effects remains lacking, often resulting in the conflation of compassion and empathy (D'Amico, 2018). Compassion extends beyond empathy in that it involves not only recognising another's distress but actively seeking to alleviate it Goetz et al. (2010). This distinction is critical in mental health research, where understanding the emotional and behavioural aspects of compassion is necessary to assess its impact on psychological resilience and interpersonal relationships (Singer & Klimecki, 2014).

Moreover, defining and measuring compassion remains a subject of debate among researchers. Some argue that compassion is best assessed through subjective self-reporting of emotions, while others advocate for objective measurement through observable prosocial actions (Mascaro et al., 2020a, 2020b). Variability in research methodologies has led to discrepancies in findings, complicating efforts to standardise compassion assessments. A systematic review of 559 studies on compassion identified diverse approaches in measurement, sample populations, and assessment tools, further reinforcing the need for a unified framework to examine its role in personal and societal well-being (Vieten et al., 2024a, 2024b).

Emerging studies in neuropsychology and social sciences suggest that compassion has profound effects on neurological functioning, social behaviours, and even organisational effectiveness. Research indicates that compassion activates neural pathways associated with positive affect, reinforcing prosocial behaviours and emotional regulation (Immordino-Yang, 2016). In professional environments, organisations that promote compassionate leadership experience higher levels of collaboration, employee satisfaction, and ethical decision-making (Worline & Dutton, 2017). Such insights underline the need to integrate compassion into broader social and institutional frameworks to promote inclusivity and long-term social sustainability.

Furthermore, cultural perspectives influence how compassion is expressed and understood. In collectivist societies, compassion is often framed as a communal duty, with individuals expected to prioritise the welfare of others. In contrast, individualist cultures tend to perceive compassion as a personal choice rooted in empathy (Markus & Kitayama, 1991). Religious traditions shape compassion differently, viewing it as a moral obligation tied to spiritual beliefs, while secular perspectives promote compassion as a fundamental aspect of ethical leadership and social justice (Dalai Lama, 1995; Nussbaum, 2001). Understanding these cultural nuances enhances global discourse on compassion and its role in human interactions.

In conclusion, compassion is more than an individual virtue—it is a social force with far-reaching implications for mental health, interpersonal dynamics, and organisational structures. Developing a comprehensive framework for measuring compassion, distinguishing it from empathy, and integrating it into health, psychological, and professional domains is essential for advancing research and improving societal well-being. Future studies must focus on refining assessment methodologies, exploring the neurological basis of compassion, and investigating its long-term effects on mental health and social equity.

We believe that the concept of compassion should be examined within its sociocultural and multicultural frameworks, particularly about how regional ethics and religious beliefs shape local interpretations and applications of compassion. For instance, religion has a significant influence on individuals' perceptions and practices of compassion. Research on this subject suggests that highly religious individuals often exhibit acts of kindness and generosity; however, their motivations tend to differ from those of less religious or non-religious individuals (Simon-Thomas, 2012). For highly religious people, altruistic behaviour is less motivated by transient feelings of compassion and more by moral obligations, communal identity, or doctrinal teachings. Conversely, individuals who are less religious or non-religious are more inclined to engage in generous actions when experiencing intense feelings of compassion. Consequently, the interpretation and application of compassion vary according to religious beliefs and practices (Simon-Thomas, 2012). In the following paragraphs, we will explore the social, psychological, religious, and secular frameworks that provide the ground for the understanding and study of compassion from others in multicultural settings.

Theoretical Frameworks of Compassion

Several psychological and philosophical frameworks provide valuable insights into the mechanisms of compassion and its profound impact on well-being. The following are some of the theoretical frameworks that support the meanings and applications of compassion in health and well-being and that can guide research on the topic. Compassion is a vital force shaping societal norms, interpersonal relationships, and organisational structures, deeply embedded in cultural, ethical, and professional frameworks. Different cultures interpret compassion through varied lenses—collectivist societies emphasise communal harmony and mutual aid, while individualist cultures view it as a personal choice based on empathy. Religious traditions frame compassion as a moral duty tied to spiritual teachings, whereas secular perspectives regard it as an essential aspect of ethical leadership and social cohesion. In organisations, compassionate leadership fosters inclusivity, emotional intelligence, and collaboration, leading to higher job satisfaction and professional growth. Understanding the diverse applications of compassion helps strengthen human connections, drive positive change, and build environments that support altruistic behaviour and well-being.

Attachment Theory

Rooted in the work of Bowlby (1969), this theory emphasises the manner in which perceived compassion fosters secure attachments, which are essential for emotional stability and resilience. Secure attachments mitigate anxiety and enhance emotional regulation by fostering a sense of safety and trust in interpersonal relationships. This framework emphasises the importance of early caregiving experiences in shaping an individual's capacity for compassion and their ability to form healthy interpersonal connections throughout their life. Cultivating trusting relationships during childhood through positive early attachment experiences with primary caregivers represents a requisite step for nurturing the acceptance of compassion from others, alongside the belief that the self is worthy of compassion from others (Lazzari & Masino, 2006). By internalising the parents as 'compassionate and loving individuals' during childhood, an individual is enabled to develop a more adaptable acceptance of the idea that others can exhibit compassion towards oneself because social trust development remains unaffected (Lazzari & Masino, 2006). Consequently, this process of internalising 'others as loving individuals' will naturally transform into genuine compassion for oneself and acceptance of compassion from others, in contrast to perceiving oneself as unworthy of love and compassion, as is often seen in various personality disorders associated with self-harming behaviours and depression (Lazzari & Rabottini, 2023).

Social Support Theory

Developed by Cohen and Wills (1985), this theory emphasises the crucial role of compassion as a protective factor against stress and mental distress. Compassionate interactions provide both emotional and practical support, thereby reinforcing psychological stability and promoting effective coping strategies. The same occurs within organisations, where fostering collateral compassion improves the well-being and professional efficiency of interprofessional teams (Lazzari et al., 2024). By cultivating a sense of belonging and reducing feelings of isolation, social support significantly enhances an individual's capacity to navigate life's challenges and maintain mental well-being (Cohen & Wills, 1985).

Neuroscientific Approach

Research conducted by Chierchia and Singer (2016) suggests that empathy for pain activates specific brain regions, including the anterior insula and the anterior midcingulate cortex, which are associated with negative emotions. Conversely, compassionate states are associated with activity in the medial orbitofrontal cortex and the ventral striatum, resulting in feelings of warmth, care, and positive emotions (Chierchia & Singer, 2016). Notably, compassion training has been correlated with various benefits, including enhanced psychological well-being, improved physical health, and increased cooperation, trust, and tolerance within interpersonal relationships (Chierchia & Singer, 2016). Compassionate interactions appear to activate the mirror neuron pathway. Two or more persons in consensual, co-compassionate interactions exhibit synchronised variations in their neurophysiological variables, including blood pressure, heart rate, and EEG waves (Lazzari & Masiello, 2016).

Social Ecological Model and Compassion

The Social Ecological Model (SEM) offers a comprehensive framework for understanding the influence of multiple interconnected levels on health and behaviour, including intrapersonal, interpersonal, institutional, communal, and public policy environments (Jacobsen, 2021). This model is particularly pertinent to the examination of compassion, as it emphasises the dynamic interplay between individual and environmental factors that shape compassionate behaviours and their subsequent impact on health and well-being. However, individuals drifting away from social interactions – either victims of loneliness, social isolation, social anxiety, or agoraphobia – become somewhat 'socially deskilled', requiring extra effort to internalise compassionate actions from others and to entrust these actions as natural and spontaneous (Lazzari & Rabottini, 2024).

Intrapersonal Level of Compassion

At the intrapersonal level, the SEM focuses on individual characteristics, including knowledge, attitudes, beliefs, and skills. Compassion, as an intrapersonal trait, is often rooted in personal values and emotional intelligence (Neff, 2003a, 2003b). Studies have shown that individuals with higher levels of self-compassion are better equipped to manage stress and exhibit empathy towards others, which contributes to improved mental health outcomes (Barnard & Curry, 2011). Self-compassion is understood to encompass three key elements: self-kindness as opposed to self-criticism, recognising shared human experiences rather than feeling isolated, and maintaining mindfulness instead of becoming overly absorbed in distress. Studies have shown that self-compassion contributes to psychological well-being and is associated with lower levels of mental health difficulties (Germer & Neff, 2013). In cross-cultural research including German and Japanese workers, Kotera et al. (2023a) compared mental health constructs among German and Japanese employees, highlighting cultural differences despite similar socio-economic development. A cross-sectional design was used, with 257 German and 165 Japanese employees completing self-report scales on mental health problems, mental health shame, self-compassion, and work motivation. The findings indicate that German employees reported higher levels of mental health issues, shame, self-compassion, and work motivation than their Japanese counterparts. Self-compassion, encompassing compassion, humanity, care, and unconditional love, was influenced by gender and age in Japanese employees but showed no similar association in Germans. Regression analysis revealed self-compassion as the strongest predictor of mental health problems in Germans, while mental health shame was the strongest predictor among Japanese employees, indicating cultural variance (Kotera et al., 2023a).

Interpersonal Level of Compassion

The interpersonal level thoroughly examines the relationships and social networks that considerably influence behaviour. Empathy is broadly understood to encompass both emotional and cognitive dimensions. Davis (2017) explores the influence of two key aspects of empathy—compassion and perspective-taking—on social relationships across three domains: overall relationship functioning, social support, and responses to partner transgressions. Research consistently indicates that perspective-taking is significantly associated with relationship quality, resulting in increased satisfaction and decreased interpersonal hostility (Davis, 2017). In contrast, compassion exhibits weaker and less consistent correlations with relationship quality. Furthermore, perspective-taking has a positive influence on the provision of social support, whereas the impact of compassion is less pronounced. Nonetheless, compassion emerges as the most substantial predictor of forgiveness following partner transgressions. Limited cross-cultural studies suggest that these patterns are applicable beyond American contexts (Davis, 2017). Embracing a social network perspective requires recognising the interpersonal context within which close relationships develop. On a broader scale, Felmlee and Sinclair (2018) present evidence indicating that interpersonal networks provide the support, information, opportunities, and structural embeddedness that frequently facilitate the initiation and maintenance of personal relationships while simultaneously tending to obstruct their dissolution (Felmlee & Sinclair, 2018).

Institutional Level

At the institutional level, the SEM considers the role of organisations and systems in influencing behaviour. The presence of compassion within healthcare institutions, for instance, is essential for facilitating patient-centred care and improving the overall quality of service delivery (Epstein & Street, 2011). Research has highlighted the importance of organisational policies and practices that emphasise compassion, including training programmes for healthcare professionals and the integration of compassionate care principles into institutional frameworks (Epstein & Street, 2011). These initiatives not only improve patient outcomes but also promote the well-being of caregivers and staff (Epstein & Street, 2011).

Communal Level

The communal level emphasises the broader community and societal norms that influence behaviour. Compassion at this level is manifested through collective actions and shared values that promote social cohesion and mutual support (Braveman & Gottlieb, 2014). Community-based initiatives, including volunteer programmes and public health campaigns, frequently utilise the principles of compassion to address social inequalities and enhance access to resources (Braveman & Gottlieb, 2014). By cultivating a sense of belonging and shared responsibility, the communal level of the Social Ecological Model emphasises the importance of compassion in building resilient and inclusive communities.

Public Policy Level

The concept of compassion within organisations aligns closely with understanding and addressing stakeholder expectations. Compassionate organisations actively seek to fulfil the needs of their diverse stakeholders, fostering a culture of empathy, care, and mutual benefit. For shareholders, compassion involves ensuring transparency and delivering consistent value-based services, recognising their trust in the organisation's ability to provide financial stability. Employees experience organisational compassion through fair treatment, safe working conditions, opportunities for growth, and support for their well-being, both personal and professional (OpenSax College, 2018). Similarly, compassion towards local communities entails respecting the environment, contributing positively to regional development, and avoiding harm to societal quality of life (OpenSax College, 2018). By embedding compassion into decision-making processes, organisations demonstrate their commitment to fostering meaningful relationships with stakeholders, creating a supportive environment where satisfaction and trust thrive (OpenSax College, 2018; Lazzari, 2004). Compassionate behaviours within organisations also promote equitable resource distribution, prioritise sustainability, and encourage collective responsibility—all essential for long-term success and ethical growth (OpenSax College, 2018; Lazzari, 2000).

Findings from Our Systematic Review

Drawing from the Social Ecological Model (SEM) and Social Support Theory, this research aimed to explore the influence of perceived compassion on personal well-being, particularly concerning the level of interpersonal interactions. In this chapter, we omit the numerical outcomes of this review but condense the narratives that highlight the global findings. To understand how perceived compassion from others shapes individual well-being, we conducted a systematic review, posing the question: What meanings do individuals assign to receiving compassion from others? The findings of our systematic review addressing this question reveal two interpretations of perceived compassion from others. Some individuals show an acceptance of compassion from others (ACO), while others experience a fear of compassion from others (FCO). We systematically reviewed eight pivotal studies on this subject, culminating in the following findings. Across all studies, a total of 2,759 participants were included. FCO demonstrated a positive correlation with anxiety, depression, stress, a fear of expressing compassion, a fear of self-compassion, obsessive–compulsive symptoms, social anxiety, and self-criticism. Conversely, ACO exhibited a positive correlation with self-compassion, compassion for others, health status, self-reassurance, resilience, flourishing, reduced psychological distress, and meaning in life (Chan et al., 2022; Carvalho et al., 2024; Gilbert, 2011; Gilbert et al., 2017; Hermanto et al., 2016; Hsieh et al., 2019; Merritt and Purdon, 2020; Trindale et al., 2018).

The theoretical framework that underpins this research is grounded in the SEM and Social Support Theory, both of which provide essential insights into the role of perceived compassion in shaping individual well-being. These models help contextualise the psychological and relational mechanisms through which interpersonal compassion influences mental health outcomes. The SEM posits that health and well-being are shaped by multiple levels of influence, including individual, interpersonal, community, and societal factors (Bronfenbrenner, 1979). SEM highlights the interaction between personal experiences and broader environmental structures, suggesting that an individual's perception of compassion from others is influenced not only by personal psychological processes but also by social networks and community support systems (McLeroy et al., 1988). In this context, Acceptance of Compassion from Others (ACO) and Fear of Compassion from Others (FCO) can be understood as responses shaped by varying levels of socioeconomic and relational dynamics.

Individuals embedded in supportive social structures are more likely to accept and integrate compassion into their self-perception, enhancing psychological resilience and overall well-being (Adler & Stewart, 2010). Conversely, those experiencing social inequalities, past trauma, or interpersonal distress may develop apprehension towards receiving compassion, reinforcing FCO and contributing to psychological challenges such as anxiety and self-criticism (Wilkinson & Pickett, 2018). Similarly, Social Support Theory suggests that interpersonal interactions, particularly emotional and instrumental support, significantly contribute to psychological and physiological well-being (Cobb, 1976). The perception of compassion from others functions as a form of social support, providing reassurance, validation, and emotional stability (House, 1981).

ACO aligns with positive social support mechanisms, where individuals perceive compassion as beneficial, reinforcing prosocial behaviours and emotional security (Sarason et al., 1987). FCO, on the other hand, may stem from negative past experiences, distrust, or unresolved emotional trauma, leading individuals to reject or struggle with receiving compassion, thereby exacerbating mental health vulnerabilities (Gilbert, 2010a, 2010b). Moreover, social support theory highlights how interpersonal connections mediate stress responses, suggesting that a strong network promoting compassion fosters adaptive coping strategies, reducing psychological distress (Thoits, 1995). When individuals experience consistent emotional validation and compassionate interactions, they are more likely to develop positive affect, resilience, and flourishing (Reis et al., 2000).

By integrating SEM and Social Support Theory, this research positions perceived compassion within a multilayered framework of psychosocial influence, illustrating how individual, relational, and structural factors interact to shape well-being. ACO and FCO emerge as distinct pathways through which compassion-related experiences either enhance or challenge psychological health, reinforcing the importance of social context, interpersonal trust, and emotional regulation in understanding well-being. Future research should further investigate how cultural variations, historical experiences, and systemic inequalities impact individuals' responses to receiving compassion, deepening the theoretical discourse surrounding interpersonal support and psychological resilience.

Multicultural Aspects of Compassion

Compassion is a universal human sentiment that is interpreted in various ways, depending on the cultural context in which it is expressed. An intriguing question arises: Do adults from different cultural backgrounds utilise a religious or secular framework to comprehend the acts of compassion shown by others?

Religious and Secular Frameworks

Religious frameworks portray compassion as a moral directive tied to divine commandments or spiritual teachings. For instance, *Christianity* emphasises compassion through the principle of loving one's neighbour (Walker, 2023). *Islam* celebrates the virtues of Rahma (mercy) (Ashfaq et al., 2024), and *Buddhism* views Karuna (compassion) as a vital step towards enlightenment (Mythology, 2024). In Mahayana Buddhism, compassion is often described through the concept of Jihi (慈悲), combining Ji (loving-kindness) and Hi (the desire to relieve suffering). Jihi reflects the dual aspects of wishing happiness for others and actively working to alleviate their suffering, guiding practitioners towards wisdom, selflessness, and, ultimately, enlightenment (Keown, 2005).

In *Hinduism,* the Upanishads, foundational texts of Hindu philosophy, emphasise compassion (*Daya*) as a core ethical principle. Compassion is defined as a deep empathy for others' suffering and a commitment to alleviate it. It plays a vital role in spiritual growth, fostering unity and higher states of consciousness. The interconnectedness of all beings, as taught in the Upanishads, underpins compassion, suggesting that harming others equates to hurting oneself. Ethical principles like *Ahimsa* (non-violence) and *Seva* (selfless service) complement compassion. By practising compassion, individuals progress towards *Moksha* (liberation), dissolving ego and ignorance to achieve unity with the ultimate reality, Brahman (Mythology, 2024).

Shintoism, the indigenous spirituality of Japan, emphasises harmony with nature and reverence for *Kami* (spirits). Compassion in Shintoism is expressed through acts of kindness, purification rituals, and community harmony (Nelson, 2000). The concept of *Magokoro,* or a sincere heart, underpins compassionate actions, fostering mutual respect and care (Breen & Teeuwen, 2010). Shinto shrines often serve as centres for community support, reflecting the faith's emphasis on collective well-being, as Shintoism practices encourage compassion as a natural expression of human and spiritual interconnectedness (Breen & Teeuwen, 2010).

Islamism places a profound emphasis on compassion, rooted in the concept of *Rahma* (mercy), as highlighted in the Quran (Ashfaq et al., 2024). Compassion is encouraged in interpersonal relationships, community welfare, and acts of charity. The teachings urge Muslims to care for the vulnerable and uphold justice (Esposito, 2002). Through practices such as *Zakat* (charitable giving) and *Sadaqah* (voluntary charity), Islam promotes a culture of empathy and altruism (Esposito, 2002).

In *Christianity,* compassion is a fundamental virtue rooted in the teachings of Jesus Christ. The principle of loving one's neighbour as oneself stresses the importance of empathy and kindness (Walker, 2023). Compassion is exemplified in the parable of the Good Samaritan, which encourages believers to aid those in need, regardless of differences (Esposito, 2002). Acts of charity and service, such as feeding the hungry and caring for the sick, reflect the Christian commitment to compassion and care. Through prayer and community engagement, Christians strive to embody compassion as a reflection of divine love (Walker, 2023).The Secular Interpretation of Compassion

Compassion, traditionally associated with religious and spiritual frameworks, has increasingly been examined through a secular lens, particularly in psychology, neuroscience, and ethics. Secular compassion is understood as an innate human trait that fosters social cohesion, emotional resilience, and ethical behaviour. Unlike religious interpretations that often link compassion to divine or moral imperatives, secular perspectives view it as a fundamental aspect of human nature, shaped by evolutionary, psychological, and social factors.

Evolutionary Basis of Compassion

From an evolutionary perspective, compassion is viewed as a survival mechanism that fosters cooperation and group cohesion. Research suggests that early human societies thrived due to their ability to support and care for vulnerable members, reinforcing social bonds and collective well-being (Goetz et al., 2010). Compassionate behaviour, such as caregiving and altruism, has been linked to increased chances of survival and reproductive success, making it a deeply ingrained aspect of human nature.

Psychological and Neuroscientific Perspectives

Modern psychology and neuroscience have provided empirical evidence supporting the impact of compassion in mental health and interpersonal relationships. Studies using functional MRI scans have demonstrated that compassionate thoughts and actions activate brain regions associated with reward and emotional regulation, such as the anterior cingulate cortex and the ventromedial prefrontal cortex (Singer & Klimecki, 2014). These findings suggest that compassion is not merely a social construct but a neurologically embedded response that enhances emotional well-being.

Furthermore, compassion-focused therapy (CFT) has emerged as a psychological intervention aimed at fostering self-compassion and reducing distress in individuals with anxiety and depression (Gilbert, 2017). CFT is grounded in the idea that cultivating compassion can mitigate self-criticism and promote psychological resilience, reinforcing the notion that compassion is a valuable tool for mental health.

Ethical and Social Dimensions

In secular ethics, compassion is regarded as a universal principle that transcends cultural and religious boundaries. Philosophers such as Martha Nussbaum and Peter Singer have argued that compassion should be the foundation of moral reasoning, advocating for policies and practices that prioritise empathy and social justice (Nussbaum, 2001; Singer, 2015). Singer's concept of 'effective altruism' emphasises the rational application of compassion to maximise positive outcomes, encouraging individuals to contribute to causes that alleviate suffering on a global scale.

Compassion also plays a crucial role in social justice movements, influencing policies related to healthcare, education, and human rights. Research indicates that societies that prioritise compassionate governance tend to exhibit lower levels of inequality and higher overall well-being (Wilkinson & Pickett, 2018). This underlines the importance of integrating compassion into secular frameworks for policymaking and social development.

Cultivating Secular Compassion

While compassion is often perceived as an innate trait, studies suggest that it can be cultivated through mindfulness and cognitive training. Secular mindfulness programs, such as Cognitively-Based Compassion Training (CBCT) and Compassion Cultivation Training (CCT), have been developed to enhance empathy and emotional regulation (Lavelle, 2017). These programs, rooted in contemplative traditions but adapted for secular use, demonstrate that compassion can be systematically developed through structured practice. Additionally, educational initiatives aimed at fostering compassion in children and young adults have gained traction. Schools incorporating social-emotional learning (SEL) curricula report improved student well-being and interpersonal relationships, highlighting the benefits of integrating compassion into secular education (Durlak et al., 2011).

Cultural Variations in the Meanings of Compassion

Research highlights that cultural norms and values shape how compassion is expressed, received, and understood. For instance, collectivist cultures, such as those in many Asian societies, often emphasise interdependence and communal harmony, framing compassion as a moral duty and a reflection of societal cohesion (Kariyawasam et al., 2022). In contrast, autonomous cultures, such as those in Western societies, may view compassion as a personal choice and an expression of individual virtue (Koopmann-Holm & Tsai, 2017). Despite these insights, there is limited research on how adults in these cultural contexts interpret compassion when they are the recipients, particularly about their spiritual or philosophical beliefs. In autonomous cultures, such as those in Western countries, people often interpret compassion as a personal act of kindness or altruism (Kotera et al., 2022b). Here, compassion is frequently associated with personal choice and moral responsibility rather than communal duty (Pogosyan, 2022). For instance, in the United States, compassion is often linked to volunteerism and charitable acts, reflecting a focus on individual agency (Pogosyan, 2022).

Gaps in Cross-Cultural and Interdisciplinary Research

Existing studies often focus on compassion within specific cultural or religious contexts, limiting the generalisability of findings. For example, research on compassion in Western societies frequently emphasises psychological well-being and individual growth, while studies in non-Western contexts may prioritise social harmony and collective welfare (Koopmann-Holm & Tsai, 2017). Cross-cultural research that examines how adults in diverse settings interpret received compassion, integrating perspectives from psychology, sociology, and theology, is needed (Kotera et al., 2023b). Additionally, interdisciplinary approaches could provide a more comprehensive understanding of how religious practices and acquired wisdom intersect with cultural norms to shape these interpretations (Gilbert, 2019; Kotera et al., 2023b).

We now present findings from four surveys. Across four anonymous online surveys conducted in the United States between 2024 and 2025, we explored how adults from diverse ethnic and multidenominational religious backgrounds interpret and experience compassion in both personal and professional contexts. One survey of 318 participants examined whether individuals primarily derive their understanding of compassion from religious or secular ethical frameworks. Another, involving 285 adults, found that receiving compassion in the workplace was central to job satisfaction. A third survey of 235 respondents investigated everyday barriers to practising compassion, while a fourth, targeting 274 employed adults, assessed the perceived importance of compassion within organisational cultures. Together, these studies offer a multidimensional view of compassion as a moral, relational, and institutional phenomenon shaping wellbeing across American society.

Findings from Our Survey No. 1

The theoretical, social, and health models underpinning this research help contextualise the interpretation of compassion across cultural and ethnic backgrounds. These models provide a framework for understanding how individuals integrate religious and secular beliefs into their perceptions of compassion and its societal applications.

Theoretical Models

1. *Social Cognitive Theory (SCT):* Bandura's (1986) Social Cognitive Theory (SCT) highlights the role of observational learning, social norms, and self-efficacy in shaping individual attitudes and behaviours. In the context of compassion, SCT suggests that individuals internalise compassionate behaviours through social interactions and cultural exposure. Whether compassion is interpreted through

religious doctrine or secular reasoning, its expression is influenced by learned experiences and the perceived social environment.

2. *Theory of Moral Development*: Kohlberg's (1981) Theory of Moral Development outlines different stages through which individuals develop ethical reasoning, ranging from pre-conventional moral judgements to post-conventional principles. Compassion, in this framework, is seen as a function of moral reasoning, where individuals may associate it with spiritual teachings or secular humanistic values. This theory helps explain why some individuals derive compassion from religious principles, while others view it as a universal ethical standard independent of faith traditions.
3. *Biopsychosocial Model:* Engel's (1977) Biopsychosocial Model integrates biological, psychological, and social dimensions in explaining human experiences. Compassion can be analysed through this model by examining how biological predispositions (such as empathy-related neural pathways), psychological influences (personal values and belief systems), and social interactions (community expectations and cultural norms) shape an individual's ability to express and receive compassion.

Social Models

4. *Social Identity Theory:* Tajfel and Turner's (1986) Social Identity Theory explains how group affiliations influence self-perception and interpersonal relationships. The interpretation of compassion may be shaped by cultural identity, religious affiliation, or communal ties. Individuals who identify strongly with religious communities may be more inclined to associate compassion with spiritual teachings. In contrast, those who engage primarily in secular settings might define it through ethical philosophy and social responsibility.
5. *Social Support Theory:* Social Support Theory (Cohen & Wills, 1985) posits that emotional and instrumental support have a significant impact on individual well-being. Compassion serves as a social support mechanism, strengthening interpersonal bonds and enhancing psychological resilience. Religious communities often institutionalise compassion through structured social support systems, such as charitable giving and pastoral care, while secular frameworks emphasise peer networks and community-driven aid initiatives.
6. *Structuration Theory*: Giddens' (1984) Structuration Theory posits that individual agency and societal structures are mutually influential. Compassion, therefore, operates within the interplay between personal interpretation and institutional influences. Whether compassion is viewed as a religious obligation or a secular ethical principle depends on an individual's engagement with societal norms and cultural institutions.

Health Models

7. *Health Belief Model (HBM):* The Health Belief Model (Becker, 1974) describes how personal beliefs influence health-related behaviours. Individuals who perceive compassion as a crucial factor in healthcare may be more likely to pursue caregiving professions or advocate for compassionate practices in medical settings. The high prioritisation of healthcare as a domain for compassion stresses the intersection of emotional support and physical well-being.
8. *Salutogenic Model of Health:* Antonovsky's (1996) Salutogenic Model of Health emphasises factors that promote well-being rather than those that merely prevent illness. Compassion serves as a protective factor, enhancing psychological resilience and social cohesion, thereby helping individuals better cope with stress and adversity. Both religious teachings and secular ethical reasoning contribute to creating compassionate environments that promote mental and emotional well-being.
9. *Ecological Systems Theory*: Bronfenbrenner's (1979) Ecological Systems Theory examines the layered influences of micro, meso, exo, and macro systems on individual behaviour. Compassion is shaped by immediate family dynamics, community interactions, institutional influences, and cultural ideologies, reinforcing the notion that its interpretation varies across different social structures.

Results from Our Survey No. 1

Regarding the topic of cultural and ethnic variations in the interpretation of compassion, we conducted an online survey to explore how cultural backgrounds influence adults' interpretations of compassion, aiming to uncover how many individuals rely on religious frameworks to understand acts of compassion, as opposed to secular perspectives. We also sought to investigate where our population of interest believed that compassion teaching should be focused. Our anonymous online survey targeted 318 adult citizens of the United States from a multidenominational religious background to ascertain whether their interpretation of compassion was primarily derived from religious or secular ethics. Among this sample, when asked where compassion was most needed, 73.90% of respondents identified healthcare, followed by 66.98% for education, 56.92% for family, 50% for community services, 47.48% for politics, and 38.06% for business. Additionally, 28.93% reported that, in their opinion, compassion derives from religious teachings, while 28.62% stated that they derive the meaning of compassion from common sense. This research demonstrates that compassion, as interpreted by a diverse group of adult citizens in the United States, transcends purely religious or secular frameworks; instead, it emerges as a multidimensional construct informed by spiritual beliefs and common sense, with significant implications for addressing urgent societal challenges.

The Conclusion from the Survey No. 1

The diverse theoretical, social, and health models outlined above provide a structured foundation for understanding how compassion is interpreted across cultural backgrounds. Compassion is not a singular concept confined to religious or secular perspectives, but rather a dynamic construct influenced by moral development, social identity, health beliefs, and cultural frameworks. The interplay between individual agency and societal expectations highlights the evolving nature of compassion, particularly in domains such as healthcare, education, and family dynamics. Future research should further explore how institutional contexts shape the integration of compassion into societal norms, policy-making, and interpersonal relationships.

Cultural Variations in the Meaning of Compassion and Its Impact on Personal Wellbeing

Research

Research indicates that genuine expressions of compassion reduce cortisol levels (the stress hormone) and foster feelings of safety and reassurance (Kirby et al., 2017). In clinical settings, compassionate interactions contribute to lower rates of anxiety and depression, improving emotional regulation and overall psychological stability (Gilbert, 2014).

A meta-analysis of 21 randomised controlled trials represents the first comprehensive review of the effects of compassion-based interventions (Kirby et al., 2017). Findings suggest that these interventions show potential for fostering compassion and self-compassion, alleviating suffering—particularly in relation to depression, anxiety, and psychological distress—and enhancing overall well-being (Kirby et al., 2017). However, the existing evidence largely relies on studies with small sample sizes. A set of recommendations has been proposed to assist evaluators in designing randomised controlled trials (RCTs) to further investigate the efficacy of compassion-based interventions (Kirby et al., 2017). Furthermore, more rigorous evidence syntheses such as component network meta-analyses and umbrella reviews need to be conducted in compassion research.

The Importance of Perceived Compassion in Mental Health

Studies have consistently demonstrated that perceived compassion correlates with improved mental health outcomes. When individuals feel supported, valued, and understood, they develop greater emotional resilience, stronger interpersonal bonds, and an enhanced ability to navigate stress and adversity (Davidson & Harrington,

2002). The presence of compassionate interactions in both professional and personal environments fosters psychological stability, reducing anxiety and depressive symptoms (Kirby et al., 2017). For example, individuals who perceive compassion from therapists, healthcare providers, friends, or family members are significantly more likely to display enhanced emotional regulation and increased trust in their relationships (Gilbert, 2014).

Moreover, perceived compassion has direct physiological effects. Studies in affective neuroscience reveal that compassion-based interactions activate brain regions associated with emotional bonding, reward processing, and stress regulation (Singer & Klimecki, 2014). Receiving compassionate gestures can stimulate the release of oxytocin, a neurochemical associated with social connection and psychological safety (Kirby et al., 2017). This biological mechanism illustrates how compassion functions as a fundamental component of human mental and emotional health.

Perceived Compassion and Social Structures

Perceived compassion refers to the experience of receiving compassion from others. Social structures, including family dynamics, community networks, and institutional frameworks shape this perception. In collectivist societies, perceived compassion is often tied to the support provided by family and community members. For example, in Sri Lanka, compassion is closely linked to social roles and expectations, with individuals often experiencing compassion through collective efforts rather than individual acts (Kariyawasam et al., 2022). This communal approach to compassion reinforces social bonds and fosters a sense of belonging.

In more autonomous societies, perceived compassion may be more closely associated with professional or institutional support. For instance, in healthcare settings in the UK, patients often perceive compassion through the quality of care provided by healthcare professionals, including their attentiveness, empathy, and communication skills (Sinclair et al., 2016). This fact highlights the role of institutional frameworks in shaping the perception of compassion and stresses the importance of professional training in fostering compassionate care.

Cultural Norms and Emotional Expression

Cultural norms play a pivotal role in shaping how compassion is expressed and received. In some cultures, overt displays of compassion may be discouraged, while in others, they are celebrated. For example, in certain Asian cultures, the concept of 'saving face' can impact how compassion is shown (Kotera et al., 2018). Rather than overtly displaying pity or sympathy, compassion may be conveyed through actions aimed at preserving dignity and offering support discreetly (Koopmann-Holm & Tsai, 2017). This subtle approach to compassion reflects a cultural emphasis on maintaining social harmony and avoiding embarrassment. In Western cultures, where emotional expression is often encouraged, compassion may be demonstrated through verbal affirmations, physical gestures, or public acts of kindness. This difference in emotional expression can affect how compassion is perceived and whether it is recognised as genuine or appropriate. For instance, a public display of compassion that is valued in one culture may be seen as intrusive or insincere in another (Koopmann-Holm & Tsai, 2017).

Findings from Our Survey No. 2

The theoretical, social, and health models underpinning perceived compassion and its impact on mental health provide a structured framework for understanding how compassion influences psychological well-being, emotional resilience, and physiological responses.

Theoretical Models

1. *Attachment Theory*: Bowlby's (1969) Attachment Theory explains how early emotional bonds shape interpersonal relationships and psychological resilience. Compassion, particularly when received from trusted individuals such as healthcare providers or family members, reinforces secure attachment, fostering emotional regulation and trust (Mikulincer & Shaver, 2007). The presence of compassionate interactions supports individuals in managing stress and adversity by activating attachment-related mechanisms associated with safety and reassurance.
2. *Self-Determination Theory (SDT)*: Deci and Ryan's (2000) Self-Determination Theory emphasises the psychological needs of autonomy, competence, and relatedness as essential for mental well-being. Perceived compassion enhances relatedness, strengthening social bonds and reinforcing self-worth. The emotional validation that stems from compassionate interactions contributes to greater intrinsic motivation, emotional security, and overall psychological stability (Ryan & Deci, 2017).
3. *Broaden-and-Build Theory of Positive Emotions*: Fredrickson's (2001) Broaden-and-Build Theory posits that positive emotions broaden cognitive and social resources, thereby promoting psychological resilience and well-being. Compassion fosters affective experiences that enhance emotional regulation, reduce distress, and improve interpersonal functioning. Compassion-induced emotional security strengthens problem-solving abilities and social support networks, further reinforcing the adaptive benefits of compassionate interactions.

Social Models

4. *Social Buffering Hypothesis*: This model posits that social support, particularly through compassionate interactions, mitigates stress responses and enhances emotional well-being (Cohen & Wills, 1985). Compassion functions as an affective buffer, mitigating the adverse effects of anxiety and depression while reinforcing psychological stability (Taylor, 2011). Individuals who experience consistent social support through compassionate gestures exhibit lower cortisol levels and increased emotional resilience (Eisenberger et al., 2007).
5. *Social Contagion Theory*: Compassion can be understood within the framework of Social Contagion Theory, which posits that emotions and behaviours spread through social networks (Christakis & Fowler, 2009). Compassionate interactions create positive emotional cycles, reinforcing psychological safety and interpersonal trust. As individuals perceive compassion from therapists, caregivers, or peers, they become more likely to reciprocate compassionate behaviours, strengthening communal bonds and reducing social distress (Hatfield et al., 1994).
6. *Collectivist and Individualist Cultural Models:* Cultural interpretations of compassion vary based on collectivist and individualist orientations. In collectivist societies, compassion is perceived as an obligation tied to social harmony (Triandis, 1995), whereas individualist cultures emphasise personal emotional regulation and relational trust (Markus & Kitayama, 1991). These cultural dimensions shape how individuals perceive and incorporate compassion into their social environments and psychological frameworks.

Health Models

7. *Polyvagal Theory*: Porges' (2007) Polyvagal Theory explains how social engagement and emotional bonding impact the nervous system. Compassion activates the parasympathetic nervous system, promoting emotional stability, stress regulation, and cognitive clarity. The release of oxytocin, stimulated by compassionate interactions, reinforces physiological relaxation, trust, and emotional openness (Kemp et al., 2017).
8. *Stress-Response Theory*: Selye's (1956) Stress-Response Theory suggests that psychological and physiological reactions to stress can be modulated by social support. Compassion functions as a protective factor, reducing sympathetic nervous system activation and mitigating cortisol responses. Compassion-driven emotional security fosters adaptive coping strategies, lowering the physiological burden of chronic stress and depressive symptoms (McEwen, 1998).
9. *Mindfulness-Based Compassion Models*: Emerging research on mindfulness and compassion indicates that practicing self-compassion enhances emotional regulation and psychological resilience (Neff, 2003a, 2003b). Mindfulness-Based Compassion Training enhances cognitive flexibility, interpersonal trust, and

stress tolerance, thereby reinforcing the neurobiological mechanisms associated with mental health stability (Singer & Ricard, 2015).

Results from the Survey No. 2

In our anonymous, cross-sectional, and online survey of 285 adults in the United States conducted in 2025, receiving compassion in the work setting was a component central to job satisfaction. Furthermore, due to the nature of multiethnicity and multidenominational representation within organisational teams, we wanted to explore whether, in this case too, secular ethics or religious ethics influenced how individuals interpreted acts of compassion from others. Although not derived from naturalistic observations, our online survey revealed that 59.95% of respondents reported that their religion or faith could offer guidance on interpreting or applying compassion in the workplace. Furthermore, when considering compassion within their organisational teams, people focus on common sense in 34.39% of cases, a religious interpretation in 30.18% of cases, personal experiences in 24.56%, and company culture in 10.18% of cases. These findings emphasise that within a specific geographical area and in our multi-ethnic society, both religious and secular ethics, as well as diverse cultural heritages, influence people's interpretation and application of compassion in their daily lives.

Regarding the origins of compassion, perspectives varied significantly across religious groups. Christians, Muslims, Jews, and Hindus tended to attribute compassion primarily to religious teachings, reinforcing the idea that spiritual frameworks shape ethical behaviour. In contrast, Buddhists more frequently considered compassion a balance between religious doctrine and common sense. Those identifying with secular or non-religious perspectives overwhelmingly viewed compassion as a product of human reasoning rather than divine instruction.

Responses also differed concerning the representation of compassion in modern media. A notable portion of Christians and Muslims believed compassion was well represented, possibly due to the visibility of charitable initiatives and humanitarian efforts tied to faith-based organisations. However, Buddhists, Hindus, Jews, and respondents from other backgrounds were more likely to argue that compassion needs greater media attention, suggesting a perceived imbalance in how kindness and ethical conduct are portrayed in public discourse.

When evaluating the areas where compassion is most needed, respondents from all faiths widely agreed that healthcare and education should be the highest priorities. However, subtle differences emerged, with Buddhists, Hindus, and Jews giving slightly greater emphasis to community services and family dynamics, reflecting their traditions' focus on interpersonal relationships and social harmony. In contrast, Christians and Muslims showed more concern for politics, indicating that compassion's role in governance and leadership might be particularly relevant in their ethical frameworks.

The question of whether compassion should be explicitly taught in educational curricula also revealed distinctions across religious perspectives. While most respondents supported formal instruction in compassion, Christians, Muslims, and Hindus were more inclined to advocate its inclusion in religious studies, reinforcing the view that faith-based teachings serve as a primary source of moral development. Buddhists and secular respondents, however, were more likely to favour its integration into ethics or philosophy courses, emphasising its broader applicability beyond religious frameworks.

These findings highlight the complex interplay between religious traditions and secular ethical perspectives in shaping interpretations of compassion. While religious teachings provide a structured foundation for altruistic behaviour, secular reasoning and philosophical principles also contribute to shaping compassionate attitudes. The responses suggest a need for a balanced approach that acknowledges both theological and non-theological influences in fostering compassion across diverse social, educational, and policy domains.

The Conclusion of the Survey No. 2

The theoretical, social, and health models outlined above illustrate the multifaceted role of compassion in mental and emotional well-being. Compassion is not simply an individual trait, but a dynamic social and physiological process that shapes stress regulation, interpersonal trust, and psychological resilience. The presence of compassionate interactions in both professional and personal environments enhances emotional security, reduces anxiety and depression, and strengthens relational bonds. Future research should investigate cultural variations in compassion perceptions, the long-term physiological effects of compassion, and effective intervention strategies to integrate compassion into mental health care practices.

Compassion in Multiethnic and Multifaith Cultures

As previously seen, religious frameworks emphasise the ethical responsibility to act compassionately, and the spiritual rewards associated with such actions. The article 'Cultural Shaping of Compassion' by Koopmann-Holm and Tsai (2017) highlights that cultural values significantly impact how compassion is perceived and enacted, with implications for counselling, healthcare, and public service settings. The authors conclude that interventions promoting compassion should consider cultural contexts to be effective (Koopmann-Holm & Tsai, 2017).

Cultural Variations

Research by Kariyawasam et al. (2022) examined cross-cultural differences in compassion between participants from the UK and Sri Lanka. Using a questionnaire-based approach, it explores the facilitators and inhibitors of compassion, including fears of compassion, self-reassurance, external shame, and social safety. Findings reveal that Sri Lankan participants exhibit higher self-compassion and self-reassurance, particularly among Buddhists, but also report greater external shame and fear of compassion. Conversely, UK participants demonstrate higher social safeness, feeling more secure and soothed by societal interactions. This research stresses the importance of considering cultural and social factors when implementing Western compassionate approaches in non-Western settings (Kariyawasam et al., 2022).

This research reflects the cultural value placed on collective responsibility and the importance of social support in promoting well-being (Hofstede, 2001). In Western cultures, compassionate care often focuses on empowering the individual patient by providing personalised care, respecting patient autonomy, and addressing emotional needs (Neff, 2003a, 2003b). Research has shown that patients who perceive compassion from healthcare providers report higher levels of satisfaction, better adherence to treatment plans, and improved health outcomes (Sinclair et al., 2016). This fact highlights the critical role of perceived compassion in enhancing patient experiences and outcomes in a multicultural context. In some contexts, neighbourhood support and assistance are part of a compassionate network where the whole community joins its efforts in assisting who is in need.

Cultural variations significantly influence how compassion is perceived, expressed, and enacted. In collectivist cultures, such as those in East Asia, compassion often emphasises group harmony and collective well-being (Kotera et al., 2024). Acts of compassion are typically directed towards maintaining social cohesion and fulfilling communal responsibilities (Koopmann-Holm et al., 2024). Conversely, in more individually independent cultures, compassion tends to focus on empowering individuals and addressing personal needs. Here, expressions of compassion are often more explicit and centred on validating individual experiences (Chang & Shin, 2021).

In research by Kariyawasam et al. (2022), the authors investigated cross-cultural differences in compassion between UK and Sri Lankan participants, focusing on facilitators and inhibitors such as fears of compassion, self-reassurance, external shame, and social safety. Sri Lankan participants, particularly Buddhists, exhibited higher levels of self-compassion and self-reassurance. However, they also reported greater external pity and fear of compassion, indicating challenges in engaging compassionately with others. In contrast, UK participants demonstrated higher social safeness, feeling more secure and soothed by societal interactions. The findings highlight the significant role of cultural and social factors in shaping experiences of compassion, suggesting the need for culturally tailored approaches when implementing compassionate practices in diverse settings (Kariyawasam et al., 2022).

Despite the benefits of compassion in the personal and interpersonal spheres, barriers to perceived compassion exist in various cultural and social contexts. Cultural norms, personal biases, and systemic factors can hinder the expression and perception of compassion. For instance, stigma surrounding mental health issues may prevent individuals from seeking or recognising compassionate support (Bracke et al., 2019). This stigma can create barriers to accessing care and exacerbate feelings of isolation and distress. Additionally, the operationalisation of cultural competency in daily mental health practice can improve how compassion is perceived across diverse populations (Mollah et al., 2018).

Using and interpreting compassion in culturally diversified settings is a complex process influenced by various social, philosophical, and ethical frameworks. Compassion is universally recognised as the ability to empathise with others and respond with kindness in the face of suffering. However, its expression and interpretation differ across cultures, shaping interpersonal relationships and psychological well-being (Singer & Klimecki, 2014). Cultural frameworks for understanding compassion vary widely. Collectivist societies, such as those in East Asia, Latin America, and Africa, emphasise interdependence and duty-based kindness, where compassionate acts are integrated into social obligations (Hofstede, 2001). In contrast, individualist societies, including those in North America and Western Europe, prioritise personal autonomy, framing compassion as an intrinsic, voluntary action. Religious and spiritual beliefs also guide the perception of compassion. In Buddhist traditions, *karuṇā* represents ethical living (Dalai Lama & Ekman, 2008), while Christian teachings frame compassion as an extension of divine mercy. Secular ethical perspectives, on the other hand, define compassion through principles of justice, equality, and human dignity (Nussbaum, 2001). Despite its universality, *challenges in cross-cultural compassion* arise from differing emotional expressions, expectations of reciprocity, and hierarchical social structures. Some cultures value emotional restraint, perceiving it as a sign of strength, while others openly express compassion through words or physical touch (Singer & Klimecki, 2014). Additionally, varying expectations regarding whether compassion should be reciprocated can create misunderstandings. Societal hierarchies further shape compassionate interactions, as deference and respect may influence how individuals receive and interpret compassion (Hofstede, 2001).

To navigate compassion in multicultural settings, individuals and organisations must foster cultural awareness, inclusive communication, and adaptable compassionate practices. Developing an understanding of cultural norms enhances empathy, ensuring that compassion is interpreted as intended rather than misinterpreted (Nussbaum, 2001). Flexibility in compassionate behaviours based on context strengthens intercultural relationships, while open ethical dialogue can broaden perspectives on kindness and altruism (Dalai Lama & Ekman, 2008).

Compassion remains an essential factor in human relationships across cultures. Recognising and adapting to cultural differences in compassionate practices contribute to the development of inclusive communities, fostering emotional well-being and social harmony (Singer & Klimecki, 2014). Sensitivity and openness to diverse interpretations of compassion enable meaningful human connections, bridging gaps between cultural perspectives.

Research by Mollah et al. (2018) addresses gaps in understanding culturally competent mental healthcare, particularly in what frontline practitioners consider culturally competent care and the factors that help or hinder its delivery. Authors findings reveal that while cultural competence is generally understood, its application varies depending on the profession, health setting, locality, and experience (Mollah et al., 2018). For example, urban psychiatrists were more functional and authoritarian in their communication compared to allied health staff in rural, non-specialist settings who had less experience. The operationalisation of cultural competence was influenced by practitioners' own cultural backgrounds and exposures, creating diverse approaches to building cultural concordance with patients (Mollah et al., 2018). Addressing these barriers requires not only awareness of systemic challenges but also targeted efforts to shift cultural stigma and improve access to compassionate care (Chumber, 2025).

Multicultural research on compassion suggests that self-compassion is conceptualised differently depending on cultural values and social contexts, aligning with the idea that collective mental programming through socialisation influences thoughts, feelings, and behaviours (Montero-Marin et al., 2018). This research highlights that the positive items of the Self-Compassion Scale (SCS) are more significant than the negative items in defining self-compassion, indicating that measuring attitudes and behaviours in positive terms better captures the construct. However, the prominence of these positive or negative items may vary based on cultural influences, such as long-term orientation and individualism (Montero-Marin et al., 2018). The research also notes that the relationship between SCS traits, and their role in forming a broader self-compassion construct, is shaped by cultural dimensions like indulgence versus restraint. The findings stress the importance of refining and contextualising the concept of self-compassion to effectively address suffering across different cultural settings (Montero-Marin et al., 2018). Among UK university students, the six-factor model was not replicated; instead, an element relevant to self-inadequacy was identified across the negative components of self-compassion (Kotera & Sheffield, 2020).

Findings from Our Survey No. 3

Theoretical Frameworks

The theoretical framework underpinning this research and its outcomes draws from multiple perspectives, including Altruism Theory, Social Learning Theory, and the Structural Functionalist Model, which together help explain the barriers and manifestations of compassion in daily life.

1. *Altruism Theory:* Altruism Theory, particularly Batson's (1991) Empathy-Altruism Hypothesis, argues that compassionate behaviour arises from genuine concern for others rather than self-interest. However, our respondents (in our

survey) who expressed cynicism about compassion as 'self-promotion' align with critiques suggesting that some acts of altruism may be motivated by social recognition rather than pure empathy (Cialdini et al., 1987). This dichotomy between intrinsic and extrinsic compassion informs our research's findings, indicating varying perceptions of what drives compassionate behaviour.

2. *Social Learning Theory:* Bandura's (1977) Social Learning Theory provides further insight into how individuals develop compassionate behaviours. According to this theory, compassionate acts are reinforced through observation, social modelling, and media influence. Many respondents in our research pointed to media as a factor shaping societal divisions, reinforcing the idea that exposure to compassionate role models—or, conversely, negative messaging—can influence one's willingness to practice altruism. Positive reinforcement of compassion, as demonstrated in participants' personal experiences of witnessing kindness, highlights the role of social environment and learned behaviour in fostering compassion.
3. *Structural Functionalist Model:* Parsons' (1951) Structural Functionalist Model explains how compassion contributes to societal stability by reinforcing cohesion and collective moral values. Acts of kindness, such as helping vulnerable individuals, strengthen social bonds and contribute to a functional society. However, barriers such as a lack of volunteering and societal cynicism highlight the challenges in maintaining compassion as an integral social norm. The data from our research on the frequency of compassion suggest that while many individuals encounter it regularly, others seldom experience or practice it, pointing to disparities in its societal distribution.

Results from the Survey No. 3

Our survey, involving 235 adults from diverse ethnic and religious backgrounds across the United States, explored barriers to practising compassion in daily life. Responses varied widely, with some participants expressing cynicism, stating that 'most compassion is self-promotion,' while others identified a lack of volunteering as a hindrance. The influence of the media was also highlighted, with one respondent commenting, 'Fake news spreads hatred and division.' When asked to describe acts of compassion they had performed, the examples were vivid and impactful. Instances included helping elderly ladies change a tyre, witnessing someone bring clothes and food to a homeless person, and a neighbour assisting with shovelling out a car stuck in the snow. Participants also recounted witnessing compassion, such as sponsoring a Ukrainian family during the war at great personal cost, with friends, family, and strangers helping the family settle and thrive. Everyday acts of kindness, like aiding homeless individuals, supporting unemployed parents, and working with developmentally disabled children, were also frequently mentioned. Our research suggests that compassion is deeply intertwined with daily life and societal progress, serving as a powerful force for meaning and connection. Participants reported encountering acts of compassion 'rarely' 44.65%, 'very often' 34.28% of the time; 'occasionally', 19.50%; and 'never' 1.57% of the time. The frequency at which individuals reported experiencing compassion further emphasises its magnitude across varying contexts.

Conclusion from the Survey No. 3

The outcomes of our survey, alongside the foundational and extractable theoretical frameworks, position compassion within both individual psychological mechanisms and broader societal structures. This demonstrates how observational learning, altruistic intent, and social functionality influence perceptions and practices of compassion. The results suggest that compassion constitutes a deeply embedded social process influenced by media representation, interpersonal relationships, and structural opportunities for engagement. Future research ought to examine how systemic inequalities and cultural norms impact compassion's role in social cohesion and human well-being.

The Role of Compassion in Organisational Life, Team Building, and Job Satisfaction

We now explore the multifaceted role of compassion in organisational life, focusing on its impact on team building and job satisfaction (Lazzari, 2004). Drawing on academic literature and real-world examples, we discuss how compassion fosters a positive organisational culture, enhances team dynamics, and contributes to overall job satisfaction (Lazzari, 2004; Lazzari, Costley & Nikolou-Walker, 2024).

Compassion in Organisational Life

Compassion in organisational life refers to the ability of individuals and groups within an organisation to notice, feel, and respond to the suffering of others. According to Kanov et al. (2004a, 2004b), organisational compassion involves collective processes where members of a system acknowledge and address the pain and distress experienced by others. This collective approach is essential for creating a supportive work environment that prioritises employee's well-being.

Organisational compassion is not merely an ethical ideal but a practical necessity. It mitigates the prevalence and costs of workplace stress, burnout, and disengagement. For instance, during the COVID-19 pandemic, organisations that demonstrated compassion through flexible work arrangements and mental health support witnessed higher levels of employee loyalty and productivity (Kanov et al., 2004a, 2004b).

Compassionate practices, such as recognising employees' challenges and providing timely support, create a culture of trust and mutual respect (Lazzari et al., 2024).

Compassion and Team Building

Team building is a critical aspect of organisational success, and compassion plays a pivotal role in fostering strong team dynamics. Compassionate leadership, characterised by empathy and understanding, sets the tone for collaborative and inclusive team environments. Leaders who exhibit compassion inspire their teams to work cohesively, resolve conflicts amicably, and achieve common goals (Lazzari et al., 2024). Miralles et al. (2024) explore the interplay between compassion, mindfulness, and servant leadership in organisational settings and found that compassion, as a response to suffering, is shown to elevate mindfulness levels, contributing to a positive work environment. Compassion also enhances psychological safety within teams. When team members feel safe to express their concerns and vulnerabilities, they are more likely to engage in open communication and collaborative problem-solving (Lazzari et al., 2024). This sense of safety is vital in diverse teams, where differences in perspectives and experiences can lead to misunderstandings. Compassionate practices, such as active listening and inclusive decision-making, bridge these gaps and strengthen team cohesion (Lazzari et al., 2024).

Role of Spiritual Training in Nursing Compassion

A study by Birimoglu Okuyan et al. (2024) examined the relationship between nursing students' religious attitudes, levels of compassion, and perceptions of spiritual care. It found a positive correlation among these factors, influenced by students' socio-demographic characteristics, professional satisfaction, and exposure to spiritual care training. Female students demonstrated higher scores in compassion and sharing, while students dissatisfied with the nursing profession scored higher in laxness and disengagement (Birimoglu Okuyan et al., 2024). Most students emphasised the importance of addressing patients' spiritual needs, although many lacked formal training in spiritual care, with a significant number expressing a desire for such education. Spiritual care training was shown to enhance students' compassion and perceptions of caregiving (Birimoglu Okuyan et al., 2024). The findings suggest that integrating spiritual care into nursing education may better prepare students for holistic patient care and enhance their levels of compassion. Despite moderate levels of spiritual care perception, students exhibited positive attitudes towards spiritual care, indicating potential for growth through targeted training. The research stresses the importance of fostering compassion and spiritual awareness in nursing to ensure professional and empathetic care, providing a valuable foundation for curriculum development and clinical interventions (Birimoglu Okuyan et al., 2024).

Furthermore, *spiritual counselling skills* in the helping professions teach how to promote reciprocal compassion –often focusing on spiritual needs of clients–, especially with patients enduring severe illnesses (Lazzari, 2009). Focusing on the process of seeking meaning in extreme and terminal illnesses, spiritual counsellors and their patients concentrate on intense compassionate relationships in the here-and-now, where compassion is communicated verbally (through compassionate words), non-verbally (through compassionate acts), and para-verbally (through tone of voice, gentle touch, and paced communication) (Lazzari, 2009).

Compassion and Job Satisfaction

Job satisfaction is a key determinant of employee performance and organisational success. Compassion significantly contributes to job satisfaction by addressing employees' emotional and psychological needs. According to Lilius et al. (2003), compassion in the workplace involves an empathetic response to others' pain or suffering, leading to actions that alleviate their distress. This empathetic approach fosters a sense of belonging and appreciation among employees.

Compassionate organisations prioritise employee well-being through initiatives such as mental health programmes, flexible work policies, and recognition of individual contributions. These initiatives not only enhance job satisfaction but also reduce turnover rates and absenteeism. For instance, research by Barghouti et al. (2023) examines the impact of compassion and altruism on organisational performance, using organisational resilience as a mediating factor. It highlights a paradigm shift in management, moving from self-centred to interconnected approaches, where employees are motivated by values like altruism. The research, conducted on innovative companies, reveals that compassion fosters a climate of altruism, enhancing resilience and enabling organisations to turn challenges into growth opportunities. This resilience indirectly boosts performance, offering a humanistic perspective on management (Barghouti et al., 2023).

Challenges and Opportunities

While the benefits of compassion in organisational life are well-documented, its implementation is not without challenges. Organisational cultures that prioritise competition and individual achievement may resist compassionate practices (Barghouti et al., 2023). Additionally, leaders may struggle to balance compassion with accountability, fearing that excessive leniency could undermine performance standards (McAllum et al., 2023).

However, these challenges present opportunities for growth and innovation. Organisations can overcome resistance by integrating compassion into their core values and practices (Barghouti et al., 2023). Training programmes that develop emotional intelligence and compassionate leadership skills can equip leaders to navigate the complexities of organisational life (Akgün et al., 2025). Furthermore, organisations can leverage technology to promote compassion, such as using digital platforms to provide mental health support and facilitate remote collaboration (McAllum et al., 2023).

Findings from Our Survey No. 4

Theoretical Frameworks

The theoretical frameworks underpinning this research are informed by Organisational Compassion Theory, Social Exchange Theory, and the Transformational Leadership Model, which provide a structured explanation for the role of compassion in professional environments.

1. *Organisational Compassion Theory*: Dutton et al. (2006) proposed Organisational Compassion Theory, which suggests that workplaces fostering compassion create stronger interpersonal connections and increase employee well-being. Compassion within organisational structures supports psychological safety, emotional resilience, and collaboration, particularly in team relationships and crises (Lilius et al., 2011). The high percentage of respondents in our research who consider compassion essential in team building aligns with the principle that compassionate organisations cultivate trust and positive social interactions, which lead to higher morale and collective support (see Kanov et al., 2004a, 2004b).
2. *Social Exchange Theory:* Blau's (1964) Social Exchange Theory elucidates how reciprocal interactions contribute to the development of workplace relationships. Employees who perceive compassion as an integral component of their work environment are likely to establish more substantial commitments to their teams, thereby enhancing cooperation and mutual support. The findings of our research suggest that compassionate exchanges among colleagues enhance team effectiveness and emotional well-being, thereby strengthening professional bonds and fostering workplace generosity (see Cropanzano & Mitchell, 2005). Conversely, the reported variability in organisational compassion during times of crisis underlines the inconsistencies inherent in reciprocal support dynamics, suggesting that the perception of workplace compassion may not be universally applicable across different organisations.
3. *Transformational Leadership Model:* Bass and Riggio (2006) delineated Transformational Leadership Theory, which asserts that leaders who exhibit empathy and emotional intelligence cultivate a more engaged and motivated workforce. Responses affirm the significance of compassion as a leadership attribute, with employees anticipating compassionate treatment in professional environments, particularly during complex or high-stress situations (Goleman, 2013). Leaders

who prioritise compassion foster inclusive workplaces, whereas the absence of compassionate responses reported by certain participants indicates that specific organisations fail to incorporate emotional intelligence into their leadership practices (Brown & Treviño, 2006).

Results from the Survey No. 4

In another survey of 274 adults in the United States that we conducted in 2025, we asked the adult population currently employed how important compassion was in their organisations. Respondents reported feeling that compassion was important in team relationships: 59.85% felt it was 'very important' and 32.12% 'Important'. When asked about moments of crisis or complex situations, respondents reported on how often their organisation treated them with compassion Forty-one per cent indicated 'Always' 23.72%, 'Often' 26.28%, 'sometimes' 7.30% and 'rarely' 1.46% 'never'. When we asked if they thought that compassion should be considered a key skill in team building, 53.65% 'Strongly agreed', 35.40% 'Agreed', while 10.22% felt 'Neutral'. When asked to define how compassion was interpreted in the context of interprofessional teams in organisations and via open-ended questions, participants responded, 'Seeking knowledge of another to help them excel', or 'emotional support' or 'concern for one another'. Another participant commented: 'Compassion is a great theological term, and since I am a Catholic Priest, I truly appreciate compassion. I am not sure that it really applies in secular groups—it would be mocked by the workerists.'

Conclusion of the Survey No. 4

The findings suggest that compassion plays a crucial role in organisational culture, fostering trust, team cohesion, and effective leadership. Employees who experience compassionate workplaces demonstrate higher levels of engagement, well-being, and resilience, whereas a lack of compassion in leadership structures fosters an emotional disconnect and workplace dissatisfaction. Future research should investigate how cultural differences, industry-specific expectations, and leadership styles affect perceptions of compassion in professional environments.

Conclusion

Social and cultural contexts profoundly shape the meanings of compassion, particularly regarding its perceived or received forms. These contexts influence the expression, understanding, and experience of compassion, as well as the expectations and norms that govern compassionate interactions. Our research findings indicate that perceptions of compassion from others, alongside its meanings, can be influenced by the social and cultural contexts in which individuals exist. Concurrently, acts of compassion towards others impart significance to individuals in their daily lives and across diverse cultures. Furthermore, compassion has been observed to positively impact personal well-being, especially when individuals are willing to cultivate compassion, receptive to compassion from others, and leverage this perception to enhance their resilience and overall outlook on life.

In conclusion, compassion represents a fundamental element that significantly influences individual well-being, social dynamics, and workplace environments across multicultural and multifaith contexts. This chapter has illuminated the multifaceted nature of compassion, demonstrating how cultural, religious, and social frameworks shape its perception and expression. The findings highlight the positive impact of compassion on mental health, emotional resilience, and interpersonal relationships, while also acknowledging the barriers that may impede its acceptance and practice. Our systematic reviews and theoretical frameworks emphasise the importance of understanding compassion within its sociocultural context, highlighting how acceptance or fear of compassion can impact psychological well-being. Furthermore, this document advocates for the development of standardised methodologies to measure compassion effectively, distinguishing it from empathy and integrating it into health, psychological, and professional domains. As societies continue to navigate diverse cultural landscapes, fostering compassion can lead to enhanced social cohesion, ethical leadership, and overall community well-being. Future research should concentrate on exploring the neurological basis of compassion, its long-term effects on mental health, and the implications of cultural variations in its interpretation. By embracing compassion as a transformative force, individuals and organisations can cultivate environments that promote trust, cooperation, and resilience, ultimately contributing to a more supportive and harmonious society.

Author Contributions Conceptualisation: CL; Investigation: CL; Resources: YK; Writing—original draft: CL; Writing—review & editing: CL, YK; Project administration: CL.

References

Adler, N. E., & Stewart, J. (2010). Health disparities across the lifespan: Meaning, methods, and mechanisms. *Annals of the New York Academy of Sciences, 1186*(1), 5–23. https://doi.org/10.1111/j.1749-6632.2009.05337.x

Akgün, A. E., Keskin, H., & Başaran, H. T. E. (2025). Organizational compassion: A conceptual extension and scale development. *Current Psychology*. https://doi.org/10.1007/s12144-025-07442-6

Antonovsky, A. (1996). The salutogenic model as a theory to guide health promotion. *Health Promotion International, 11*(1), 11–18. https://doi.org/10.1093/heapro/11.1.11

Ashfaq, M., Iqbal, A., & Hussain, S. (2024). Locating Islamic concept of mercy (*al-Raḥmah*) vis-à-vis the doctrine of salvation (*Soteriology*): A qualitative review. *ResearchGate*. https://www.researchgate.net/publication/379150670_Locating_Islamic_Concept_of_Mercy_al-Rahmah_vis-a-vis_the_Doctrine_of_Salvation_Soteriology_A_Qualitative_Review

Babaei, S., & Taleghani, F. (2019). Compassionate care challenges and barriers in clinical nurses: A qualitative research. *Iranian Journal of Nursing and Midwifery Research, 24*(3), 213–219. https://doi.org/10.4103/ijnmr.IJNMR_100_18

Bandura, A. (1977). Self-efficacy: Toward a unifying theory of behavioral change. *Psychological Review, 84*(2), 191–215. https://doi.org/10.1037/0033-295X.84.2.191

Bandura, A. (1986). *Social foundations of thought and action: A social cognitive theory*. Prentice-Hall.

Barghouti, Z., Guinot, J., & Chiva, R. (2023). Compassion and altruism in organizations: A path for firm survival. *International Journal of Manpower, 44*(9), 1–19. https://doi.org/10.1108/ijm-05-2021-0266

Barnard, L., & Curry, J. F. (2011). Self-compassion: Conceptualizations, correlates, & interventions. *Review of General Psychology, 15*(4), 289–303. https://self-compassion.org/wp-content/uploads/publications/barnard.review.pdf

Bass, B. M., & Riggio, R. E. (2006). *Transformational leadership*. Lawrence Erlbaum Associates.

Batson, C. D. (1991). *The altruism question: Toward a social psychological answer*. Lawrence Erlbaum Associates.

Batson, C. D. (2011). *Altruism in humans*. Oxford University Press.

Becker, M. H. (1974). The health belief model and personal health behavior. *Health Education Monographs, 2*(4), 324–473. https://doi.org/10.1177/109019817400200407

Birimoglu Okuyan, C., Akgul, E., & Gurcay, B. (2024). The relationship between religious attitude, compassion and spiritual care in nursing students: The case of Türkiye. *Journal of Religion and Health, 63*(3), 1802–1817. https://doi.org/10.1007/s10943-023-01969-3

Blau, P. M. (1964). *Exchange and power in social life*. Wiley.

Bowlby, J. (1969). *Attachment and loss: Volume 1. Attachment*. Basic Books.

Bracke, P., Delaruelle, K., & Verhaeghe, M. (2019). Dominant cultural and personal stigma beliefs and the utilization of mental health services: A cross-national comparison. *Frontiers in Sociology, 4*. https://doi.org/10.3389/fsoc.2019.00040

Braveman, P., & Gottlieb, L. (2014). The social determinants of health: It is time to consider the causes of the causes. *Public Health Reports, 129*(Suppl 2), 19–31. https://doi.org/10.1177/00333549141291s206

Breen, J., & Teeuwen, M. (2010). *A new history of Shinto*. Wiley-Blackwell.

Bronfenbrenner, U. (1979). *The ecology of human development: Experiments by nature and design*. Harvard University Press.

Brown, M. E., & Treviño, L. K. (2006). Ethical leadership: A review and future directions. *The Leadership Quarterly, 17*(6), 595–616. https://doi.org/10.1016/j.leaqua.2006.10.004

Cacioppo, J. T., & Patrick, W. (2008). *Loneliness: Human nature and the need for social connection*. W.W. Norton & Company.

Cambridge Dictionary. (2025). *Compassion*. (2025). https://dictionary.cambridge.org/dictionary/english/compassion

Carvalho, S. A., Matos, M., Ferreira, N., & Graham, C. D. (2024). Contextual-behavioral approaches to improving well-being and mental health in chronic physical illness. *Frontiers in Psychology, 15*, Article 1497106. https://doi.org/10.3389/fpsyg.2024.1497106

Chan, K. K. S., Lee, J. C. K., Yu, E. K. W., Chan, A. W. Y., Leung, A. N. M., Cheung, R. Y. M., et al. (2022). The impact of compassion from others and self-compassion on psychological distress, flourishing, and meaning in life among university students. *Mindfulness, 13*, 1490–1498. https://doi.org/10.1007/s12671-022-01891-x

Chang, J.-J., & Shin, S.-H. (2021). A path model for burnout in community mental health professionals. *International Journal of Environmental Research and Public Health, 18*(18), 9763. https://doi.org/10.3390/ijerph18189763

Chierchia, G., & Singer, T. (2016). The neuroscience of compassion and empathy and their link to prosocial motivation and behavior. In *Elsevier eBooks* (pp. 247–257). https://doi.org/10.1016/b978-0-12-805308-9.00020-8

Christakis, N. A., & Fowler, J. H. (2009). *Connected: The surprising power of our social networks and how they shape our lives.* Little, Brown.

Chumber, H. (2025). Stigma in mental health care: A catalyst for change. *The Psychologist*. https://www.bps.org.uk/psychologist/stigma-mental-health-care-catalyst-change

Cialdini, R. B., Brown, S. L., Lewis, B. P., Luce, C., & Neuberg, S. L. (1987). Reinterpreting the empathy–altruism relationship: When one into one equals oneness. *Journal of Personality and Social Psychology, 52*(4), 749–758. https://doi.org/10.1037/0022-3514.52.4.749

Cobb, S. (1976). Social support as a moderator of life stress. *Psychosomatic Medicine, 38*(5), 300–314. https://doi.org/10.1097/00006842-197609000-00003

Cohen, S., & Wills, T. A. (1985). Stress, social support, and the buffering hypothesis. *Psychological Bulletin, 98*(2), 310–357. https://doi.org/10.1037/0033-2909.98.2.310

Cropanzano, R., & Mitchell, M. S. (2005). Social exchange theory: An interdisciplinary review. *Journal of Management, 31*(6), 874–900. https://doi.org/10.1177/0149206305279602

D'Amico, L. (2018). Empathy and compassion in the health-related literature: Disciplinary and topic trends and gaps. *Journal of Compassionate Health Care, 5*(1). https://doi.org/10.1186/s40639-018-0049-3

Dalai Lama. (1995). *The power of compassion: A collection of lectures.* HarperOne.

Dalai Lama, & Ekman, P. (2008). *Emotional awareness: Overcoming the obstacles to psychological balance and compassion.* Henry Holt and Co.

Davidson, R., & Harrington, A. (2002). *Visions of compassion: Western scientists and Tibetan Buddhists examine human nature.* Oxford University Press.

Davis, M. H. (2017). *Empathy, compassion, and social relationships.* Oxford University Press eBooks. https://doi.org/10.1093/oxfordhb/9780190464684.013.23

Deci, E. L., & Ryan, R. M. (2000). The 'what' and 'why' of goal pursuits: Human needs and the self-determination of behavior. *Psychological Inquiry, 11*(4), 227–268. https://doi.org/10.1207/S15327965PLI1104_01

Di Bello, M., Carnevali, L., Petrocchi, N., Thayer, J. F., Gilbert, P., & Ottaviani, C. (2020). The compassionate vagus: A meta-analysis on the connection between compassion and heart rate variability. *Neuroscience & Biobehavioral Reviews, 116*, 21–30. https://doi.org/10.1016/j.neubiorev.2020.06.016

Durlak, J. A., Weissberg, R. P., Dymnicki, A. B., Taylor, R. D., & Schellinger, K. B. (2011). The impact of enhancing students' social and emotional learning: A meta-analysis of school-based universal interventions. *Child Development, 82*(1), 405–432.

Dutton, J. E., Worline, M. C., Frost, P. J., & Lilius, J. M. (2006). Explaining compassion organizing. *Administrative Science Quarterly, 51*(1), 59–96. https://doi.org/10.2189/asqu.51.1.59

Eisenberger, N. I., Lieberman, M. D., & Williams, K. D. (2007). Does rejection hurt? An fMRI research of social exclusion. *Science, 302*(5643), 290–292. https://doi.org/10.1126/science.1089134

Engel, G. L. (1977). The need for a new medical model: A challenge to biomedicine. *Science, 196*(4286), 129–136. https://doi.org/10.1126/science.847460

Epstein, R. M., & Street, R. L. (2011). The values and value of patient-centred care. *Annals of Family Medicine, 9*(2), 100–103. https://doi.org/10.1370/afm.1239

Esposito, J. L. (2002). *What everyone needs to know about Islam* (2nd ed.). Oxford University Press.

Felmlee, D. H., & Sinclair, H. C. (2018). *Social networks and personal relationships.* Cambridge University Press eBooks (pp. 467–480). https://doi.org/10.1017/9781316417867.036

Fredrickson, B. L. (2001). The role of positive emotions in positive psychology. *American Psychologist, 56*(3), 218–226. https://doi.org/10.1037/0003-066X.56.3.218

Germer, C. K., & Neff, K. D. (2013). Self-compassion in clinical practice. *Journal of Clinical Psychology, 69*(8), 856–867. https://doi.org/10.1002/jclp.22021

Giddens, A. (1984). *The constitution of society: Outline of the theory of structuration.* University of California Press.

Gilbert, P. (2009a). Introducing compassion-focused therapy. *Advances in Psychiatric Treatment, 15*(3), 199–208. https://doi.org/10.1192/apt.bp.107.005264

Gilbert, P. (2009b). *The compassionate mind: A new approach to life's challenges.* New Harbinger Publications.

Gilbert, 2010a Gilbert, P. (2010). Compassion focused therapy. In *Routledge eBooks.* https://doi.org/10.4324/9780203851197

Gilbert, P. (2010). *Compassion focused therapy: Distinctive features.* Routledge.

Gilbert, P. (2011). *Shame in psychotherapy and the role of compassion focused therapy* (pp. 325–354). American Psychological Association eBooks. https://doi.org/10.1037/12326-014

Gilbert, P. (2014). The origins and nature of compassion focused therapy. *British Journal of Clinical Psychology, 53*(1), 6–41. https://doi.org/10.1111/bjc.12043

Gilbert, P. (2017). *Compassion: Concepts, research and applications.* Routledge.

Gilbert, P. (2019). Explorations into the nature and function of compassion. *Current Opinion in Psychology, 28,* 108–113. https://doi.org/10.1016/j.copsyc.2018.12.002

Gilbert, P., Catarino, F., Duarte, C., Matos, M., Kolts, R., Stubbs, J., Ceresatto, L., Duarte, J., Pinto-Gouveia, J., & Basran, J. (2017). The development of compassionate engagement and action scales for self and others. *Journal of Compassionate Health Care, 4*(1). https://doi.org/10.1186/s40639-017-0033-3

Goetz, J. L., Keltner, D., & Simon-Thomas, E. (2010). Compassion: An evolutionary analysis and empirical review. *Psychological Bulletin, 136*(3), 351–374. Available at: https://doi.org/10.1037/a0018807

Goleman, D. (2013). *Emotional intelligence: Why it can matter more than IQ.* Bantam.

Hermanto, N., Zuroff, D. C., Kopala-Sibley, D. C., Kelly, A. C., Matos, M., Gilbert, P., & Koestner, R. (2016). Ability to receive compassion from others buffers the depressogenic effect of self-criticism: A cross-cultural multi-research analysis. *Personality and Individual Differences, 98,* 324–332. https://doi.org/10.1016/j.paid.2016.04.055

Hofstede, G. (2001). *Culture's consequences: Comparing values, behaviors, institutions, and organizations across nations.* Sage.

House, J. S. (1981). *Work stress and social support.* Addison-Wesley.

Hsieh, C.-C., Yu, C.-Y., Chen, H.-J., Chen, Y.-W., Chang, N.-T., & Fei-Hsiu Hsiao, F.-H. (2019). Dispositional mindfulness, self-compassion, and compassion from others as moderators between stress and depression in caregivers of patients with lung cancer. *Psycho-Oncology, 28*(7), 1498–1505. https://doi.org/10.1002/pon.5106

Immordino-Yang, M. H. (2016). *Emotions, learning, and the brain: Exploring the educational implications of affective neuroscience.* Norton.

Jacobsen, K. H. (2021). *Introduction to global health.* Jones & Bartlett Learning.

Kanov, J. M., Maitlis, S., Worline, M. C., Dutton, J. E., Frost, P. J., & Lilius, J. M. (2004a). Compassion in organizational life. *American Behavioral Scientist, 47*(6), 808–827. https://doi.org/10.1177/0002764203260211

Kanov, J. M., Maitlis, S., Worline, M. C., Dutton, J. E., Frost, P. J., & Lilius, J. M. (2004b). Compassion in organizational life. *American Behavioral Scientist, 47*(6), 808–827.

Kariyawasam, L., Ononaiye, M., Irons, C., & Kirby, S. E. (2022). A cross-cultural exploration of compassion, and facilitators and inhibitors of compassion in UK and Sri Lankan people. *Cambridge Prisms: Global Mental Health, 9,* 99–110. https://doi.org/10.1017/gmh.2022.10

Kemp, A. H., Arias, J. A., & Fisher, Z. (2017). Social environment and the nervous system. *Frontiers in Psychology, 8,* 1641. https://doi.org/10.3389/fpsyg.2017.01641

Keown, D. (2005). *Buddhism: A very short introduction.* Oxford University Press.

Kirby, J. N., Tellegen, C. L., & Steindl, S. R. (2017). A meta-analysis of compassion-based interventions: Current state of knowledge and future directions. *Behavior Therapy, 48*(6), 778–792. https://doi.org/10.1016/j.beth.2017.06.003

Kohlberg, L. (1981). *The philosophy of moral development: Moral stages and the idea of justice.* Harper & Row.

Koopmann-Holm, B., & Tsai, J. L. (2017). The cultural shaping of compassion. In S. M. Brown & M. R. Brown (Eds.), *The Oxford handbook of compassion science* (pp. 273–286). Oxford University Press.

Koopmann-Holm, B., Beccari, A., & Oosthuizen, M. (2024). Individual and cultural differences in compassion, noticing suffering, and well-being: Consequences of wanting to avoid feeling negative. *Social and Personality Psychology Compass, 18*(9). https://doi.org/10.1111/spc3.70000

Kotera, Y., & Sheffield, D. (2020). Revisiting the self-compassion scale-short form: Stronger associations with self-inadequacy and resilience. *SN Comprehensive Clinical Medicine, 2*(6), 761–769. https://doi.org/10.1007/s42399-020-00309-w

Kotera, Y., & Van Gordon, W. (2021). Effects of self-compassion training on work-related well-being: A systematic review. *Frontiers in Psychology, 12.* https://doi.org/10.3389/fpsyg.2021.630798

Kotera, Y., Gilbert, P., Asano, K., Ishimura, I., & Sheffield, D. (2018). Self-criticism and self-reassurance as mediators between mental health attitudes and symptoms: Attitudes towards mental health problems in Japanese workers. *Asian Journal of Social Psychology, 22*(2), 183–192. https://doi.org/10.1111/ajsp.12355

Kotera, Y., Lieu, J., Kirkman, A., Barnes, K., Liu, G. H. T., Jackson, J., Wilkes, J., & Riswani, R. (2022a). Mental wellbeing of Indonesian students: Mean comparison with UK students and relationships with self-compassion and academic engagement. *Healthcare, 10*(8), 1439. https://doi.org/10.3390/healthcare10081439

Kotera, Y., Mayer, C., & Vanderheiden, E. (2023a). Self-compassion, mental health shame, and work motivation in German and Japanese employees. *International Review of Psychiatry, 35*(1), 113–124. https://doi.org/10.1080/09540261.2022.2148829

Kotera, Y., Ozaki, A., Miyatake, H., Tsunetoshi, C., Nishikawa, Y., Kosaka, M., & Tanimoto, T. (2022b). Qualitative investigation into the mental health of healthcare workers in Japan during the COVID-19 pandemic. *International Journal of Environmental Research and Public Health, 19*(1), 568. https://doi.org/10.3390/ijerph19010568

Kotera, Y., Ronaldson, A., Hayes, D., Hunter-Brown, H., McPhilbin, M., Dunnett, D., Jebara, T., Takhi, S., Masuda, T., Camacho, E., Bakolis, I., Repper, J., Meddings, S., Stergiopoulos, V., Brophy, L., De Ruysscher, C., Okoliyski, M., Kubinová, P., Eplov, L., Toernes, C., Narusson, D., Tinland, A., Puschner, B., Hiltensperger, R., Lucchi, F., Miyamoto, Y., Castelein, S., Borg, M., T, G., Meng, R., Sornchai, C., Tiengtom, K., Farkas, M., Moreland, H., Moore, E., Butler, A., Mpango, R., Tse, S., Kondor, Z., Ryan, M., Zuaboni, G., Elton, D., Grant-Rowles, J., McNaughton, R., Hanlon, C., Harcla, C., Vanderplasschen, W., Arbour, S., Silverstone, D., Bejerholm, U., Ling, C., Ochoa, S., Garcia-Franco, M., Tolonen, J., Yeo, C., Charles, A., Henderson, C., & Slade, M. (2024). How culture impacts recovery intervention: 28-country global research on associations between cultural characteristics and Recovery College fidelity. *npj Mental Health Research.* https://doi.org/10.1038/s44184-024-00092-9

Kotera, Y., Taylor, E., Brooks-Ucheaga, M., & Edwards, A. M. (2023). Need for a tool to inform cultural adaptation in mental health interventions. *International Society for the Research of Behavioural Development Bulletin.* https://issbd.org/wp-content/uploads/2023/06/JBD_47_3S_Combined-pdf.pdf

Lavelle, B. D. (2017). Compassion in context: Tracing the Buddhist roots of secular, compassion-based contemplative programs. In *The Oxford handbook of compassion science* (pp. 17–26).

Lazzari, C., & Masiello, I. (2016). Communication neurosciences for interprofessional teams in healthcare. In B. L. Wright (Ed.), *Communication skills: Challenges, importance for health care professionals and strategies for improvement.* NOVA Publisher.

Lazzari, C. (2000). *Ethical economy* [It. *Economia Etica*]. Pitagora.
Lazzari, C. (2004). *Work and organizational psychology: From mobbing to corporate ethics [*It. *Psicologia ed etica del lavoro e delle organizzazioni. Dal mobbing all"etica aziendale*]. Armando Editore. Retrieved from https://www.ibs.it/psicologia-ed-etica-del-lavoro-libro-carlo-lazzari/e/9788883586019
Lazzari, C. (2009). *Spiritual counselling in medicine: Theories and techniques of conuseling during stressful life event, severe illnesses, and palliative care.* iUniverse
Lazzari, C., & Masino, M. A. (2006). *Loves that cure. A guide to the helping relationships. [It: L'Amore che cura. Guidal alla relazione d'aiuto].* FrancoAngeli.
Lazzari, C., & Rabottini, M. (2023). Biopsychosocial theories of borderline personality disorder: A meta-synthesis and psychopathological network model from a systematic review. *Rivista di Psichiatria, 58*(6), 258–270.
Lazzari, C., & Rabottini, M. (2024). Socially ill: The new generation of medical and psychiatric patients. *Minerva Psychiatry, 65*(2), 250–252.
Lazzari, C., Costley, C., & Nikolou-Walker, E. (2024). *Interprofessional and intraprofessional practice in healthcare.* Libri.
Lazzari, C., Crawford, P., Ashmore, A., & Kotera, Y. (2024). Psychological effects of receiving compassion and its interpretation via secular or religious frameworks: A systematic review and meta-analysis. PROSPERO Registration CRD420251107986. (Registered protocol; publication forthcoming.)
Lilius, J. M., Worline, M. C., Dutton, J. E., Kanov, J., & Maitlis, S. (2003). What good is compassion at work? *Academy of Management Proceedings, 2003*(1), A1–A6.
Lilius, J. M., Worline, M. C., Dutton, J. E., Kanov, J., & Maitlis, S. (2011). Understanding compassion capability. *Human Relations, 64*(7), 873–899. https://doi.org/10.1177/0018726710396250
Markus, H. R., & Kitayama, S. (1991). Culture and the self. *Psychological Review, 98*(2), 224–253. https://doi.org/10.1037/0033-295X.98.2.224
Mascaro, J. S., Florian, M. P., Ash, M. J., Palmer, P. K., Frazier, T., Condon, P., & Raison, C. (2020). Ways of knowing compassion: How do we come to know, understand, and measure compassion when we see it? *Frontiers in Psychology, 11.* https://doi.org/10.3389/fpsyg.2020.547241
Mascaro, J., Rilling, J., Tenzin Negi, L., & Raison, C. (2020). Compassion and its measurement: A review of psychological and neuroscientific approaches. *Frontiers in Psychology, 11*, 587. Available at: https://doi.org/10.3389/fpsyg.2020.00587/full
McAllum, K., Fox, S., Ford, J. L., & Roeder, A. C. (2023). Communicating compassion in organizations: A conceptual review. *Frontiers in Communication, 8.* https://doi.org/10.3389/fcomm.2023.1144045
McEwen, B. S. (1998). Protective and damaging effects of stress mediators. *New England Journal of Medicine, 338*(3), 171–179. https://doi.org/10.1056/NEJM199801153380307
McLeroy, K. R., Bibeau, D., Steckler, A., & Glanz, K. (1988). An ecological perspective on health promotion programs. *Health Education Quarterly, 15*(4), 351–377. https://doi.org/10.1177/109019818801500401
Merritt, O. A., & Purdon, C. L. (2020). Scared of compassion: Fear of compassion in anxiety, mood, and non-clinical groups. *British Journal of Clinical Psychology, 59*(3), 354–368. https://doi.org/10.1111/bjc.12250
Mikulincer, M., & Shaver, P. R. (2007). *Attachment in adulthood: Structure, dynamics, and change.* Guilford Press.
Miralles, S., Pessi, A. B., Pozo-Hidalgo, M., & Rodríguez-Sánchez, A. (2024). Leading matters! Linking compassion and mindfulness in organizations through servant leadership. *Frontiers in Psychology, 15.* https://doi.org/10.3389/fpsyg.2024.1346751
Mollah, T. N., Antoniades, J., Lafeer, F. I., & Brijnath, B. (2018). How do mental health practitioners operationalise cultural competency in everyday practice? A qualitative analysis. *BMC Health Services Research, 18*(1). https://doi.org/10.1186/s12913-018-3296-2

Montero-Marin, J., Kuyken, W., Crane, C., Gu, J., Baer, R., Al-Awamleh, A. A., Akutsu, S., Araya-Véliz, C., Ghorbani, N., Chen, Z. J., Kim, M., Mantzios, M., Santos, D. N. R. D., López, L. C. S., Teleb, A. A., Watson, P. J., Yamaguchi, A., Yang, E., & García-Campayo, J. (2018). Self-compassion and cultural values: A cross-cultural research of self-compassion using a multitrait-multimethod (MTMM) analytical procedure. *Frontiers in Psychology, 9*. https://doi.org/10.3389/fpsyg.2018.02638

Mythology, H. (2024, October 3). The *Upanishads* and the philosophy of compassion. *Hindu Mythology*. https://hindu.mythologyworldwide.com/the-upanishads-and-the-philosophy-of-compassion/

Neff, K. (2003a). Self-compassion: An alternative conceptualization of a healthy attitude toward oneself. *Self and Identity, 2*(2), 85–101. https://doi.org/10.1080/15298860309032

Neff, K. D. (2003b). The development and validation of a scale to measure self-compassion. *Self and Identity, 2*(3), 223–250. https://doi.org/10.1080/15298860309027

Nelson, J. (2000). *Enduring identities: The guise of Shinto in contemporary Japan*. University of Hawaii Press.

Nussbaum, M. C. (2001). *Upheavals of thought: The intelligence of emotions*. Cambridge University Press.

Online Etymology Dictionary. (2025). *Definition of Compassion*. https://www.etymonline.com/

OpenStax College. (2018, September 20). Ethical decision-making and prioritizing stakeholders. *Pressbooks*. https://ecampusontario.pressbooks.pub/businessethicsopenstax/chapter/ethical-decision-making-and-prioritizing-stakeholders/

Parsons, T. (1951). *The social system*. Routledge.

Pogosyan, M. (2022). How culture affects compassion. *Psychology Today*. Retrieved from https://www.psychologytoday.com

Porges, S. W. (2007). The polyvagal perspective. *Biological Psychology, 74*(2), 116–143. https://doi.org/10.1016/j.biopsycho.2006.06.009

Reis, H. T., Sheldon, K. M., Gable, S. L., Roscoe, J., & Ryan, R. M. (2000). Daily well-being: The role of autonomy, competence, and relatedness. *Personality and Social Psychology Bulletin, 26*(4), 419–435. https://doi.org/10.1177/0146167200266002

Ryan, R. M., & Deci, E. L. (2017). Self-determination theory: Basic psychological needs in motivation, development, and wellness. Guilford Press.

Sarason, I. G., Levine, H. M., Basham, R. B., & Sarason, B. R. (1987). Assessing social support: The social support questionnaire. *Journal of Personality and Social Psychology, 52*(4), 813–825. https://doi.org/10.1037/0022-3514.52.4.813

Selye, H. (1956). The stress of life. McGraw-Hill.

Selye, H. (1976). Stress in health and disease. Butterworths.

Seppälä, E. M., Simon-Thomas, E., Brown, S. L., Worline, M. C., Cameron, C. D., & Doty, J. R. (Eds.). (2017). *The Oxford handbook of compassion science*. Oxford University Press.

Simon-Thomas, E. R. (2012). How does religion shape compassion? *Greater Good*. Retrieved from https://greatergood.berkeley.edu/article/item/how_does_religion_shape_compassion

Sinclair, S., McClement, S., Raffin-Bouchal, S., Hack, T. F., Hagen, N. A., McConnell, S., & Chochinov, H. M. (2015). Compassion in health care: An empirical model. *Journal of Pain and Symptom Management, 51*(2), 193–203. https://doi.org/10.1016/j.jpainsymman.2015.10.009

Sinclair, S., Norris, J. M., McConnell, S. J., Chochinov, H. M., Hack, T. F., Hagen, N. A., McClement, S., & Bouchal, S. R. (2016). Compassion: A scoping review of the healthcare literature. *BMC Palliative Care, 15*, Article 6. https://doi.org/10.1186/s12904-016-0080-0

Singer, P. (2015). *The most good you can do: How effective altruism is changing ideas about living ethically*. Yale University Press.

Singer, T., & Klimecki, O. M. (2014). Empathy and compassion. *Current Biology, 24*(18), R875–R878. https://www.cell.com/current-biology/fulltext/S0960-9822(14)01054-1, https://doi.org/10.1016/j.cub.2014.06.054

Singer, T., & Ricard, M. (2015). Compassion: Bridging practice and science. *Current Opinion in Psychology, 6*, 108–113. https://doi.org/10.1016/j.copsyc.2015.07.002

Stellar, J. E., Cohen, A., Oveis, C., & Keltner, D. (2015). Affective and physiological responses to the suffering of others: Compassion and vagal activity. *Journal of Personality and Social Psychology, 108*(4), 572–585. https://doi.org/10.1037/pspi0000010

Tajfel, H., & Turner, J. C. (1986). The social identity theory of intergroup behavior. *Psychology of Intergroup Relations, 7*(1), 33–47.

Taylor, S. E. (2011). Social support and resilience. *Advances in Experimental Social Psychology, 45*, 1–57.

Thoits, P. A. (1995). Stress, coping, and social support processes: Where are we? What next? *Journal of Health and Social Behavior, 36*(1), 53–79. https://doi.org/10.2307/2626957

Triandis, H. C. (1995). Individualism and collectivism. Westview Press.

Trindale, I. A., Ferreira, C., Borrego, M., Ponte, A., Carvalho, C., & Pinto-Gouveia, J. (2018). Going beyond social support: Fear of receiving compassion from others predicts depression symptoms in breast cancer patients. *Journal of Psychosocial Oncology, 36*(4), 520–528. https://doi.org/10.1080/07347332.2018.1440275

Vieten, C., Rubanovich, C. K., Khatib, L., Sprengel, M., Tanega, C., Polizzi, C., et al. (2024). Measures of empathy and compassion: A scoping review. *PLOS ONE, 19*(1), Article e0297099. https://doi.org/10.1371/journal.pone.0297099

Vieten, C., Wahbeh, H., Cahn, B., MacLean, K., & Estrada, M. (2024). Systematic review of compassion research: Measurement, constructs, and population analyses. *Journal of Compassion Studies, 12*(1), 21–45. Available at: https://compassionstudies.org/review2024.

Walker, A. T. (2023). The moral meaning of loving one's neighbor. *Ethics & Public Policy Center*. Retrieved from https://eppc.org/publication/the-moral-meaning-of-loving-ones-neighbor/

Wilkinson, R., & Pickett, K. (2018). *The inner level: How more equal societies reduce stress, restore sanity and improve everyone's well-being*. Penguin Books.

WHO (World Health Organization). (2025a). *Health and Well-Being*. https://www.who.int/Data/Gho/Data/Major-Themes/Health-and-Well-Being

World Health Organization. (2025b). *The determinants of health and well-being: Global perspectives*. WHO. Available at: https://www.who.int/publications/determinants2025

Worline, M. C., & Dutton, J. E. (2017). *Awakening compassion at work: The quiet power that elevates people and organizations*. Berrett-Koehler Publishers.

Chapter 3
Culturally Sensitive Compassion-Focused Therapy for Adult ADHD in Latin America: Integrating Familismo and Attachment Perspectives

Carolina Eugenia Cáceres Videla and Rosemary Sibley

Background

Attention Deficit and Hyperactivity Disorder (ADHD)

Attention deficit-hyperactivity disorder (ADHD) is defined as a neurodevelopmental disorder characterized by difficulties with impulsivity, hyperactivity, and inattention, which are prevalent across different environments, causing different degrees of functional impairment (American Psychiatric Association, 2013; Biederman & Faraone, 2005). The American Psychiatric Association (2013) states that ADHD features must be present by the age of 12 years old (Polanczyk et al., 2007). The ICD-10, an alternative classification system used in Europe, provides a similar operational definition and symptom criteria for the disorder, and describes ADHD as hyperkinetic disorder (HD) (World Health Organization, 1993). This neurodevelopmental condition is one of the most investigated in medical science and is linked to several negative outcomes, such as mood disorders, for affected individuals (Dulcan, 1997; Goldman et al., 1998; Swanson et al., 1998).

Descriptions of the diagnosis and management of ADHD in the current diagnostic manuals emerged in the second half of the twentieth century (Swanson, 1998). Since

C. E. C. Videla (✉)
Universidad Gabriela Mistral, Providencia, Chile
e-mail: carolina.caceres@academico.ugm.cl

Coventry and Warwickshire NHS Trust, Coventry, UK

R. Sibley
Derbyshire Community Health Services NHS Foundation Trust, Derbyshire, UK

Y. Kotera et al. (eds.), *Compassion-Focused Therapy for Mental Health: International Perspectives*, Advances in Mental Health and Addiction,
https://doi.org/10.1007/978-3-032-12438-8_3

then, efforts have been made to understand the disorder, disseminating the knowledge across societies and extending the identification and treatment of those affected (Singh, 2008; Timimi & Taylor, 2004).

There is conflicting data regarding the prevalence of ADHD in school-age children, with estimates ranging from as low as 1% to as high as almost 20% (Bird, 2002; Faraone et al., 2003). Nonetheless, a report of JAMA Paediatrics (2013) stated that ADHD has been one of the most common persistent childhood psychiatric disorders in the last decade, affecting up to 8% of all children among pre-school and adolescence, remaining into adulthood in nearly 66–85% of individuals who presented with ADHD in childhood or adolescence (Elia et al., 1999; Faraone et al., 2003; Millichap, 2007). Polanczyk et al. (2007) summarized 102 worldwide studies where a prevalence of 5.3% was found among the 171,756 children sampled from schools, communities, or birth registers.

Gender Differences in ADHD

ADHD is present in boys and girls, even though the evidence shows a higher prevalence in boys. Whereas females are more prone to be identified as predominantly inattentive (Biederman et al., 2002), research has demonstrated that boys with ADHD showed more hyperactivity and impulsivity than girls with ADHD (Gershon, 2002; Jacobson, 2017; Rucklidge & Tannock, 2002). According to the authors, boys tend to be physically aggressive, showing externalized symptoms, whereas girls are more prone to be verbally aggressive, showing internalized symptoms, such as mind-wandering and self-esteem issues (Jacobson, 2017; Rucklidge & Tannock, 2002). Although there is limited evidence of gender differences in individuals diagnosed with ADHD and some studies reported incongruent fluctuations among males and females with this disorder (Biederman et al., 2005; Gaub & Carlson, 1997).

Psychological Treatment of ADHD

The National Institute for Health and Care Excellence (NICE) (2019) suggests that suitable psychological treatment interventions in children and young people (CYP) are parent-training groups, psychoeducation on the causes and impact of ADHD, advice on parenting strategies, and cognitive behavioural therapy (CBT). In adults, the NICE (2019) guidelines recommend medication in addition to elements of, or a full course of CBT. The latter becomes more significant when clients opt for non-pharmacological treatments due to personal preferences, difficulties with adherence and tolerance. Overall, CBT is referred to as evidence-based treatment for individuals diagnosed with ADHD.

As developed by Beck (1976/1989), CBT is an evidence-based model of psychological therapy built on the assumption that cognitions, emotions, behaviours, and physical sensations are interlinked in the creation of a vicious cycle that perpetuates the main problem. Because each of these four factors influences each other, if one of them were to be intervened, the others would most likely change in their presentation (Wills & Sanders, 2013). CBT specifically aims to identify and modify thoughts and their associated behaviours based on the assumption that an event's interpretation generates an emotion instead of the event by itself causing a particular emotion (Kennerley et al., 2007). However, due to a substantial number of clients who reported self-critical thoughts finding the application of CBT difficult, another treatment emerged to emphasize eliciting feelings of contentment, safeness, and warmth (Petrocchi et al., 2024).

Compassion-Focused Therapy (CFT)

Compassion-focused therapy (CFT) integrates elements from CBT with concepts from evolutionary psychology, attachment theory and Buddhism to move towards an integrated biopsychosocial science of psychotherapy (Gilbert, 2009). Whilst evolutionary psychology aligns with understanding fight, flight or freeze mechanisms; early attachment experiences cement the basis of future interpersonal relations (Petrocchi et al., 2024). CFT seeks to cultivate secure attachments and care motivated behaviour, which are characterized by a desire to alleviate suffering, promote well-being and connection. Attachment describes the foundation for the formation of affectional bonds among the infant and significant others, and emerged from research, ethology, and developmental psychology (Sable, 1997; Van Rosmalen et al., 2014). To date, two models of attachment remain dominant, the ABC model, which then evolved into the ABC+D model in Table 3.1; and the Dynamic Maturational Model (DMM) in Fig. 3.1 (Farnfield & Stokowy, 2014; Main & Solomon, 1986).

CFT supports individuals who are captured in trans-diagnostic patterns of self-criticism and shame to understand their reactivity within the context of the old brain, new brain, and three affect system (drive, threat and soothe). The aim is to strengthen their soothing system through mindfulness and imagery (Gilbert, 2009). Although

Table 3.1 ABC+D patterns of attachment (Main & Solomon, 1986)

Attachment classification	Behaviour description
Secure attachment	Seek proximity, communicate need for comfort, and contact is effective
Avoidant attachment	Avoids contact and minimizes expressions of need for contact
Resistant attachment	Intense expression of distress, angry upon contact and contact not effective
Disorganised attachment	Contradictory, fragmented, disoriented, or fearful behaviour upon contact

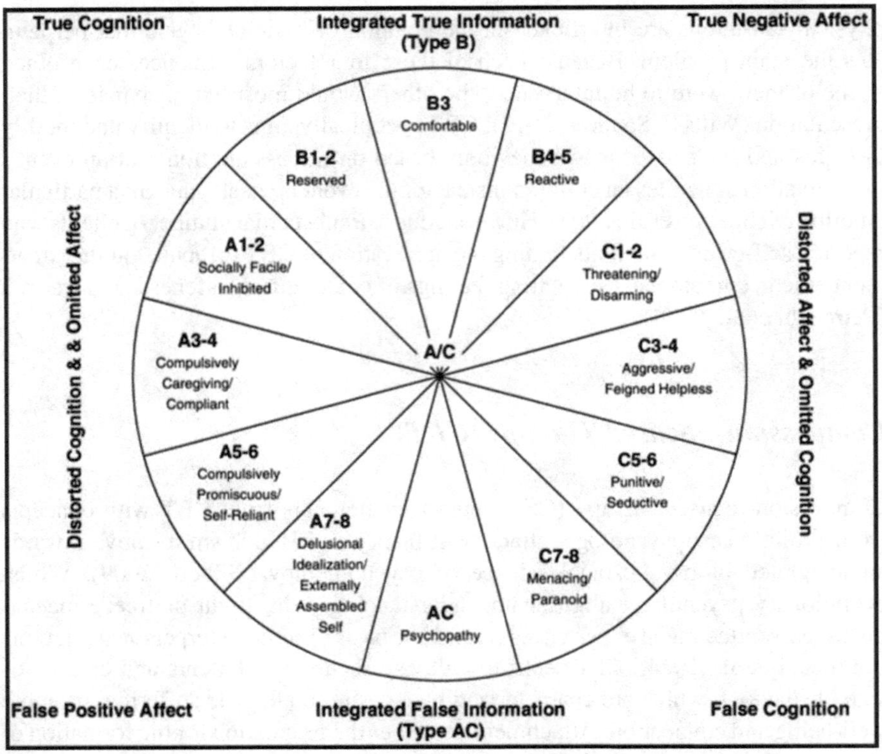

Fig. 3.1 Dynamic Maturational Model (DMM) of attachment in adolescence and adulthood (Farnfield & Stokowy, 2014)

some CFT exercises are also practiced in the context of CBT or Mindfulness-based Cognitive Therapy (MBCT), others are tailored particularly to the purpose of activating attachment systems (Segal et al., 2013). For instance, the "safe place imagery", and the "flows of compassion" practice are used in CBT, and MBCT, respectively (Segal et al., 2013). However, "the perfect nurturer", and "the multiple selves imagery" focuses on managing interpersonal conflicts in a contained space that allows the validation of the clients' anger, sadness, and fear to eventually build a response motivated by compassion (The Compassionate Mind Foundation, 2024).

The NICE guidelines do not include suggestions for the use of CFT in psychological treatments beyond the assessment and management of depressive episodes or self-harm (NICE, 2022a, 2022b). However, The Compassionate Mind Foundation (2024) offers training for mental health professionals focused on perinatal distress in post-partum depression, parenting, and care for vulnerable children or adults.

Attachment Studies in Latin American Populations

The terms Latin American, South American and Hispanic are used interchangeably as synonyms to report findings where the participants identified with these three terms. A recent review supports the key theoretical assumptions of attachment theory in urban middle-class non-risk Latin American samples, with Chile being the main producer of research on attachment theory and attachment-based interventions to promote socio-emotional development in children (Fourment et al., 2022). Despite an increase in studies in the last decades, the continent is still underrepresented. Key points for improvement stated by Fourment et al. (2022) were the incorporation of local insights independent from Western researchers; rural populations, non-maternal caregivers; and at-risk presentations, such as institutionalized, and forensic samples.

Attachment can be particularly important in the treatment of Hispanic populations, where familismo emerges as a cultural value or belief. The concept of familismo is defined as for the importance of maintaining close connection to immediate and extended family, which stems from a collectivist worldview that promotes relationships of mutual support (Sabogal et al., 1987). Namely, familismo is a cultural value prominent in Latin American and Hispanic communities that emphasizes strong identification with, loyalty to, and interdependence among nuclear and extended family members (Sabogal et al., 1987). It reflects a collectivist orientation in which family well-being often takes precedence over individual needs or goals (Sabogal et al., 1987). Familismo encompasses expectations of emotional closeness, reciprocal support, and a sense of obligation to uphold family unity and cohesion across generations (Sabogal et al., 1987). Within Sabogal et al. (1987)'s Familismo Scale, three distinctive factors have been found: Familial obligations, perceived support from the family, and family as referents. Abate et al. (2022) confirmed that Latin Americans who present familismo tend to experience higher levels of social support regardless of their attachment security, thus reinforcing the relevance of the concept. Subsequently, culturally modified cognitive-behavioural interventions have indicated that using a systemic approach in therapeutic interventions might be a protective factor for this client group (De Arellano et al., 2012).

Furthermore, in the context of immigration, Zamudio et al. (2020) stated that familismo served as a moderator between adult attachment insecurity, social self-efficacy, and psychological distress. When preventing psychological distress, identifying attachment patterns has been found crucial, with adult attachment avoidance being directly linked to acculturative distress (Wang et al., 2021).

Compassion in the Treatment of Attention Deficit and Hyperactivity Disorder (ADHD) and Attachment Difficulties

Studies addressing the link between compassion and ADHD have shown that the latter is associated with higher self-criticism, and lower levels of self-compassion (Beaton et al., 2020; Farmer et al., 2023). In previous research, compassionate responses were measured using the Self-Compassion Scale (2003) through self-kindness, common humanity, and mindfulness in opposition to self-judgement, isolation, and overidentification with negative feelings. According to Beaton et al. (2020) higher levels of self-criticism or self-judgement in those with ADHD might be related to the negative feedback perceived from others in comparison to adults without ADHD.

A review conducted by McCarthy et al. (2023) concluded that self-compassion may mediate ADHD related risks, such as the emergence of borderline personality disorder (BPD) in adolescence or adulthood. BPD is characterized by emotional lability, identity integration problems, and feelings of inner emptiness, self-harm, and suicidality (American Psychiatric Association, 2013). Some of the overlapping symptoms between ADHD and BPD include emotion dysregulation with or without impulsivity, early attachment problems and trauma with subsequent interpersonal relationship difficulties due to poor mentalization (McCarthy et al., 2023). According to Bateman and Fonagy (2010), mentalization entails exercising self-observation and perspective taking abilities with sufficient effectiveness to be able to simultaneously consider one's own feelings and those of others, particularly in interpersonal interactions.

Case Study Rationale

There is limited evidence of gender differences for those diagnosed with ADHD. Given that difficulties experienced by females may not be observed as clearly as hyperactivity and impulsivity more often seen in males, it could result in a delayed diagnosis of ADHD

(Biederman et al., 2005; Gaub & Carlson, 1997). Moreover, there is no conclusive evidence regarding the link between attachment and ADHD, whether considering the ABC+D or the DMM in terms of attachment.

Within the field of CFT, little research has been conducted about its effects in the reduction of self-critical thoughts, and shame in individuals diagnosed with ADHD, with or without attachment difficulties. The challenges faced by this population are still unknown due to the impact of stimulant medication on the activation of the drive system (NICE, 2019).

Despite the increase in research on cultural adaptations from Latin America, given the significance of acculturation, the region remains under-represented in attachment studies (Fourment et al., 2022; Wang et al., 2021). Therefore, using a case study may provide further evidence on the association between ADHD, attachment styles, and highlight the benefits of compassion interventions to reduce distressing experiences for a clinical population and their support systems.

Objectives

The present case study seeks to contribute to the limited body of literature addressing the psychological experiences of female Latin American adults diagnosed with Attention-Deficit/Hyperactivity Disorder (ADHD). Given the exploratory nature of this investigation and the current paucity of empirical research examining the application of Compassion-Focused Therapy (CFT) in the treatment of ADHD, no specific hypotheses were formulated. Instead, this study adopts a descriptive and exploratory stance to examine the therapeutic impact of CFT within this underrepresented population. The primary objectives are threefold:

1. to evaluate the effectiveness of a culturally adapted CFT intervention in alleviating symptoms of low mood,
2. to explore the extent to which the intervention can reduce maladaptive behavioural patterns associated with attachment difficulties, and
3. to assess the potential of CFT techniques in enhancing self-compassion, particularly in the context of shame and self-critical internal dialogues.

By addressing these aims, the study endeavours to generate clinically relevant insights that may inform culturally sensitive adaptations of CFT for adults with ADHD, particularly those with complex attachment histories and experiences of marginalization related to gender and ethnicity.

Methods

A single case two-phased (AB) design was used. Phase A consisted of assessment, and phase B comprised a twelve-session intervention, with outcome measures taken at three points in time: before commencing the treatment, at the mid-session review and after the treatment had ended. The participant accessed psychotherapy due to recurrent symptoms of low mood after a course of cognitive behavioural therapy in combination with stimulant medication prescribed for ADHD. During the assessment, three core symptoms of depression were identified: low mood, anhedonia, and reduced energy (World Health Organization, 1993).

Introduction to the Case

Sra. A, a Latin American female in her late 20s, self-referred to remote private psychotherapy on an individual basis. Her presentation was complex due to a late neurodevelopmental diagnosis two years before the present treatment, and the process of acculturation she was experiencing as the first generation of immigrants from her family of origin. No risk was identified to herself or others, nor was the client at risk from others. She did not consume other substances or caffeine except alcohol on social occasions that did not exceed the recommended units (National Health Service, 2021). The client had no other long-term conditions (LTCs) or physical impairments. Her protective factors included previously learned CBT techniques to manage symptoms associated to ADHD, such as physical activity, behavioural activation, and cognitive restructuring as coping mechanisms (Young & Bramham, 2012). There were no concerns in terms of eligibility to proceed with a CBT-based intervention, according to the ten criteria suggested by Safran and Segal (1990).

Sra. A had experienced episodes of intrafamilial abuse—including sexual, physical, and emotional abuse—during her childhood and adolescence, in addition to neglect. These adverse experiences are understood to contribute significantly to an elevated risk of developing attachment-related difficulties. Sra. A wanted to address her self-critical thoughts of "not having accomplished enough" in terms of educational achievements and close relationships across her lifetime coupled with feelings of shame for the perceived errors made in interpersonal interactions before been able to manage her ADHD diagnosis.

Outcome Measures

Since one of the objectives of the case study is to present the impact of the intervention in unhelpful behaviours that stem from attachment, the client completed the short version of the Experiences in Close Relationships Scale (ECR-S) designed to explore attachment styles. The measure demonstrates a high degree of internal consistency, as indicated by a Cronbach's alpha coefficient of 0.90, which is considered excellent according to psychometric standards (Gilbert et al., 2017). This suggests that the items within the scale are highly interrelated and reliably assess the underlying construct it was designed to measure.

To measure the client's increase in self-compassion, changes were measured through the Fears of Compassion Scale (FOCS), and the Self-Compassion Engagement and Action Subscale (CEAS-SC) of the Compassionate Engagement and Action Scale (Gilbert et al., 2011, 2017; Wei et al., 2007). The internal consistency of the scale is considered acceptable to good, with reported Cronbach's alpha coefficients ranging from approximately 0.78 to 0.86 for the anxiety subscale and from 0.77 to 0.88 for the avoidance subscale. These reliability estimates, as documented by Wei et al. (2007) and Lafontaine et al. (2016), indicate that the items within each subscale are sufficiently interrelated to reliably measure the underlying constructs of attachment-related anxiety and avoidance, respectively.

In addition to the previous forms, and to measure the client's improvement in mood and functioning, the following questionnaires were completed: Patient Health Questionnaire (PHQ-9) to measure symptoms of depression, and Generalized Anxiety Disorder (GAD-7) were completed on a five-point Likert scale ranging from 0 ("not at all"), 1 ("several days"), 2 ("more than half days"), to 3 ("nearly every day") (Kroenke et al., 2001; Spitzer et al., 2006). The internal consistency for both scales is good with Cronbach's alpha ~0.86–0.91, and ~0.89–0.92, respectively (Kroenke et al., 2001; Löwe et al., 2004; Spitzer et al., 2006). The Work and Social Adjustment (W&SAS) self-reported questionnaire was answered, using an 8-point Likert scale that measures the level of impairment across the following activities: Work, home management, social leisure activities, private leisure.

Intervention

The intervention was facilitated by a trainee mindfulness practitioner and qualified cognitive behavioural therapist with two years post-qualification experience. There was no specific training in CFT for ADHD; however, the therapist had been trained in CFT at a foundation level. All sessions were conducted using video calls. The assessment comprised three sessions with the purpose of conducting an initial screening, exploration of Sra. A's background and formulating from a CFT perspective. A twelve-module intervention followed with a final session for relapse prevention. Thus, a total of sixteen sessions were delivered over 4–6 months. Table 3.2 describes an adaptation of Petrocchi et al. (2024)'s treatment plan with the main content and sub-contents of each session outlined for the purpose of description and replication. Mindfulness and imagery were introduced at early stages of the intervention and then referred to as "practices" within the sub-contents. Chair work was not utilized due to the restraints of telehealth.

Additional material or sub content for each session is listed in Table 3.2 and constituted a practice agreed with the client as homework for habit building. It stemmed from the session to troubleshoot for task non-completion when providing the handouts suggested by Petrocchi et al. (2024). The sessions lasted 50 min and followed a CBT structure, commencing with an agenda, feedback gathering, moving to homework revision, introduction of new content, and homework agreement (Blackburn et al., 2001).

Table 3.2 Treatment plan adapted from Petrocchi et al. (2024)

Module	Main content	Sub-contents
1–3	Assessment	Information gathering, rapport building and co-creation of a formulation of the main problem
4	Introduction to compassion	Noticing old brain and new brain loops
5	Three-affect regulation system	Introduction of the three circles. Different versions of the self. Soothing rhythm breathing
6	Mindfulness	Mindfulness of breathing, and other practices
7	Exploring safety and safeness	Distinguishing safety from safeness. Bringing others into a family-oriented safe place imagery to include "*familismo*"
8	The compassionate self	The flows of compassion practice. Perfect nurturer imagery. Compassionate behaviour record
9	The multiple selves	The multiple selves practice. Compassionate self-integration practice. Writing from the multiple selves to significant others after conflicts are experienced to problem-solve within a communitarian environment
10	Self-criticism	Origins and functional analysis of self-criticism practices. The compassionate self meets the critic and criticized selves practices. Monitoring self-criticism
11	Shame and guilt	Origins of shame practice. Shifting from self-critical shame to reparative guilt practice. Compassionate imagery with rescripting
12	Deepening compassion for the self	Compassionate letter writing practice
13	Compassionate assertiveness	Approaching fears, blocks, and resistances to assertiveness practice. Receiving appreciation practice
14	Compassionate forgiveness	Memory of forgiveness, compassionate forgiveness, and deepening self-empathy practices
15	Envisioning a compassionate future	Compassionate future self, Metta, and Mudita practices
16	Ending preparation	Relapse prevention plan and blueprint

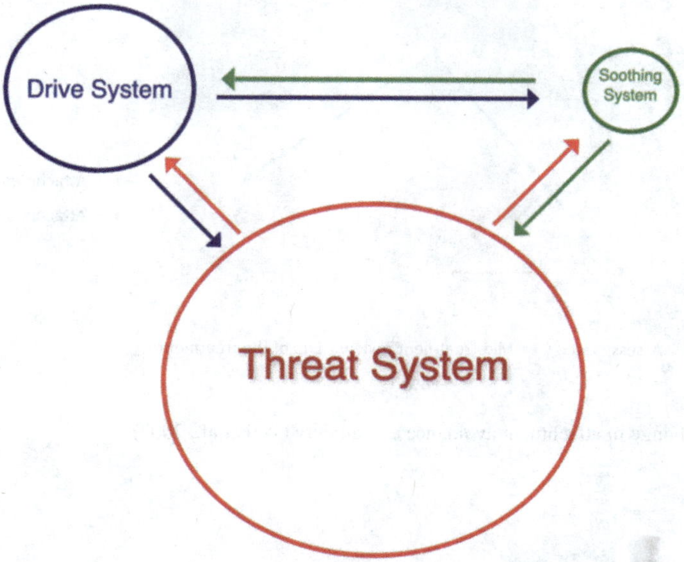

Fig. 3.2 Three affect regulation system with the threat system imbalanced (Gilbert, 2005)

Results

Case Conceptualization

The three-affect regulation system drawn by the Sra. A can be found in Fig. 3.2 (Gilbert, 2005). Table 3.2 presents a case conceptualization from compassion-focused therapy (Petrocchi et al., 2024).

Changes in Attachment; Fears of Compassion; Compassionate Engagement and Action; and Symptomatology from Pre-to Post-intervention

Although changes in attachment scores were moderate, the ECR item that demonstrated significant positive change was: "*I am nervous when another person gets too close to me*", indicating (a reduction in avoidance strategies such as maintaining rigid emotional boundaries or defensive strategies to protect against perceived relationship threats). Figure 3.3 represents the change in attachment avoidance and anxiety (Wei et al., 2007). Figures 3.4 and 3.5 represent the changes in fears of self-compassion and fears of extending compassion. No changes were reported in terms of receiving compassion or compassionate engagement and action as stated in the FOCS and CEAS-SC, respectively (Gilbert et al., 2011, 2017). Figure 3.6 provides detailed

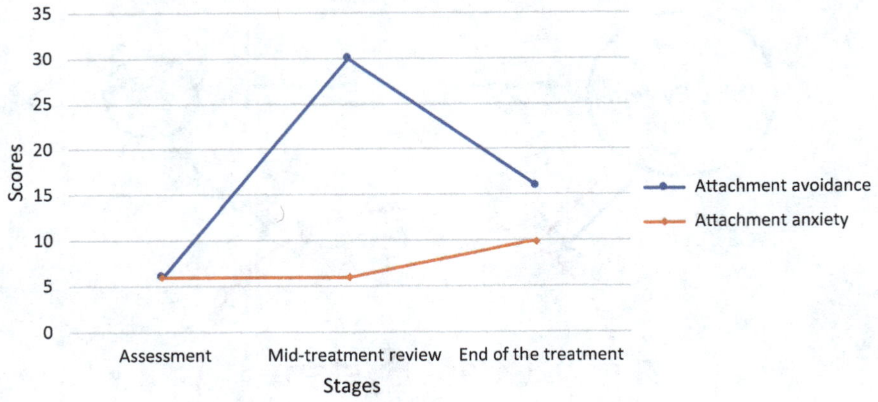

Fig. 3.3 Change in attachment avoidance and anxiety (Wei et al., 2007)

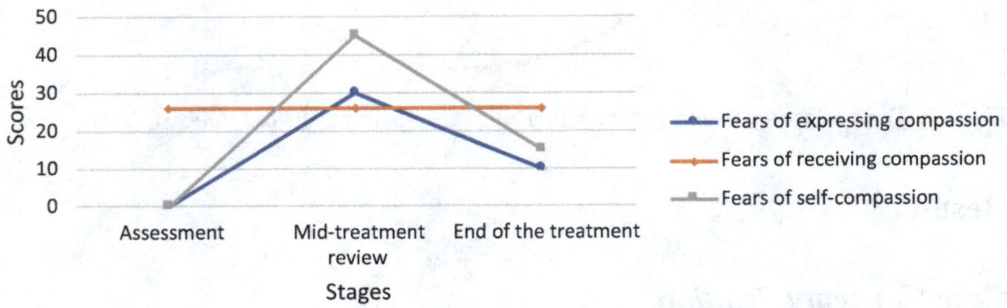

Fig. 3.4 Change in fears of compassion from self to self, self to others, and others to self (Gilbert et al., 2011)

information on the client's low mood, anxiousness, and overall functioning across the treatment (Kroenke et al., 2001; Mundt et al., 2022; Spitzer et al., 2006). This demonstrates that the client's overall aims to reduce symptoms of depression were achieved.

Safe Place Imagery

Sra. A found the creation of an image particularly helpful, incorporating different figures that embodied the compassionate qualities of previous caregivers, such as being protective, nurturing, and wise (Parnell, 2013; Petrocchi et al., 2024). Imagery prompted a compassionate intention to forgive in view of internalizing further qualities from significant others and building on her sense of security. Thus, it helped the client to counteract self-criticism that had been internalized based on her upbringing, whilst incorporating self-compassion and self-regulation at the same time.

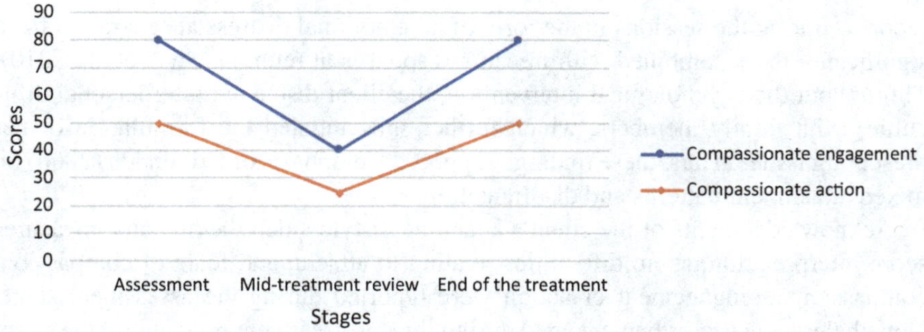

Fig. 3.5 Change in self-compassionate engagement and action (Gilbert et al., 2017)

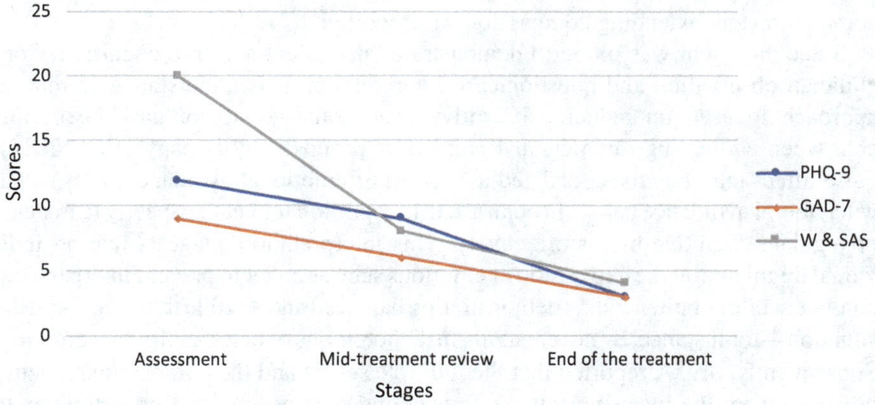

Fig. 3.6 Change in emotional symptoms and adjustment (Kroenke et al., 2001; Mundt et al., 2022; Spitzer et al., 2006)

Discussion

Given that there is no literature on this topic, the case study outcomes are promising in terms of adapting CFT approaches for use with Latin American adults presenting with ADHD. In addition, it raises the importance of addressing attachment patterns and culture when implementing interventions, recognizing possible implications for treatment. Specifically, findings suggest that activating the soothing system using CFT could be beneficial. This may help to promote a secure attachment when clients have reported detrimental experiences that might be impacting on their present interpersonal relationships.

In the present case study, the outcome measures suggested an avoidant pattern enacted by Sra. A (compulsively caregiving/compliant or A3-4) by demonstrating false affect and true cognition according to the DMM. However, occasional behaviours associated with disorganization from the ABC+D perspective were reported during the sessions in the form of no emotional distress at separation from significant others combined with freezing responses at reunion (Shah et al., 2010). Throughout the psychological intervention, the client discussed interpersonal difficulties with family members, which further substantiated the formulation of her presenting issues. Thus, these findings support the emphasis of Crittenden (2006) on mixed attachment patterns and disorientation.

Acknowledgements of the client's attachment style aided the outcome measures score interpretation, as no difficulties relating to attachment, fears of compassion, compassionate engagement or action were reported during the assessment stage. Nonetheless, the scores had changed during the mid-treatment review, and the client reported that the content covered in the initial sessions collaborated with overcoming the shame experienced at the assessment stage when reporting her difficulties. At the mid-session review a predominantly avoidant attachment style with fears of self-compassion and extending compassion was reported.

Since the client was prone to demonstrate false affect and true cognition, from clinician observation and questionnaire interpretation it is understandable that an approach focused on reducing cognitive distortions would not have been suitable when addressing interpersonal conflict as proposed by Fonagy et al. (2014). False affect may be conceptualized as a form of emotional avoidance, rather than behavioural avoidance per se. In contrast, true cognition reflects a capacity to manage or regulate cognitive biases effectively. This interpretation suggests that an individual might inhibit the expression of emotions such as anger to prevent interpersonal conflict, while simultaneously demonstrating balanced and flexible thinking about the situation—for instance, by not engaging in dichotomous or black-and-white thinking. Subsequently, Sra. A reported that the multiple selves and the compassionate letter practices were the most impactful interventions as they provided opportunities to elicit true affect in view of a compassionate intention. When writing from the multiple selves, it might be suggested that fear functioned as a key organizing affect in the client's approach to conflict resolution, in line with the DMM (Crittenden, 2006).

Historical factors that contributed to Sra. A's strategies prior to the intervention include the loss and bereavement of her mother, and qualities that did not favour the activation of the soothing system in her remaining caregivers, including her dad and siblings, such as competitiveness and criticism (Table 3.3). Thus, prompting the inhibition of forbidden negative affect and the development of low mood (Farnfield & Stokowy, 2014). Therefore, compassionate assertiveness involved approaching a difficult interaction by both providing and receiving feedback from a significant other. Positive outcomes from these interactions demonstrated that acceptance towards others' negative feedback collaborated with self-regulation and belonging.

With regard to Latin American attachment studies, the current findings align with the interpersonal difficulties found in terms of social and prosocial behaviour when paternal alienation emerged. However, internalizing symptoms were the most predominantly present in the form of inattention, low mood, anhedonia, and reduced energy (Venta et al., 2022). The incorporation of the concept of familismo, in the form of a cultural adaptation, to CFT interventions, such as the safe place, and the multiple selves imagery, was proven beneficial to promote self-regulation and problem solving

Table 3.3 CFT formulation (Petrocchi et al., 2024)

Historical influences		Key fears or threats	Safety or defensive behaviours	Unintended or unwanted consequences	Self-to-self relating
Memories: Abusive and blaming paternal figure Loss and bereavement of a maternal figure Competitive siblings		**External:** Being put down and blamed by others Having limited time available with significant others Being used for the sake of others' needs without receiving retribution	**External:** Withdrawal from social situations Focused on protection instead of connection Over-working and altruism	**External:** Isolation Superficial relations Impoverishment	**Style:** Blaming, attacking, criticizing
Self as: Naïve Disadvantaged Striving	**Others as:** Predative and self-indulging Limited Consuming	**Internal:** Feeling an outsider within a group who follows societal norms Feeling alone Never feeling enough	**Internal:** Difficulties to concentrate on the others' strengths Self-reliance Rumination	**Internal:** Self-fulling prophecies in terms of beliefs	**Emotions and Feelings:** Low motivation Anger Resentment Shame

in the context of community building (Sabogal et al., 1987). The former involved the construction of a collective safe place before progressing into further stages of the treatment (Parnell, 2013; Petrocchi et al., 2024). The latter involved replacing handouts for behavioural practices to be maintained in the context of habit building, and the use of visual aids to consolidate the collective safe place evoked by imagery (Pagán et al., 2023).

Implications for Practice

The case study provides promising outcomes for a female Latin American adult and is useful to consider when assessing clients who may have previously completed CBT treatment with limited success. In particular, clinicians may find a similar approach useful when working with individuals from Latin American heritage. Furthermore, if the client's attachment pattern inclines towards false affect and true cognition, incorporating mindfulness, imagery, and compassionate assertiveness could provide opportunities to elicit true affect. Hence, the incorporation of an attachment evaluation tool, such as the ECR-S, might help in the recognition of an appropriate treatment in ADHD.

Limitations and Recommendations for Future Research

More research is warranted about the effectiveness of CFT in individuals diagnosed with ADHD to generalize the findings obtained. Conducting research with larger samples and from other cultures could add to the evidence gathered in this case study and progress towards a randomized controlled trial (RCT).

The limitations of the present study include time constraints, as it was required that baseline data was collected over the assessment period. However, as the assessment process can be considered an intervention, this method weakens the likelihood of collecting a truly valid baseline measure. Another limitation of the study is measuring symptoms of low mood, anxiety, impairment, attachment, and compassion without evaluating self-criticism and shame directly, such as the Forms of Self-Criticizing/Attacking and Self-Reassuring Scale (FSCSR) (Gilbert et al., 2004); and the Other as Shamer Scale (OAS) (Goss et al., 1994). It would be beneficial for future research to address this by including these scales.

Conclusion

Findings support the use of CFT for adults with ADHD and attachment difficulties that experience persistent self-criticism and shame after a course of CBT. Furthermore, the present case provides support for adapting use for those from Latin American heritage and reinforces the findings of the DMM, which state that sentinel life events may catalyse a change, although moderate, in attachment classification (Crittenden, 2004; Shah et al., 2010).

Author Contributions Conceptualisation: CECV, RS; Investigation: CECV; Resources: CECV; Writing—original draft: CECV; Writing—review & editing: RS; Project administration: CECV.

References

Abate, A., Bailey, C., & Venta, A. (2022). Attachment and social support in Latinx young adults: Investigating the moderating role of familismo. *Journal of Cross-Cultural Psychology, 53*(3–4), 327–343. https://doi.org/10.1177/00220221221077378

American Psychiatric Association. (2013). *Diagnostic and statistical manual of mental disorders* (5th ed.). American Psychiatric Publishing.

Bateman, A. W., & Fonagy, P. (2010). Mentalization based treatment for borderline personality disorder. *World Psychiatry, 9*(1), 11–15. https://doi.org/10.1002/j.2051-5545.2010.tb00255.x

Beaton, D. M., Sirois, F., & Milne, E. (2020). Self-compassion and perceived criticism in adults with attention deficit hyperactivity disorder (ADHD). *Mindfulness, 11*, 2506–2518. https://doi.org/10.1007/s12671-020-01464-w

Beck, A. T. (1976/1989). *Cognitive therapy and the emotional disorders*. Penguin. (Original work published 1976)

Biederman, J., Mick, E., Faraone, S. V., Braaten, E., Doyle, A., & Spencer, T. (2002). Influence of gender on attention deficit hyperactivity disorder in children referred to a psychiatric clinic. *American Journal of Psychiatry, 159*, 39–42. https://doi.org/10.1176/appi.ajp.159.1.36

Biederman, J., & Faraone, S. V. (2005). Attention-deficit hyperactivity disorder. *Lancet, 366*, 237–248. https://doi.org/10.1016/S0140-6736(05)66915-2

Biederman, J., Kwon, A., Aleardi, M., Chouinard, V. A., Marino, T., Cole, H., Mick, E., & Faraone, S. V. (2005). Absence of gender effects on attention deficit hyperactivity disorder: Findings in nonreferred subjects. *American Journal of Psychiatry, 162*, 1083–1089. https://doi.org/10.1176/appi.ajp.162.6.1083

Bird, H. R. (2002). The diagnostic classification, epidemiology and cross-cultural validity of ADHD. In P. S. Jensen & J. R. Cooper (Eds.), *Attention deficit hyperactivity disorder: State of the science-best practices* (pp. 2-1–2-12). Civic Research Institute Inc.

Blackburn, I.-M., James, I. A., Milne, D. L., Baker, C., Standart, S., Garland, A., & Reichelt, F. K. (2001). The revised cognitive therapy scale (CTS-R): Psychometric properties. *Behavioural and Cognitive Psychotherapy, 29*(4), 431–446. https://doi.org/10.1017/S1352465801004040

Crittenden, P. (2006). A dynamic-maturational model of attachment. *Australian and New Zealand Journal of Family Therapy, 27*(2), 105–115. https://doi.org/10.1002/j.1467-8438.2006.tb00704.x

Crittenden, P. M. (2004). *Raising parents: Attachment, parenting and child safety*. Willan Publishing.

De Arellano, M. A., Danielson, C. K., & Felton, J. W. (2012). Children of Latino descent: Culturally modified TF-CBT. In J. A. Cohen, A. P. Mannarino, & E. Deblinger (Eds.), *Trauma-focused CBT for children and adolescents: Treatment applications* (pp. 253–279). The Guilford Press.

Dulcan, M. (1997). Practice parameters for the assessment and treatment of children, adolescents, and adults with attention-deficit/hyperactivity disorder. *Journal of the American Academy of Child & Adolescence Psychiatry, 36*(10), 85–121. https://doi.org/10.1097/00004583-199710001-00007

Elia, J., Ambrosini, P. J., & Rapoport, J. L. (1999). Treatment of attention-deficit/hyperactivity disorder. *The New England Journal of Medicine, 340*(10), 780–788. https://doi.org/10.1056/NEJM199903113401007

Faraone, S. V., Sergeant, J., Gillberg, C., & Biederman, J. (2003). The worldwide prevalence of ADHD: Is it an American condition? *World Psychiatry, 2*, 104–113.

Farmer, G. M., Ohan, J. L., Finlay-Jones, A. L., & Bayliss, D. M. (2023). Well-being and distress in university students with ADHD traits: The mediating roles of self-compassion and emotion regulation difficulties. *Mindfulness, 14*(2), 448–459. https://doi.org/10.1007/s12671-022-02051-x

Farnfield, S., & Stokowy, M. (2014). The Dynamic-Maturational Model (DMM) of attachment. In S. Farnfield & P. Holmes (Eds.), *The Routledge handbook of attachment: Theory* (pp. 49–72). Routledge.

Fonagy, P., Lorenzini, N., Campbell, C., & Luyten, P. (2014). Why are we interested in attachments? In P. Holmes & S. Farnfield (Eds.), *The Routledge handbook of attachment: Theory* (Vol. 1, pp. 31–48). Routledge.

Fourment, K., Espinoza, C., Ribeiro, A. C. L., & Mesman, J. (2022). Latin American attachment studies: A narrative review. *Infant Mental Health Journal, 43*(4), 653–676. https://doi.org/10.1002/imhj.21995

Gaub, M., & Carlson, C. L. (1997). Gender differences in ADHD: A meta-analysis and critical review. *Journal of the American Academy of Child and Adolescent Psychiatry, 36*, 36–45. https://doi.org/10.1097/00004583-199708000-00011

Gershon, J. (2002). A meta-analytic review of gender differences in ADHD. *Journal of Attention Disorders, 5*, 143–154. https://doi.org/10.1177/108705470200500302

Gilbert, P. (2005). *Compassion: Conceptualisations, research and use in psychotherapy*. Routledge.

Gilbert, P. (2009). Introducing compassion-focused therapy. *Advances in Psychiatric Treatment, 15*(3), 199–208. https://doi.org/10.1192/apt.bp.107.005264

Gilbert, P., Catarino, F., Duarte, C., Matos, M., Kolts, R., Stubbs, J., Ceresatto, L., Duarte, J., Pinto-Gouveia, J., & Basran, J. (2017). The development of compassionate engagement and action scales for self and others. *Journal of Compassionate Health Care, 4*(4). https://doi.org/10.1186/s40639-017-0033-3

Gilbert, P., Clarke, M., Hempel, S., Miles, J. N., & Irons, C. (2004). Criticizing and reassuring oneself: An exploration of forms, styles and reasons in female students. *The British Journal of Clinical Psychology, 43*(1), 31–50. https://doi.org/10.1348/014466504772812959

Gilbert, P., McEwan, K., Matos, M., & Rivis, A. (2011). Fears of compassion: Development of three self-report measures. *Psychology and Psychotherapy, 84*(3), 239–255. https://doi.org/10.1348/147608310X526511

Goldman, L. S., Genel, M., Bezman, R. J., & Slanetz, P. J. (1998). Diagnosis and treatment of attention-deficit/hyperactivity disorder in children and adolescents. *JAMA, 279*, 1100-1107. https://doi.org/10.1001/jama.279.14.1100

Goss, K., Gilbert, P., & Allan, S. (1994). An exploration of shame measures—I: The other as Shamer scale. *Personality and Individual Differences, 17*(5), 713–717. https://doi.org/10.1016/0191-8869(94)90149-X

Jacobson, R. (2017). *How girls with ADHD are different*. https://childmind.org/article/how-girls-with-adhd-are-different/. Accessed June17, 2025.

Kennerley, H., Kirk, J., & Westbrook, D. (2007). *Introduction to cognitive behavior therapy*. Sage.

Kroenke, K., Spitzer, R. L., & Williams, J. B. (2001). The PHQ-9: Validity of a brief depression severity measure. *Journal of General Internal Medicine, 16*(9), 606–613. https://doi.org/10.1046/j.1525-1497.2001.016009606.x

Lafontaine, M.-F., Brassard, A., Lussier, Y., Valois, P., Shaver, P. R., & Johnson, S. M. (2016). Selecting the best items for a short-form of the Experiences in Close Relationships Questionnaire. *European Journal of Psychological Assessment, 32*(2), 140–154. https://doi.org/10.1027/1015-5759/a000243

Löwe, B., Spitzer, R. L., Gräfe, K., Kroenke, K., Quenter, A., Zipfel, S., Buchholz, C., Witte, S., & Herzog, W. (2004). Comparative validity of three screening questionnaires for DSM-IV depressive disorders and physicians' diagnoses. *Journal of Affective Disorders, 78*(2), 131–140. https://doi.org/10.1016/S0165-0327(02)00237-9

Main, M., & Solomon, J. (1986). Discovery of a new insecure disorganised/disoriented attachment pattern. In T. B. Brazelton & M. W. Yogman (Eds.), *Affective development in infancy* (pp. 95-124). Ablex Publishing Company.

McCarthy, J. B., Conway, F., Kastin, J. D., & Seabrook, F. H. (2023). Attention deficit hyper-activity disorder in childhood, resilience, compassion, mentalization, and the prevention of borderline personality disorder in adulthood: A review. *Journal of Infant, Child, and Adolescent Psychotherapy, 22*(4), 323–335. https://doi.org/10.1080/15289168.2023.2266673

Millichap, J. (2007). Etiologic classification of attention-deficit hyperactivity disorder. *Pediatrics, 121*(2), e358–e365. https://doi.org/10.1542/peds.2007-1332

Mundt, J. C., Marks, I. M., Shear, M. K., & Greist, J. H. (2002). The work and social adjustment scale: A simple measure of impairment in functioning. *British Journal of Psychiatry, 180*, 461–464. https://doi.org/10.1192/bjp.180.5.461

National Health Service. (2021). *Alcohol units.* https://www.nhs.uk/live-well/alcohol-advice/calculating-alcohol-units/. Accessed June17, 2025.

Pagán, A. F., Mumma, G. H., & Littlefield, A, K. (2023). Using visual displays in a manualized cognitive-behavioral treatment for adults with ADHD and comorbid mood or anxiety disorders: A pilot study. *Cognitive and Behavioral Practice.* https://doi.org/10.1016/j.cbpra.2023.08.003.

Parnell, L. (2013). *Attachment-focused EMDR: Healing relational trauma.* W. W. Norton.

Petrocchi, N., Kirby, J., & Baldi, B. (2024). *Essentials of compassion focused therapy: A practice manual for clinicians.* Routledge.

Polanczyk, G., Lima, M. S., Horta, B. L., Biederman, J., & Rohde, L. A. (2007). The worldwide prevalence of ADHD: A systematic review and meta-regression analysis. *American Journal of Psychiatry, 164*, 942–948. https://doi.org/10.1176/ajp.2007.164.6.942

Rucklidge, J., & Tannock, R. (2002). Neuropsychological profiles of adolescent with ADHD: Effects of reading difficulties and gender. *Journal of Child Psychology and Psychiatry, and Allied Disciplines, 43*, 988–1003. https://doi.org/10.1111/1469-7610.00227

Sable, P. (1997). Disorders of adult attachment. *Psychotherapy: Theory, Research, Practice, Training, 34*(3), 286–296. https://doi.org/10.1037/h0087678

Sabogal, F., Marín, G., Otero-Sabogal, R., Marín, B. V., & Perez-Stable, E. J. (1987). Hispanic familism and acculturation: What changes and what doesn't? *Hispanic Journal of Behavioral Sciences, 9*(4), 397–412. https://doi.org/10.1177/07399863870094003

Safran, J., & Segal, Z. (1990). *Interpersonal process in cognitive therapy.* Basic Books.

Segal, Z. V., Williams, J. M. G., & Teasdale, J. D. (2013). *Mindfulness-based cognitive therapy for depression.* Guilford Press.

Shah, P. E., Fonagy, P., & Strathearn, L. (2010). Is attachment transmitted across generations? The plot thickens. *Clinical Child Psychology and Psychiatry, 15*(3), 329–346. https://doi.org/10.1177/1359104510365449

Singh, I. (2008). Beyond polemics: Science and ethics of ADHD. *Nature Reviews Neuroscience, 9*, 957–964. https://doi.org/10.1038/nrn2514

Spitzer, R. L., Kroenke, K., Williams, J. B., & Löwe, B. (2006). A brief measure for assessing generalized anxiety disorder: The GAD-7. *Archives of Internal Medicine, 166*(10), 1092–1097. https://doi.org/10.1001/archinte.166.10.1092

Swanson, J. M., Sergeant, J. A., Taylor, E., Sonuga-Barke, E. J., Jensen, P. S., & Cantwell, D. P. (1998). Attention-deficit hyperactivity disorder and hyperkinetic disorder. *Lancet, 351*, 429-433. https://doi.org/10.1016/S0140-6736(97)11450-7

The Compassionate Mind Foundation. (2024). *Compassionate mind training.* Retrieved from www.compassionatemind.co.uk. Accessed June17, 2025.

The National Institute for Health and Care Excellence. (2019). *Attention deficit hyperactivity disorder: Diagnosis and management (NG87).* https://www.nice.org.uk/guidance/ng87. Accessed June17, 2025.

The National Institute for Health and Care Excellence. (2022a). *Depression in adults: Treatment and management (NG222).* Retrieved from https://www.nice.org.uk/guidance/ng222

The National Institute for Health and Care Excellence. (2022b). *Self-harm: Assessment, management and preventing recurrence (NG225).* Retrieved from https://www.nice.org.uk/guidance/ng225

Timimi, S. M., & Taylor, E. (2004). ADHD is best understood as a cultural construct. *British Journal of Psychiatry, 184*, 8-9. https://doi.org/10.1192/bjp.184.1.8

Van Rosmalen, L., Van IJzendoorn, M., & Bakermans-Kranenburg, M. J. (2014). ABC+D of attachment theory: The strange situation procedure as the gold standard of attachment assessment. In P. Holmes & S. Farnfield (Eds.), *The Routledge handbook of attachment: Theory* (pp. 11–30). Routledge.

Venta, A., Walker, J., Bailey, C., Long, T., Mercado, A., & Colunga-Rodríguez, C. (2022). The importance of attachment to fathers in Latinx mental health. *Journal of Social and Personal Relationships, 39*(5), 1508–1528. https://doi.org/10.1177/02654075211059444

Wang, C. D., Carbajal, I., Barajas-Munoz, I. A., Julio, K., Gomez, A., Trummer, M., & Scalise, D. (2021). Adult attachment, acculturation, acculturative stress, and psychological distress of first-generation Latinx immigrants. *Counselling Psychology Quarterly, 35*(3), 634–651. https://doi.org/10.1080/09515070.2021.1933910

Wei, M., Russell, D. W., Mallinckrodt, B., & Vogel, D. L. (2007). The Experiences in Close Relationship Scale (ECR)-short form: Reliability, validity, and factor structure. *Journal of Personality Assessment, 88*(2), 187–204. https://doi.org/10.1080/00223890701268041

Wills, F., & Sanders, D. (2013). *Cognitive behavior therapy*. Sage.

World Health Organization. (1993). *The ICD-10 classification of mental and behavioral disorders: Diagnostic criteria for research.* Author.

Young, S., & Bramham, J. (2012). *Cognitive-behavioural therapy for ADHD in adolescents and adults: A psychological guide to practice.* Wiley Blackwell. https://doi.org/10.1002/9781119943440

Zamudio, G., Wang, C. D., & Jin, L. (2020). Adult attachment, social self-efficacy, familismo, and psychological wellbeing: A cross-cultural comparison. *The Counseling Psychologist, 48*(7), 922–952. https://doi.org/10.1177/0011000020930637

Chapter 4
West Meets East in Compassion: Exploring CFT for Individuals with Dyslexia Across Cultures

Dana Abu Omar

Introduction

In a world where academic performance is often equated with self-worth, individuals with dyslexia frequently navigate systems that misunderstand their needs and underestimate their potential (Fawcett, 2022; Tanner, 2009). As a result of these systemic shortcomings, this lack of understanding leads to significant emotional challenges, including anxiety, shame, and internalised stigma (Riddick & Fawcett, 2012). In response to these emotional and psychological burdens, Compassion-Focused Therapy (CFT), developed by Gilbert (2010a), offers a transformative approach to supporting individuals with dyslexia by addressing not only cognitive difficulties but also the emotional struggles that hinder both their academic and personal growth. CFT, which focuses on fostering self-compassion and emotional regulation, is particularly effective for individuals who experience chronic self-criticism and emotional distress (Gilbert, 2009). Given that these emotional struggles are common among individuals with dyslexia, often because of repeated academic failures and negative social comparisons, CFT offers a therapeutic framework that is well-suited to their needs. When applied in this context, CFT goes beyond addressing learning challenges to also alleviate the emotional burdens that often accompany them (e.g., shame and low self-esteem; Beaumont & Hollins Martin, 2015). Through the cultivation of a more compassionate inner dialogue and the development of emotional resilience, individuals with dyslexia can begin to reframe their experiences, reduce internalised stigma, and foster a more positive sense of self (Butler & Edmonson, 2009). Building on this foundation, this chapter explores the intersection of CFT and dyslexia highlighting its potential to reshape the lived experience of individuals

D. A. Omar (✉)
The Unit for English As a Foreign Language, The Faculty of Humanities, The Hebrew University of Jerusalem, Jerusalem, Israel
e-mail: dana.abuomar@mail.huji.ac.il

Y. Kotera et al. (eds.), *Compassion-Focused Therapy for Mental Health: International Perspectives*, Advances in Mental Health and Addiction,
https://doi.org/10.1007/978-3-032-12438-8_4

with dyslexia across diverse cultural contexts. By doing so, it aims to underscore the broader applicability of compassion-focused approaches in educational and therapeutic settings worldwide, where stigma and misunderstanding of learning differences continue to persist. In examining this intersection further, the chapter also seeks to bridge the gap in current research by exploring how CFT can be adapted to fit the unique cultural, societal, and educational dynamics of both Western and Eastern contexts. These regions have differing perceptions of dyslexia, and their distinct educational and social frameworks present both challenges and opportunities for integrating CFT into local therapeutic practices (Eltyeb et al., 2024). By addressing these cultural nuances, the chapter aims to expand the applicability of CFT beyond a Western clinical model, promoting more inclusive and context-sensitive interventions for individuals with dyslexia worldwide. To guide this exploration in a structured and comprehensive manner, the chapter is organised as follows:

- Overview of Dyslexia
- The Role of Emotional Well-being in Dyslexia
- The Intersection of CFT and Dyslexia
- Dyslexia and CFT Across Cultures: Case Studies from West and East
- The Role of Education in Facilitating CFT
- Challenges and Opportunities
- Conclusion

This structure is designed to build a layered understanding, beginning with foundational concepts and moving towards a critical analysis of how CFT can be meaningfully adapted across cultural settings to support individuals with dyslexia more effectively.

Overview of Dyslexia

Understanding the multifaceted nature of dyslexia is crucial, as it lays the groundwork for exploring how emotional well-being is intricately linked to the learning experience (Xu, 2024). This connection becomes especially relevant in the context of therapeutic interventions like CFT, which aim not only to support academic skills but also to address the psychological challenges that often accompany a dyslexia diagnosis (Snowling, 2019).

To lay this foundation, it is important to first define and contextualise dyslexia within both educational and psychological frameworks. Dyslexia is a specific learning disability of neurological origin that affects reading fluency, spelling, phonological awareness, verbal memory, and processing speed, despite average or above-average intelligence (the International Dyslexia Association [IDA], 2025; the British Dyslexia Association [BDA], n.d.). This discrepancy between cognitive ability and academic performance often results in a cycle of frustration and failure, particularly when educational systems are ill-equipped to recognise and support the needs of dyslexic learners.

Adding to the complexity of dyslexia is its global variability in prevalence, which reflects differences in linguistic, diagnostic, and cultural contexts (Aldakhil et al., 2023; Aldakhil, 2024; Farghaly et al., 2022; Lin et al., 2020; Sakhai et al., 2025; Uno, 2022; Uno et al., 2009; Xu et al., 2019; Zhang et al., 2019). Rates range from 3.4 to 24%, are often reported as higher in boys. These gender disparities are thought to arise from a combination of neurological, behavioural, and diagnostic biases (Aboudan et al., 2011; Elbeheri, 2022; Margulies et al., 2025; Willcutt & Pennington, 2000; Yang et al., 2022). Recognising these variations is essential, not only for accurately identifying dyslexia across populations but also for tailoring interventions to diverse sociocultural contexts.

Moreover, the persistent difficulties encountered by individuals with dyslexia can have far-reaching emotional and psychological consequences, including anxiety, low self-worth, and chronic self-criticism, challenges that extend well beyond the classroom. As such, understanding dyslexia not merely as a learning issue, but as a condition with complex emotional implications, is critical for designing interventions that support the whole individual, not just their academic performance (Snowling, 2019). This connection becomes especially relevant in the context of therapeutic interventions like CFT, which aim not only to support academic skills but also to address the psychological challenges that are often associated with a dyslexia diagnosis.

The Role of Emotional Well-being in Dyslexia

Expanding on this emotional dimension, it is important to recognise that beyond its cognitive and academic challenges, dyslexia often carries significant emotional burdens that can persist into adulthood. In traditional educational environments, individuals with dyslexia frequently encounter repeated failure, negative feedback, and social comparison, which can lead to entrenched feelings of inadequacy and shame (Carawan et al., 2016). These experiences frequently foster heightened self-criticism and contribute to a range of mental health concerns, including anxiety, depression, and a persistent fear of judgement in both academic and social spheres (Nalavany et al., 2011).

Over time, many individuals begin to internalise these struggles, avoiding tasks that might expose their difficulties. This withdrawal further limits their engagement in educational and social opportunities, reinforcing a negative self-concept and perpetuating cycles of low self-esteem and underachievement (Alexander-Passe, 2015). The need for interventions that address these psychological dimensions beyond academic remediation is therefore critical, particularly approaches that foster emotional resilience and self-compassion (Sako, 2016).

This emotional toll often deepens during adolescence, a period when academic performance heavily influences self-concept and social belonging. In cultures where educational achievement is closely linked to family honour, such as in parts of the Middle East, the stigma surrounding dyslexia can be particularly acute, intensifying feelings of shame and isolation (Burden, 2008). To avoid judgement or disappointing expectations, many adolescents conceal their struggles, withdrawing from potential sources of support. This concealment not only limits access to help but also increases psychological vulnerability, reinforcing patterns of distress and disconnection (Wilmot et al., 2023).

These entrenched emotional struggles can have far-reaching effects on overall mental well-being, particularly when left unacknowledged or unsupported. Beyond general feelings of anxiety and depression, individuals with dyslexia may develop chronic emotional distress marked by low self-worth, a diminished sense of agency, and difficulty trusting their own abilities. Over time, the internalisation of academic failure and negative social feedback can lead to a deeply ingrained sense of hopelessness. This psychological burden is not only linked to increased rates of depressive symptoms but, in more severe cases, to self-harming behaviours and suicidal ideation, especially when emotional isolation is compounded by co-existing psychological vulnerabilities (Dolan, 2023; Georgiou et al., 2024). These outcomes highlight the critical importance of early, emotionally attuned interventions that extend beyond literacy support to include the cultivation of resilience, self-compassion, and psychological safety (Livingston et al., 2018).

This complex psychological burden is further intensified by the role of shame and social stigma, which often serve to amplify emotional distress. For some individuals, particularly those lacking supportive environments, self-harm may emerge as a maladaptive coping mechanism. Adolescents and young adults are especially susceptible, as heightened sensitivity to peer evaluation and societal expectations during these formative years can exacerbate feelings of inadequacy and isolation (Mastorci et al., 2024). These vulnerabilities underscore the need for interventions that not only target academic support but also directly address the social-emotional challenges that dyslexic individuals face in navigating their identities (Evans, 2014).

Given the emotional complexities associated with dyslexia, ranging from internalised shame and low self-worth to the use of self-harm as a coping strategy, it becomes evident that academic interventions alone are insufficient. Despite advances in inclusive education, emotional support is often treated as secondary, leaving a critical gap in care for individuals who struggle not only with learning but also with profound psychological challenges (Nalavany et al., 2011). Addressing these needs calls for a more holistic, integrative approach. This is where CFT becomes particularly relevant. Developed to reduce self-criticism and foster emotional resilience, CFT aims to cultivate self-kindness and an inner sense of safety, essential tools for individuals navigating the compounded stressors of dyslexia. By targeting emotional patterns such as shame, fear of failure, and hypervigilance to judgement, CFT helps individuals build a more compassionate relationship with themselves. In doing so, it reframes support for dyslexia as not merely academic but deeply emotional, setting the stage for individuals to thrive rather than merely cope.

The Intersection of Compassion-Focused Therapy (CFT) and Dyslexia

Dyslexia extends beyond reading difficulties, often manifesting early in life as significant psychological distress well before formal diagnoses are made. Persistent academic struggles can lead to frustration, diminished self-esteem, and social withdrawal, with many children internalising their challenges and developing a negative self-concept (Riddick, 2001; Snowling, 2019; Snowling et al., 2020). These early emotional wounds, if left unaddressed, can evolve into more severe psychological issues in adolescence and adulthood, including chronic self-criticism, shame, and even self-harm (Alexander-Passe, 2015). Without timely support, individuals with dyslexia face heightened risks of anxiety, depression, and behavioural problems, particularly when co-occurring conditions like Attention deficit hyperactivity disorder (ADHD) or Oppositional defiant disorder (ODD) are present (Brimo et al., 2021; Kurushi et al., 2024).

The emotional impact of dyslexia is not only shaped by the condition itself but also profoundly influenced by the sociocultural context in which it is experienced. The perception and management of dyslexia differ markedly between Western and Eastern cultural settings. In Western societies, dyslexia is broadly recognised as a neurodevelopmental disorder, grounded in medical and psychological research. This scientific framing has contributed to the development of support systems that include tailored educational interventions, therapeutic approaches, and accommodations designed to reduce barriers and promote inclusion (Shaywitz & Shaywitz, 2003). Crucially, the recognition of dyslexia as a legitimate neurological condition helps reduce stigma, enabling individuals to seek support and fostering a culture of self-advocacy. Dyslexia is typically viewed as a challenge to be addressed rather than a personal shortcoming (Colenbrander et al., 2018).

In contrast, many Eastern societies continue to hold significant misconceptions about dyslexia, often attributing it to laziness, lack of discipline, or even moral weakness rather than recognising it as a cognitive difference (Eltyeb et al., 2024). These views are deeply rooted in cultural values that prize academic excellence, conformity, and collective honour. As a result, individuals with dyslexia may face heightened stigma, social marginalisation, and psychological distress, particularly in environments where academic failure reflects poorly on both the individual and the family (Wissell et al., 2025). In collectivist cultures, the emphasis on group harmony and fulfilling societal expectations can cause individuals to suppress their difficulties for fear of bringing shame upon their families. This may lead to internalised shame, emotional withdrawal, and low self-worth. Furthermore, such stigma can discourage families from pursuing diagnosis or intervention, contributing to widespread underdiagnosis and a lack of appropriate support systems (Elbeheri, 2022).

Family and societal roles are central to how dyslexia is perceived and managed across cultures. In individualist societies, such as those in the West, dyslexia is often framed as a personal challenge, addressed through individualised education plans and personal therapeutic work (Shaywitz & Shaywitz, 2003). In collectivist cultures, however, a diagnosis of dyslexia can be perceived as a familial failure, sometimes leading to concealment or denial of the condition to preserve family honour. This dynamic can significantly delay diagnosis and intervention, further entrenching emotional and educational difficulties.

In this context, CFT emerges as a promising intervention. Indeed, CFT targets the core emotional challenges often associated with dyslexia, such as shame, self-criticism, and emotional distress by cultivating self-compassion and activating the brain's soothing system. It encourages individuals to shift their internal dialogue away from self-blame and towards kindness and understanding, which is particularly beneficial for those with long-standing experiences of failure and social rejection (Gilbert, 2009, 2010b; Hofmann et al., 2010). Although direct research on the application of CFT to dyslexia is limited, findings from broader psychological contexts suggest its effectiveness in enhancing self-concept and emotional well-being (Beaumont & Hollins Martin, 2015; Kurian, 2025).

For individuals with dyslexia, especially in cultural contexts where academic struggles are heavily stigmatised, CFT may offer a powerful means of reframing self-perceptions and mitigating the emotional toll of societal expectations. However, its implementation must be culturally sensitive. In collectivist societies, adapting CFT to incorporate family and community involvement may enhance its resonance and effectiveness. Group-based therapeutic formats and interventions that emphasise shared compassion and collective healing may not only align with cultural values but also reduce stigma and encourage broader engagement with mental health support (Kariyawasam et al., 2023).

To foster more inclusive and effective support systems worldwide, it is essential to develop culturally tailored interventions that address both the emotional and social dimensions of dyslexia. This includes expanding awareness, challenging misconceptions, and integrating therapeutic approaches like CFT that honour cultural values while addressing the unique psychological needs of individuals with dyslexia. By bridging the gap between cultural perceptions and psychological intervention, we can create more supportive environments that promote resilience, self-worth, and long-term well-being for people with dyslexia across diverse cultural contexts.

Dyslexia and CFT Across Cultures: Case Studies from West and East

CFT is increasingly being explored as a supportive intervention for individuals with learning disabilities, including dyslexia. While direct case studies on dyslexia and CFT remain limited, a growing body of research on compassion-based therapies underscores CFT's potential in alleviating emotional difficulties frequently experienced by individuals with dyslexia, such as shame, low self-esteem, and anxiety

(Wakelin et al., 2022). CFT works by reducing self-criticism and fostering self-compassion, helping individuals shift their internal dialogue and engage the brain's soothing system to manage stress and build resilience (Gilbert, 2009; Hofmann et al., 2010). Its core emphasis on compassion and emotional regulation aligns well with the psychological needs of those facing persistent academic challenges and social stigma. In collectivist cultures, where family and social harmony are central, adapting CFT to include communal and family-based elements may enhance its cultural relevance and therapeutic impact (Rajaei, 2025). By bridging clinical insights with cultural sensitivity, CFT offers a promising framework for improving the mental health and emotional well-being of individuals with dyslexia across diverse cultural contexts.

Building on this foundation, CFT, which is originated in Western contexts, is grounded in cultural norms that emphasise autonomy, emotional regulation, and self-acceptance (Germer & Neff, 2013; Heine & Ruby, 2010). These values align well with CFT's core focus on reducing self-criticism and cultivating a kinder internal dialogue (Viou & Georgaca, 2021). This approach has proven particularly effective in addressing internalised stigma and emotional distress, which are common among individuals with dyslexia due to repeated academic struggles and negative self-perceptions (Burden, 2008). By fostering self-compassion, CFT offers a framework through which individuals with dyslexia can reframe their experiences, reduce psychological distress, and build emotional resilience. However, as Kotera et al., (2024a, 2024b) emphasise, the expression and reception of compassion are deeply shaped by cultural frameworks, particularly those that value interdependence, hierarchy, and collective identity. In non-Western, collectivist cultures, where familial duty and social harmony are central, interventions rooted purely in individualistic notions of self-compassion may not fully resonate.

Therefore, adapting CFT to reflect these cultural dimensions is critical. For individuals with dyslexia in such contexts, CFT may be more effective when it emphasises relational harmony, shared resilience, and compassion as communal values rather than solely personal pursuits. Incorporating family involvement, community-based therapeutic formats, and culturally relevant metaphors of compassion can enhance engagement and reduce stigma around both dyslexia and mental health. By integrating cross-cultural insights into its practice, CFT can become a more accessible and psychologically meaningful intervention for neurodivergent individuals across diverse cultural settings.

Thus, effectively applying CFT in non-Western contexts necessitates cultural sensitivity and thoughtful adaptation. As discussed, while the therapy's Western origins emphasise individual autonomy and self-acceptance, many Eastern societies view emotional experiences through a collective lens, prioritising familial harmony and social cohesion over individual expression (Chentsova-Dutton & Tsai, 2010). In these settings, framing compassion not merely as a personal virtue but as a relational or moral responsibility that contributes to family well-being or societal balance, can enhance the relevance and acceptance of the intervention (Roomy, 2017). For individuals with dyslexia, who may already face cultural stigma and internalised shame, group-based compassion practices and the integration of culturally resonant values such as perseverance, duty, and social contribution can increase the therapy's impact. As Kotera et al., (2024a, 2024b) note, CFT has been associated with improved psychological flexibility, emotional resilience, and overall well-being, highlighting its potential to empower marginalised individuals, particularly when adapted to align with their sociocultural frameworks.

Building on this culturally sensitive approach, cross-cultural applications of CFT further highlight its adaptability and promise in addressing the socio-emotional dimensions of dyslexia beyond Western paradigms. As initial adaptations demonstrate, compassion-based interventions when embedded within culturally relevant frameworks, can effectively complement traditional academic and psychological support systems (Kirby et al., 2017). In educational and clinical settings, pilot programmes suggest that integrating culturally informed CFT enhances both emotional and academic resilience by empowering individuals with dyslexia to navigate challenges through shared understanding and psychological strength. This aligns with Kotera et al. (2022), who emphasise the role of common humanity in peer support, underscoring the therapeutic value of recognising shared experience and mutual support in promoting well-being. When CFT is framed within cultural narratives that emphasise collective identity, perseverance, and duty, individuals are more likely to view self-compassion not as a solitary act, but as a socially meaningful practice (Golojuch et al., 2025). Importantly, Kotera et al., (2024a, 2024b) argue that a lack of cultural alignment in mental health interventions often leads to disengagement and lower efficacy, particularly among populations who experience stigma or marginalisation. Therefore, tailoring CFT to reflect both cultural values and the lived experiences of neurodivergent individuals not only enhances relevance and uptake but also broadens its capacity to support diverse populations through a strengths-based, compassionate lens (Lucre et al., 2021). Expanding on this, Kotera et al. (2023) stress the urgent need for structured, evidence-based tools to guide and evaluate the cultural adaptation of such interventions. Without systematic frameworks, adaptations risk being inconsistent or superficial, limiting their long-term impact. Therefore, developing robust models for culturally responsive CFT not only ensures fidelity and effectiveness but also strengthens its role as an inclusive, global mental health strategy for neurodivergent individuals such as those with dyslexia.

Western Context

This section builds on the preceding analysis by presenting case examples that illustrate how CFT has been applied to support individuals with dyslexia, particularly within Western cultural contexts. Given the emotional challenges commonly associated with dyslexia, such as shame, self-criticism, anxiety, and self-harm. CFT offers a promising framework for fostering resilience, self-acceptance, and emotional regulation. In Western settings, CFT interventions often centre on individual transformation through the cultivation of self-compassion. In contrast, adaptations in Eastern contexts are increasingly designed to align with cultural values that prioritise collective well-being, family cohesion, and social harmony (Tirch & Vogel, 2024). By comparing these culturally informed approaches, this section underscores the flexibility of CFT and its capacity to address the diverse emotional and sociocultural needs of neurodivergent individuals, ultimately supporting the development of more inclusive and contextually responsive therapeutic strategies.

United Kingdom

In the UK, emerging case studies indicate that CFT holds promise as an effective intervention for addressing the emotional challenges commonly experienced by individuals with dyslexia, including shame, self-criticism, and low self-esteem (Gibby-Leversuch et al., 2021). One illustrative case presented by Cooper and Frearson (2017) involved "Joe," an adult with dyslexia whose struggles with low mood and disordered eating were closely linked to deeply entrenched self-critical thought patterns (e.g., Jeong, 2024). The CFT intervention was carefully adapted to accommodate Joe's cognitive profile, placing emphasis on cultivating self-compassion and dismantling internalised stigma. Over the course of 13 sessions, Joe reported developing a more compassionate inner dialogue and a greater sense of emotional clarity. While quantitative outcome measures showed only modest change, qualitative feedback revealed meaningful improvements in self-understanding and psychological relief underscoring CFT's potential to support emotional recovery in dyslexic individuals.

Although published case studies specific to dyslexia remain sparse, clinical practice increasingly reflects the broader applicability of CFT principles. Practitioners working with dyslexic students frequently observe pervasive emotional distress, often fuelled by repeated academic setbacks, negative feedback, and social comparison (Bazen et al., 2023).

Informal integration of compassion-based techniques, such as guided imagery, self-kindness exercises, and reframing failure through a non-judgemental lens, has shown promise in helping dyslexic students to reduce self-criticism, improve coping, and enhance emotional resilience. These approaches not only support academic engagement but also contribute to a healthier sense of self-worth. While systematic empirical research is still needed to substantiate these findings, existing evidence and practitioner reports suggest that CFT offers a valuable complement to conventional dyslexia interventions by addressing the often-overlooked emotional toll of dyslexia (Cowles, 2017; Hardiman, 2015). Its emphasis on kindness, acceptance, and inner reassurance represents a powerful counterbalance to the shame and self-doubt that many individuals with dyslexia internalise over time.

Malta

In a culturally specific context, Falzon and Camilleri (2010) investigated the role of school counsellors in Malta in supporting students with dyslexia. Their research highlights the emotional toll experienced by these students, who often face repeated academic failure and social misunderstanding. Common emotional responses included low self-worth, anxiety, and frustration, indicators of a broader psychological impact that extends beyond academic challenges. While the intervention did not draw explicitly on CFT, the authors advocated for emotionally supportive and attuned counselling practices, underscoring a need for interventions that promote psychological safety. This emphasis on compassionate engagement aligns with CFT's core principles, particularly its focus on soothing the threat system and reducing self-criticism. As such, their findings point to the potential value of culturally grounded, compassion-based approaches in school settings, an essential consideration for adapting CFT across international educational contexts.

Collectively, these findings highlight a growing international awareness that dyslexia involves not only cognitive and academic challenges but also profound emotional impacts. Compassion-Focused Therapy offers a promising framework for addressing these needs by equipping individuals with emotional regulation strategies to cope with academic stress, reduce self-critical thinking, and foster psychological well-being. Research by Kotera et al. (2021) further supports this approach, demonstrating that self-compassion can moderate the relationship between extrinsic and intrinsic motivation in postgraduate students. This suggests that interventions grounded in compassion, such as those within the CFT model, not only alleviate emotional distress but also promote deeper, more autonomous engagement with learning. In the context of dyslexia, where learners frequently face diminished motivation due to repeated setbacks and external evaluation, cultivating intrinsic motivation through self-compassion may enhance both resilience and academic perseverance. These insights underscore the relevance of compassion-based strategies as part of a holistic, culturally adaptable approach to supporting neurodivergent individuals in educational and therapeutic settings.

Eastern Context

Japan

At present, there are no documented applications of Compassion-Focused Therapy (CFT) specifically tailored to individuals with dyslexia in Japan. Nonetheless, emerging clinical evidence suggests that CFT holds considerable promise for addressing the emotional dimensions of dyslexia within collectivist cultural contexts. Asano and Shimizu (2018), for example, reported on a Japanese client diagnosed with recurrent depressive disorder, marked by chronic self-criticism and pervasive shame, emotional experiences that closely parallel those frequently observed in individuals with dyslexia. The intervention incorporated core CFT practices such as compassionate imagery and soothing rhythm breathing, leading to significant improvements in emotional regulation and relational functioning. Although the client was not neurodivergent, the therapeutic focus on reducing shame and self-blame is highly relevant for dyslexic individuals, particularly in cultures where academic performance is closely tied to social identity and familial expectations. This case underscores the potential of compassion-based interventions to address culturally mediated experiences of distress, supporting the broader applicability of CFT in neurodiversity-informed, cross-cultural care.

Considered alongside the cases from the UK and Malta, the Japanese example further illustrates the cultural adaptability of CFT across diverse emotional landscapes. Considered alongside the cases from the UK and Malta, the Japanese example further illustrates the cultural adaptability of Compassion-Focused Therapy across diverse emotional landscapes. In the UK, CFT was employed to support an adult with dyslexia in reducing internalised stigma and cultivating a more compassionate inner dialogue. In Malta, school counsellors advocated for more emotionally attuned interventions within educational settings, implicitly aligning with the principles of compassion-based care. The Japanese case extends this trajectory by demonstrating how CFT techniques can be sensitively adapted to collectivist cultural values such as social harmony, relational obligation, and group cohesion. Taken together, these cases provide cross-cultural evidence that, although the emotional impact of dyslexia is shaped by sociocultural norms, common psychological themes emerge, particularly around self-criticism, diminished self-worth, and shame. These are precisely the domains in which CFT has shown strong clinical efficacy, reinforcing its relevance as a globally responsive intervention for neurodivergent individuals.

Collectively, these cases underscore the importance of culturally responsive applications of CFT that address the emotional impact of dyslexia while aligning with local values and norms. In collectivist contexts such as Japan, positioning compassion as a relational or moral duty, rather than solely an act of self-kindness, may enhance therapeutic resonance. These findings reinforce CFT's adaptability as a culturally attuned intervention for dyslexia-related distress across both Western and non-Western settings.

China

While no documented case studies currently exist on the direct application of CFT to individuals with dyslexia in China, emerging evidence suggests its potential relevance. A randomised controlled trial by Gu et al. (2022) examined a CFT-based online intervention for Chinese international students experiencing high levels of self-criticism, a core emotional difficulty frequently reported among individuals with dyslexia. The intervention resulted in significant reductions in self-criticism, depression, anxiety, and shame, pointing to the efficacy of compassion-focused approaches within Chinese cultural contexts. When considered alongside similar findings from

Japan (Asano & Shimizu, 2018), this study contributes to a growing body of evidence supporting the cultural adaptability of CFT for addressing emotional challenges, such as shame and self-blame, that are central to the dyslexic experience across global settings. The following table provides an overview of how CFT has been applied to dyslexia-related emotional issues across different regions, highlighting both direct applications and broader emotional health interventions. By comparing these case studies, we can gain insights into the ways CFT can be adapted to fit the unique needs of neurodivergent individuals, while considering the cultural frameworks that influence emotional experiences (Table 4.1).

As reflected in the table above, the application of Compassion-Focused Therapy varies across cultural contexts, with differing degrees of specificity to dyslexia. In Western contexts such as the UK, case studies like that of Joe (Cooper & Frearson, 2017) demonstrate the direct use of CFT to reduce self-criticism and enhance both emotional well-being and academic engagement in individuals with dyslexia. In Western contexts such as the UK, case studies like that of Joe (Cooper & Frearson, 2017) demonstrate the direct use of CFT to reduce self-criticism and enhance both emotional well-being and academic engagement in individuals with dyslexia. Similarly, the Maltese example (Falzon & Camilleri, 2010) illustrates how emotionally attuned, compassion-based strategies can be integrated into school counselling to support dyslexic students. In contrast, studies from Eastern contexts such as China and Japan have applied CFT more broadly to emotional issues like shame, anxiety, and self-criticism, without specific reference to dyslexia. These differences underscore the importance of culturally sensitive adaptation: while emotional challenges such as low self-worth and internalised self-blame are common across settings, tailoring CFT to align with local cultural values, such as collectivist norms of social harmony and familial obligation, is essential for its relevance and effectiveness.

This contrast underscores the critical need for culturally sensitive adaptations of CFT. In collectivist societies such as Japan and China, where social conformity, family honour, and interdependence are deeply embedded in the cultural fabric, framing CFT within the values of communal responsibility, family harmony, and social cohesion may significantly enhance its acceptance and therapeutic effectiveness. These cultural considerations are crucial when developing interventions that resonate with local emotional landscapes, as they can foster stronger engagement and improved outcomes. Moreover, the findings from these Eastern contexts also highlight a notable gap in the availability of compassion-based interventions, particularly in regions where access to psychotherapy is limited. This gap suggests the potential value of online and community-based adaptations of CFT, which could broaden accessibility and make culturally attuned interventions more widely available. By comparing the diverse models and outcomes of CFT across cultural settings, we can identify pathways to make CFT more inclusive and relevant to individuals with dyslexia worldwide. Such comparisons ensure that compassion-based approaches are not only culturally appropriate but also effective in addressing the emotional and academic challenges faced by neurodivergent learners, irrespective of their geographic or cultural background.

Table 4.1 Cross-cultural applications and relevance of CFT to dyslexia-related emotional challenges

Country/region	Population studied	Emotional focus	CFT application/method	Relevance to dyslexia	Cultural considerations
UK	Adult with dyslexia	Self-stigma, negative self-narrative	Full CFT protocol, including imagery and compassionate mind training	Direct application; reduced self-criticism and improved self-concept	Individualistic framing of self-compassion effective
Malta	School counsellors supporting dyslexic students	Low self-esteem, anxiety, frustration	Not formal CFT, but advocacy for emotionally supportive practices	Indirect support for CFT; emphasis on emotional responsiveness in schools	Mediterranean cultural context with emphasis on relational support
Japan	Client with depression (non-dyslexic)	Shame, self-criticism	Compassionate imagery, soothing rhythm breathing	Mechanisms align with dyslexia-related emotional needs	Compassion reframed as relational/moral duty in collectivist context
China	Chinese international students (non-dyslexic)	High self-criticism, shame, anxiety	Online CFT-based intervention (RCT)	Strong relevance due to shared emotional themes	Emphasis on social face, familial expectations, and emotional restraint

The Role of Education in Facilitating CFT

Educational Frameworks for Dyslexia in West and East

In Western contexts such as the UK, significant strides have been made in supporting students with dyslexia, with comprehensive systems in place for early identification, individualised education plans (IEPs), and evidence-based, multisensory instructional methods grounded in psychological and neuroscientific research (Snowling et al., 2020). These frameworks have not only focused on mitigating the academic challenges associated with dyslexia but have also increasingly addressed its emotional implications. Within this context, CFT has emerged as a promising complementary intervention. By targeting self-criticism and fostering emotional resilience, CFT helps dyslexic students cultivate self-compassion, which in turn supports improvements in both emotional well-being and academic outcomes. This integrated approach highlights the potential of CFT to enhance traditional educational models, ensuring that dyslexic students receive holistic support that nurtures both their cognitive and emotional development.

In contrast, many Eastern countries continue to face significant challenges in addressing dyslexia, including persistent stigma, insufficient teacher training, and centralised, inflexible curricula that hinder the adoption of inclusive educational practices (Ho & Fong, 2005). These systemic barriers often result in the marginalisation of dyslexic students, reinforcing feelings of shame and social exclusion. The integration of CFT into these educational contexts could offer a transformative shift, moving from a deficit-oriented approach to one that emphasises strengths and resilience. When implemented in schools or community programs, CFT has the potential to foster emotional resilience in dyslexic students while simultaneously cultivating empathy, compassion, and collaboration among educators, caregivers, and the broader community.

Furthermore, the experience of countries such as Japan and China, where CFT has been successfully applied to address self-criticism and emotional distress, underscores the potential for culturally adapted versions of CFT to be particularly effective in collectivist societies. By integrating cultural values such as family harmony, duty, and social cohesion, CFT could resonate more deeply with local norms, enhancing its acceptance and facilitating its incorporation into educational frameworks. This culturally attuned approach not only supports the emotional well-being of neurodivergent students but also contributes to the development of more inclusive, compassionate educational environments that recognise and nurture both cognitive and socio-emotional needs.

Training Educators in CFT

Building on the increasing recognition of CFT as an effective approach for supporting students with dyslexia, its successful implementation is closely tied to the preparedness of educators. It is essential that teachers are equipped with a thorough understanding of CFT's psychological foundations, particularly the cultivation of self-compassion, the activation of the soothing system, and the reduction of shame (Gilbert, 2014). These components are of particular relevance to students with dyslexia, who often encounter emotional challenges such as anxiety, low self-esteem, and internalised stigma (Kirby et al., 2017; Lawrence & Lee, 2014). In Western contexts, where teacher training often includes elements of child psychology and social-emotional learning, CFT-informed strategies can be seamlessly incorporated into professional development through workshops, reflective practices, and collaboration with school psychologists. These approaches not only cultivate teacher empathy but also enhance trauma-informed and inclusive pedagogical practices (Jennings et al., 2013). By training educators to recognise and address the emotional dimensions of dyslexia, they are better prepared to respond with compassion, reduce classroom stigma, and foster psychologically safe, inclusive learning environments.

This perspective reinforces earlier discussions on the importance of culturally responsive applications of CFT across both Western and Eastern educational contexts. While systemic challenges such as rigid curricula, limited teacher autonomy, and persistent stigma around learning differences may hinder implementation in some Eastern settings, culturally attuned adaptations, framed around values such as familial obligation, social cohesion, and collective well-being, can facilitate CFT's gradual integration into educational practice (Feng et al., 2025). Across cultural contexts, equipping educators with compassion-based strategies offers a scalable and pragmatic approach to strengthening emotional resilience, enriching student–teacher relationships, and fostering inclusive learning environments. Such approaches not only support the cognitive development of neurodivergent learners but also promote their emotional well-being, aligning with broader educational goals of equity, engagement, and psychological safety (Neff & Germer, 2018).

Holistic Approach to Learning

An effective educational framework for students with dyslexia must extend beyond the development of cognitive and literacy skills to encompass the emotional, psychological, and social dimensions of learning. A holistic approach recognises that emotional well-being, positive self-concept, and supportive social relationships are foundational to sustained academic engagement and long-term educational outcomes (Ecclestone & Hayes, 2009). In many Western educational systems, the integration of Social and Emotional Learning (SEL) into mainstream curricula reflects this understanding, promoting competencies such as emotional regulation, self-awareness, and empathy. Robust evidence indicates that SEL programmes contribute not only to improved academic achievement but also to enhanced mental health and interpersonal functioning (Durlak et al., 2011). These developments hold particular relevance for students with dyslexia, who frequently contend with elevated levels of anxiety, shame, and reduced self-efficacy as a result of recurring academic difficulties (Burden, 2008; Nalavany et al., 2011). Addressing these emotional challenges is essential for creating inclusive environments that support both the cognitive and affective needs of neurodivergent learners.

As recognition grows around the role of CFT in supporting neurodivergent learners, its successful integration into educational contexts relies on the preparedness and emotional competence of educators. For students with dyslexia, who often experience chronic self-doubt, shame, and internalised stigma, teachers equipped with a foundational understanding of compassion-based psychology are better positioned to respond to these emotional needs. In Western educational systems, where frameworks for social-emotional learning and child development are already embedded, CFT can be introduced through targeted professional development that emphasises experiential practice, reflective dialogue, and interdisciplinary collaboration (Gilbert, 2014; Kirby et al., 2017). Such initiatives help cultivate emotionally responsive teaching, enabling educators to create classroom environments that are attuned not only to cognitive diversity but also to the psychological well-being of learners. By fostering compassion within educational relationships, these approaches promote more inclusive, resilient, and humanising learning spaces.

In many Eastern educational contexts, longstanding philosophical traditions rooted in Confucianism, Buddhism, and collectivist ethics promote holistic development and moral cultivation. However, the prevailing emphasis on standardised assessment and academic performance often limits the adoption of emotionally responsive pedagogies (Feng et al., 2025). Within this landscape, CFT offers a culturally consonant framework for integrating emotional well-being into education. Practices such as mindfulness, compassionate teacher-student interactions, and emotionally inclusive dialogue align with core Eastern values of self-discipline, relational harmony, and communal responsibility (Neff & Pommier, 2013). By contextualising CFT within culturally embedded ideals, such as filial piety, group interdependence, and the moral development of the self, its incorporation into educational systems becomes not only feasible but also meaningful. Across both Western and Eastern settings, empowering educators with compassion-based strategies enhances their capacity to respond to student diversity with sensitivity and care. Such approaches foster trust, emotional resilience, and inclusive classroom environments where neurodivergent learners are recognised, supported, and affirmed (Neff & Germer, 2018).

Challenges and Opportunities

Expanding on earlier discussions of holistic and emotionally responsive education, the integration of CFT into support frameworks for students with dyslexia highlights both region-specific barriers and strategic opportunities. In Western contexts, where inclusive education policies and Social and Emotional Learning (SEL) are well established, CFT aligns closely with prevailing psychological paradigms that emphasise self-compassion, affect regulation, and the mitigation of shame (Durlak et al., 2011). This conceptual compatibility facilitates the incorporation of CFT into teacher education, school-based mental health services, and digitally mediated interventions. Nonetheless, despite these infrastructural strengths, many students with dyslexia continue to experience enduring emotional challenges, including anxiety, low self-worth, and internalised stigma, which often remain unaddressed within standard pedagogical models. The core challenge, therefore, lies not in infrastructural access, but in cultivating deeper educator competencies and embedding compassion-informed practices systematically across learning environments. Such integration is critical for fostering emotionally safe, inclusive settings where neurodivergent learners can thrive both academically and psychologically.

In Eastern contexts, the landscape presents a more intricate interplay of cultural values and systemic constraints. Traditions grounded in Buddhism and collectivist philosophies underscore the importance of compassion, ethical development, and relational attunement (Asano et al., 2022). However, practical obstacles, including persistent stigma surrounding learning differences, limited public and professional awareness of dyslexia, inflexible curricular frameworks, and a scarcity of specialised support services, continue to hinder the provision of timely and emotionally attuned interventions. Despite these challenges, there exists a strong conceptual resonance between the principles of CFT and culturally embedded ideals such as self-cultivation, filial responsibility, and social cohesion. This philosophical congruence creates a promising foundation for adaptation. Furthermore, increasing regional interest in mindfulness, emotional well-being, and inclusive education, amplified by global policy initiatives, provides momentum for the integration of compassion-based approaches. By embedding CFT-informed strategies into teacher training, school-based mental health services, and community-driven educational programmes, Eastern systems can move towards more culturally responsive and emotionally supportive environments for neurodivergent learners.

Across both Western and Eastern contexts, the successful implementation of CFT hinges on the ability to integrate core psychological principles with culturally grounded values. Such alignment not only enhances emotional resilience and learning engagement among students with dyslexia but also contributes to the development of an inclusive global education framework, one that honours individual neurodiversity while remaining sensitive to collective sociocultural priorities.

Conclusion

Compassion-Focused Therapy (CFT) presents a compelling, emotionally attuned framework for supporting individuals with dyslexia, extending beyond the cognitive challenges to address the emotional distress often intertwined with academic struggles. By nurturing self-compassion and enhancing emotional resilience, CFT not only mitigates internalised stigma but also fosters a healthier self-concept, an essential factor for sustained well-being and active engagement in learning. This approach is particularly valuable in promoting positive psychological outcomes for neurodivergent learners, reinforcing their capacity to navigate both academic and emotional challenges.

With its adaptability, CFT holds cross-cultural relevance: it aligns with inclusive practices in Western education and resonates with Eastern values of relational harmony and self-cultivation. Despite systemic differences, integrating CFT through teacher training and culturally responsive school programmes presents a practical path towards more empathetic, inclusive learning environments worldwide where neurodiverse students are supported both academically and emotionally.

Call to Action

Given the emotional challenges dyslexia poses for individuals and families across cultures, there is a clear need for interventions that address its psychological impact. CFT, which promotes self-acceptance and reduces shame, offers a promising, evidence-based approach to support emotional well-being. Yet, its potential remains underutilised, particularly in regions where dyslexia is misunderstood or stigmatised.

To harness CFT's benefits globally, cross-cultural research and adaptation are crucial. Culturally sensitive training for therapists, school-based implementation, and awareness campaigns can help integrate CFT into diverse educational systems. By fostering collaboration between educators and mental health professionals, CFT can help reframe dyslexia, not as a deficit, but as a difference, supporting resilience, inclusion, and human potential.

Author Contributions Conceptualisation: DAO; Investigation: DAO; Resources: DAO; Writing—original draft: DAO; Writing—review & editing: DAO; Project administration: DAO.

References

Aboudan, R., Eapen, V., Bayshak, M., Al-Mansouri, M., & Al-Shamsi, M. (2011). Dyslexia in the United Arab Emirates University—A study of prevalence in English and Arabic. *International Journal of English Linguistics, 1*(2), 64.

Aldakhil, A. F. (2024). Prevalence of developmental dyslexia among primary school children in Arab countries: A systematic review and meta-analysis. *Research in Developmental Disabilities, 152,* Article 104812.

Aldakhil, A. F., Ebrahim, M. T., & Gadelrab, H. F. (2023). Diagnostic survey of dyslexia and accompanying behavioural indicators in primary school students in Saudi Arabia. *Research in Developmental Disabilities, 134,* Article 104424.

Alexander-Passe, N. (2015). The dyslexia experience: Difference, disclosure, labelling, discrimination and stigma. *Asia Pacific Journal of Developmental Differences, 2*(2), 202–233.

Asano, K., Tsuchiya, M., Okamoto, Y., Ohtani, T., Sensui, T., Masuyama, A., Isato, A., Shoji, M., Shiraishi, T., Shimizu, E., Irons, C., & Gilbert, P. (2022). Benefits of group compassion-focused therapy for treatment-resistant depression: A pilot randomized controlled trial. *Frontiers in Psychology, 13,* 903842.

Asano, K., & Shimizu, E. (2018). A case report of compassion focused therapy (CFT) for a Japanese patient with recurrent depressive disorder: The importance of layered processes in CFT. *Case Reports in Psychiatry, 2018*(1), 4165434.

Bazen, L., de Bree, E. H., van den Boer, M., & de Jong, P. F. (2023). Perceived negative consequences of dyslexia: The influence of person and environmental factors. *Annals of Dyslexia, 73*(2), 214–234.

Beaumont, E., & Hollins Martin, C. J. (2015). A narrative review exploring the effectiveness of Compassion-Focused Therapy. *Counselling Psychology Review, 30*(1), 21–32.

Brimo, K., Dinkler, L., Gillberg, C., Lichtenstein, P., Lundström, S., & Åsberg Johnels, J. (2021). The co-occurrence of neurodevelopmental problems in dyslexia. *Dyslexia, 27*(3), 277–293.

British Dyslexia Association [BDA]. (n.d.). *Dyslexia.* https://www.bdadyslexia.org.uk/dyslexia

Burden, R. (2008). Is dyslexia necessarily associated with negative feelings of self-worth? A review and implications for future research. *Dyslexia, 14*(3), 188–196.

Butler, C., & Edmonson, S. L. (2009). Fostering resiliency: Making schools a better place for students with dyslexia. *Remember Our Mission, 109,* 109–118.

Carawan, L. W., Nalavany, B. A., & Jenkins, C. (2016). Emotional experience with dyslexia and self-esteem: The protective role of perceived family support in late adulthood. *Aging & Mental Health, 20*(3), 284–294.

Chentsova-Dutton, Y. E., & Tsai, J. L. (2010). Self-focused attention and emotional reactivity: The role of culture. *Journal of Personality and Social Psychology, 98*(3), 507.

Colenbrander, D., Ricketts, J., & Breadmore, H. L. (2018). Early identification of dyslexia: Understanding the issues. *Language, Speech, and Hearing Services in Schools, 49*(4), 817–828.

Cooper, R., & Frearson, J. (2017). Adapting compassion focused therapy for an adult with dyslexia—A case study. *British Journal of Learning Disabilities, 45*(2), 142–150.

Cowles, M. (2017). Compassion-focused therapy for trauma in people with learning disabilities: A conceptual review. *Research Portfolio Submitted in Part Fulfilment of the Requirements for the Degree of Doctorate in Clinical Psychology, 15.*

Dolan, A. (2023). Dealing with the trauma of undiagnosed dyslexia. *Journal of Franco-Irish Studies, 7*(1), 5.

Durlak, J. A., Weissberg, R. P., Dymnicki, A. B., Taylor, R. D., & Schellinger, K. B. (2011). The impact of enhancing students' social and emotional learning: A meta-analysis of school-based universal interventions. *Child Development, 82*(1), 405–432.

Ecclestone, K., & Hayes, D. (2009). *The dangerous rise of therapeutic education.* Routledge.

Elbeheri, G. (2022). Dyslexia in Egypt. In *The Routledge international handbook of dyslexia in education* (pp. 64–72). Routledge.

Eltyeb, E. E., Gohal, G. A., Al-Makramani, A. A., Humedi, A. M., Shubayli, S. M., Thurwi, S. A., Zaalah, S. A., Kariri, T. M., Majhali, A. Y., Ghalibi, A. T., & Mujarribi, M. H. (2024). Dyslexia in primary schools' children: A study to explore Saudi teachers' knowledge and attitudes in the Jazan region. *Hail Journal of Health Sciences, 6*(2), 98–103.

Evans, W. (2014). 'I am not a dyslexic person I'm a person with dyslexia': Identity constructions of dyslexia among students in nurse education. *Journal of Advanced Nursing, 70*(2), 360–372.

Falzon, R., & Camilleri, S. (2010). Dyslexia and the school counsellor: A Maltese case study. *Counselling and Psychotherapy Research, 10*(4), 307–315.

Farghaly, W. M., El Tallawy, S. H., Ramadan, A. S., Abdelrasol, R. B., Omar, M. S., Eltallawy, H. N., & Mohamed, K. O. (2022). Training second-grade dyslexic students using a computerised program in Asyut, Egypt. *The Egyptian Journal of Neurology, Psychiatry and Neurosurgery, 58*(1), 50.

Fawcett, A. J. (2022). Dyslexia world-wide: A view of emerging themes. In *The Routledge international handbook of dyslexia in education* (pp. 371–385). Routledge.

Feng, X., Zhang, N., Yang, D., Lin, W., & Maulana, R. (2025). From awareness to action: Multicultural attitudes and differentiated instruction of teachers in Chinese teacher education programmes. *Learning Environments Research, 28*(2), 345–386.

Georgiou, G. K., Parrila, R., & McArthur, G. (2024). Dyslexia and mental health problems: Introduction to the special issue. *Annals of Dyslexia, 74*(1), 1–3.

Germer, C. K., & Neff, K. D. (2013). Self-compassion in clinical practice. *Journal of Clinical Psychology, 69*(8), 856–867.

Gibby-Leversuch, R., Hartwell, B. K., & Wright, S. (2021). Dyslexia, literacy difficulties and the self-perceptions of children and young people: A systematic review. *Current Psychology, 40*(11), 5595–5612.

Gilbert, P. (2009). Introducing compassion-focused therapy. *Advances in Psychiatric Treatment, 15*(3), 199–208.

Gilbert, P. (2010a). An introduction to compassion focused therapy in cognitive behaviour therapy. *International Journal of Cognitive Therapy, 3*(2), 97–112.

Gilbert, P. (2010b). *Compassion-focused therapy: Distinctive features.* Routledge.

Gilbert, P. (2014). The origins and nature of compassion focused therapy. *British Journal of Clinical Psychology, 53*(1), 6–41.

Golojuch, L. A., Morgan, A. A., & Mittal, M. (2025). "As therapists, we get to be quietly subversive": A qualitative exploration of CFTs' social justice practices. *Journal of Marital and Family Therapy, 51*(2), Article e70006.

Gu, X., Li, S., & Hyun, M. H. (2022). Does compassion-focused therapy-based online intervention work for Chinese international students with high self-criticism? A randomized controlled trail. *SAGE Open, 12*(3).

Hardiman, M. (2015). *A mixed methods evaluation of the experiences of adults with learning difficulties and anxiety undertaking compassion focussed therapy* (Doctoral dissertation, University of East London).

Heine, S. J., & Ruby, M. B. (2010). Cultural psychology. *Wiley Interdisciplinary Reviews: Cognitive Science, 1*(2), 254–266.

Ho, C. S. H., & Fong, K. M. (2005). Do Chinese dyslexic children have difficulties learning English as a second language? *Journal of Psycholinguistic Research, 34*, 603–618.

Hofmann, S. G., Sawyer, A. T., Witt, A. A., & Oh, D. (2010). The effect of mindfulness-based therapy on anxiety and depression: A meta-analytic review. *Journal of Consulting and Clinical Psychology, 78*(2), 169.

International Dyslexia Association [IDA]. (2025). Dyslexia. https://or.dyslexiaida.org/about-dyslexia/

Jennings, P. A., Frank, J. L., Snowberg, K. E., Coccia, M. A., & Greenberg, M. T. (2013). Improving classroom learning environments by cultivating awareness and resilience in education (CARE): Results of a randomised controlled trial. *School Psychology Quarterly, 28*(4), 374.

Jeong, M. L. (2024). *Parental descriptions of eating patterns and executive function in children with dyslexia* (Doctoral dissertation, Grand Canyon University).

Kariyawasam, L., Ononaiye, M., Irons, C., & Kirby, S. E. (2023). Compassion-based interventions in Asian communities: A meta-analysis of randomised controlled trials. *Psychology and Psychotherapy: Theory, Research and Practice, 96*(1), 148–171.

Kirby, J. N., Tellegen, C. L., & Steindl, S. R. (2017). A meta-analysis of compassion-based interventions: Current state of knowledge and future directions. *Behavior Therapy, 48*(6), 778–792.

Kotera, Y., Ozaki, A., Miyatake, H., Tsunetoshi, C., Nishikawa, Y., & Tanimoto, T. (2021). Mental health of medical workers in Japan during COVID-19: Relationships with loneliness, hope and self-compassion. *Current Psychology, 40*(12), 6271–6274.

Kotera, Y., Richardson, M., & Sheffield, D. (2022). Effects of shinrin-yoku (forest bathing) and nature therapy on mental health: A systematic review and meta-analysis. *International Journal of Mental Health and Addiction, 20*(1), 337–361.

Kotera, Y., Beaumont, J., Edwards, A. M., Cotterill, M., Kirkman, A., Tofani, A. C., Kirkman, A., Tofani, A. C., McPhilbin, M., Takhi, S., Barnes, K., Todowede, O., Ingall, B. R., Asano, K., Arimitsu, K. (2024). A Narrative Review of Compassion Focused Therapy on Positive Mental Health Outcomes. *Behavioral Sciences, 14*(8), 643.

Kotera, Y., Llewellyn-Beardsley, J., Charles, A., & Slade, M. (2024b). Common humanity as an under-acknowledged mechanism for mental health peer support. *International Journal of Mental Health and Addiction, 22*(3), 1096–1102.

Kotera, Y., Taylor, E., Fido, D., Williams, D., & Tsuda-McCaie, F. (2023). Motivation of UK graduate students in education: Self-compassion moderates pathway from extrinsic motivation to intrinsic motivation. *Current Psychology, 42*(12), 10163–10176.

Kurian, S. (2025). Compassionate trauma-informed counselling for cancer patients based on compassion-focused therapy in the post-COVID era. *Vinayasādhana, 16*(1), 30–43.

Kurushi, R., Omer, M., Hussein, O., Ali, M., & Auf, A. I. (2024). Synergistic interventions for silencing oppositional defiant disorder and dyslexia in a child with attention-deficit/hyperactivity disorder: A case report from Albania. *Cureus, 16*(6).

Lawrence, V. A., & Lee, D. (2014). An exploration of people's experiences of compassion-focused therapy for trauma, using interpretative phenomenological analysis. *Clinical Psychology & Psychotherapy, 21*(6), 495–507.

Lin, Y., Zhang, X., Huang, Q., Lv, L., Huang, A., Li, A.,... & Huang, Y. (2020). The prevalence of dyslexia in primary school children and their Chinese literacy assessment in Shantou, China. *International Journal of Environmental Research and Public Health, 17*(19), 7140.

Livingston, E. M., Siegel, L. S., & Ribary, U. (2018). Developmental dyslexia: Emotional impact and consequences. *Australian Journal of Learning Difficulties, 23*(2), 107–135.

Lucre, K., & Clapton, N. (2021). The Compassionate Kitbag: A creative and integrative approach to compassion-focused therapy. *Psychology and Psychotherapy: Theory, Research and Practice, 94*, 497–516.

Margulies, R., Somodevilla, A., & Chen, S. (2025). Policy approaches to improving coverage of Dyslexia screening, testing and treatment. *Policy.*

Mastorci, F., Lazzeri, M. F. L., Vassalle, C., & Pingitore, A. (2024). The transition from childhood to adolescence: Between health and vulnerability. *Children, 11*(8), 989.

Nalavany, B. A., Carawan, L. W., & Rennick, R. A. (2011). Psychosocial experiences associated with confirmed and self-identified dyslexia: A participant-driven concept map of adult perspectives. *Journal of Learning Disabilities, 44*(1), 63–79.

Neff, K. D., & Pommier, E. (2013). The relationship between self-compassion and other-focused concern among college undergraduates, community adults, and practicing meditators. *Self and Identity, 12*(2), 160–176.

Neff, K., & Germer, C. (2018). The mindful self-compassion workbook: A proven way to accept yourself, build inner strength, and thriveÿ ÿ. Guilford Publications.

Rajaei, A. (2025). Exploring couple and family therapy approaches for addressing intergenerational trauma in Iran: A mixed-methods study. *The American Journal of Family Therapy*, 1–23.

Riddick, B. (2001). Dyslexia and inclusion: Time for a social model of disability perspective? *International Studies in Sociology of Education, 11*(3), 223–236.

Riddick, B., & Fawcett, A. (2012). *Living with dyslexia: The social and emotional consequences of specific learning difficulties/disabilities.* Routledge.

Roomy, A. J. (2017). Self-Compassion: Integrating Buddhist philosophy and practices with Western psychotherapy and a group counselling curriculum.

Sako, E. (2016). The emotional and social effects of dyslexia. *European Journal of Interdisciplinary Studies, 2*(2), 175–183.

Sakhai, F., Mazaheri, S., Golmohammadi, G., & Asadollahpour, F. (2025). Prevalence of developmental dyslexia among primary school children in Iran: A systematic review and meta-analysis. *Iranian Journal of Psychiatry, 20*(2), 223.

Shaywitz, S. E., & Shaywitz, B. A. (2003). Dyslexia (specific reading disability). *Pediatrics in Review, 24*(5), 147–153.

Snowling, M. J. (2019). *Dyslexia: A very short introduction.* Oxford University Press.

Snowling, M. J., Hulme, C., & Nation, K. (2020). Defining and understanding dyslexia: Past, present and future. *Oxford Review of Education, 46*(4), 501–513.

Tanner, K. (2009). Adult dyslexia and the 'conundrum of failure.' *Disability & Society, 24*(6), 785–797.

Tirch, D., & Vogel, T. (2024). Compassion focused therapy for the treatment of Trauma. In *Experiential Therapies for Treating Trauma* (pp. 241–255). Routledge.

Uno, A. (2022). Japan: Developmental Dyslexia in two writing systems using three scripts. In *The Routledge International Handbook of Dyslexia in Education* (pp. 169–174). Routledge.

Uno, A., Wydell, T. N., Haruhara, N., Kaneko, M., & Shinya, N. (2009). Relationship between reading/writing skills and cognitive abilities among Japanese primary-school children: Normal readers versus poor readers (dyslexics). *Reading and Writing, 22*(7), 755–789.

Viou, M., & Georgaca, E. (2021). "Enriching our inner dialogue": An activity to explore compassionate voices. *Journal of Constructivist Psychology, 34*(2), 207–217.

Wakelin, K. E., Perman, G., & Simonds, L. M. (2022). Effectiveness of self-compassion-related interventions for reducing self-criticism: A systematic review and meta-analysis. *Clinical Psychology & Psychotherapy, 29*(1), 1–25.

Willcutt, E. G., & Pennington, B. F. (2000). Comorbidity of reading disability and attention-deficit/hyperactivity disorder: Differences by gender and subtype. *Journal of Learning Disabilities, 33*(2), 179–191.

Wilmot, A., Pizzey, H., Leitão, S., Hasking, P., & Boyes, M. (2023). Growing up with dyslexia: Child and parent perspectives on school struggles, self-esteem, and mental health. *Dyslexia, 29*(1), 40–54.

Wissell, S., Hudson, J., Flower, R. L., & Goh, W. (2025). 'I hate calling it a disability': Exploring how labels impact adults with dyslexia through an intersectional lens. *Neurodiversity, 3*, 27546330241308540.

Xu, Y. (2024). Early pathogenesis, risks, and interventions of Dyslexia. *Theoretical and Natural Science, 35*, 102–111.

Xu, M., Tan, L. H., & Perfetti, C. (2019). 10 Developmental Dyslexia in Chinese. *Developmental Dyslexia Across Languages and Writing Systems, 200.*

Yang, L., Li, C., Li, X., Zhai, M., An, Q., Zhang, Y.,... & Weng, X. (2022). Prevalence of developmental dyslexia in primary school children: A systematic review and meta-analysis. *Brain Sciences, 12*(2), 240.

Zhang, L., Xia, Z., Zhao, Y., Shu, H., & Zhang, Y. (2023). Recent advances in Chinese developmental dyslexia. *Annual Review of Linguistics, 9*(1), 439–461.

Chapter 5
Culturally Sensitive Applications of Compassion-Focused Therapy for Perfectionism: Conceptual and Clinical Perspectives

Naoki Kawasaki

Perfectionism has been widely associated with a range of mental health problems, including depression, anxiety, disordered eating, obsessive–compulsive symptoms, and suicidality (Limburg et al., 2017; Patterson et al., 2021); it has even been regarded as a "transdiagnostic" factor underlying various psychological disorders (Egan et al., 2011). Moreover, many clients with perfectionistic tendencies have difficulty forming therapeutic alliances, which can negatively affect treatment outcomes (Miller et al., 2017; Van Der Kaap-Deeder et al., 2016; Zuroff et al., 2000). Additionally, perfectionists are known to experience not only challenges in therapeutic relationships but also general interpersonal difficulties that often lead to isolation and disconnection, which in turn are associated with increased risks of depression and suicidality (Hewitt et al., 2006, 2017; Roxborough et al., 2012; Smith et al., 2020).

As suggested by their tendency to struggle with emotional connection and receiving psychological support, perfectionists are often characterised by a lack of compassion (Ferrari et al., 2018; Kawamoto et al., 2023; Linnett & Kibowski, 2020; Stoeber et al., 2020) along with a heightened fear of it (Asano et al., 2017; Kawasaki et al., 2023). Furthermore, given the strong link between perfectionism and self-criticism (Dunkley et al., 2006; Gilbert et al., 2006; James et al., 2015), compassion-focused therapy (CFT; Gilbert, 2010a; Gilbert & Simos, 2022) appears to be a promising approach for working with perfectionists. The first half of this chapter will explore the rationale and implications of applying CFT to perfectionism.

Meta-analyses have shown that culturally adapted psychotherapy interventions tend to be quite effective (Griner & Smith, 2006). As there are various perspectives on

This work was supported by JSPS KAKENHI, Grant Number JP24K06534.

N. Kawasaki (✉)
Department of Psychology, Japan Women's University, Tokyo, Japan
e-mail: kawasakin@fc.jwu.ac.jp

Y. Kotera et al. (eds.), *Compassion-Focused Therapy for Mental Health: International Perspectives*, Advances in Mental Health and Addiction,
https://doi.org/10.1007/978-3-032-12438-8_5

the relationship between perfectionism and culture (Chang et al., 2012; DiBartolo & Rendón, 2012; Smith et al., 2016), it is essential to consider cultural sensitivity in therapeutic approaches to perfectionism. Hence, the second half of this chapter will discuss applying CFT to perfectionism, with a focus on cultural context.

Models of Intervention for Perfectionism

In contemporary clinical practice, two major approaches have emerged for treating perfectionism: cognitive behavioural therapy for perfectionism (CBT-P; Egan & Shafran, 2017; Shafran et al., 2018, 2023) and dynamic-relational therapy (DRT; Hewitt et al., 2017, 2023; Mikail et al., 2022). Both approaches are supported by a growing body of empirical evidence. Meta-analyses have further demonstrated their respective efficacies and allowed for detailed comparisons (Galloway et al., 2022; Lloyd et al., 2015; Smith et al., 2023; Suh et al., 2019). While both have proven effective, they differ significantly in their theoretical foundations and modes of intervention.

Cognitive Behavioural Therapy

CBT-P centres on the tendency of perfectionists to impose rigid standards upon themselves—standards they feel must be met through relentless effort and achievement (Egan & Shafran, 2017; Shafran et al., 2018, 2023). CBT-P draws attention to how excessive striving and checking behaviours aimed at achieving such standards can cause mental health to deteriorate, while in other cases, the fear of failure may result in counterproductive behaviours such as avoidance or procrastination. At the beginning of treatment, clients are invited to explore the costs and benefits of their perfectionistic patterns, helping them clarify their motivation for change. Then, based on the cognitive-behavioural model, the therapist and client collaboratively develop a case formulation of the client.

Therapeutic intervention is then used to target the underlying cognitive aspects of the client's rigid standards, such as "all-or-nothing" thinking and attentional bias that prioritises failure over success. Behavioural strategies are also employed, including "surveys" where clients explore how other people set and approach standards, as well as "behavioural experiments" where clients attempt to act imperfectly on purpose and reflect on the outcomes (Shafran et al., 2018).

CBT-P conceptualises perfectionism as involving an over-reliance of self-worth on achievement and effort. As a result, failure to meet internal standards or follow personal rules often triggers harsh self-criticism. Therefore, therapy aims to enhance clients' awareness of self-critical tendencies and introduce compassion as a viable and healthier alternative. Perfectionists also tend to overgeneralise failure in specific contexts to a global judgement of self-worth. Addressing these cognitive patterns and how self-worth is constructed becomes another vital aspect of intervention.

Dynamic-Relational Therapy and the Social Disconnection Model

In contrast, DRT (Hewitt et al., 2017; Mikail et al., 2022) is characterised by its conceptualisation of perfectionism as an interpersonal issue. DRT is grounded in the hypothesis known as the social disconnection model (SDM; Hewitt et al., 2017). The SDM posits a developmental process in which, when early attachment relationships fail to meet the child's needs synchronously, the individual develops an incoherent and wounded sense of self. In an attempt to compensate for this, perfectionistic behaviours emerge that are driven by an underlying belief: "If I am perfect, there will be nothing to criticise, to judge or to reject—nothing to be ashamed of—and I will be accepted, I will be whole, and I will have worth" (Hewitt et al., 2017, p. 101). This represents the individual striving to construct a flawless and non-rejected self.

The SDM also suggests that perfectionistic behaviours, shaped by past developmental experiences, contribute to social disconnection in current relationships. Individuals with early attachment injuries often form internal representations of themselves as "flawed and unworthy" and of others as "incapable and/or unavailable to respond to attachment needs" (Hewitt et al., 2017). These representations serve as a "perceptual lens" through which they interpret current relationships (Hewitt et al., 2017). As a result, they may experience subjective disconnection, believing that their flawed selves have no value and will be disliked and rejected by others. At the same time, distrust and hostility towards others may lead to real difficulties in interpersonal relationships, creating objective disconnection as well. Through both of these subjective and objective processes, perfectionists end up experiencing disconnection and rejection they try to avoid. This cycle has been shown to contribute to a range of psychological difficulties, including depression (see Smith et al., 2020 for a meta-analysis).

Based on the SDM, a key therapeutic goal of DRT is to increase clients' awareness of their interpersonal tendencies, such as expecting perfection of themselves and others. Therapy places strong emphasis on insight and understanding, particularly with regard to the developmental origins of perfectionism. Ultimately, DRT aims to help clients discover and internalise more adaptive, flexible ways of meeting their needs for safety, connection, and self-worth (Hewitt et al., 2017).

To facilitate insight, DRT incorporates case formulation as an important therapeutic approach through which therapists collaborate with clients to clarify their interpersonal needs rooted in early attachment relationships, the emotional pain experienced when those needs were unmet, and the coping strategies developed in response. This process includes identifying how current relational patterns may echo past experiences, including how such patterns might emerge in the therapeutic relationship. Prior to treatment, a comprehensive assessment explores the client's attachment history, trauma, emotional functioning, and relational dynamics. Therapists provide feedback on these patterns to build a cooperative alliance. Through this process, clients begin to examine the protective functions of perfectionism, the costs it has imposed on their lives, and the fears that underpin it. Although emotionally challenging, this work is foundational to therapeutic change (Hewitt et al., 2017).

The therapist's role is to attune to these emotional states and create a space where clients feel safe enough to express them. The work proceeds through a trial-and-error process that involves progress as well as setbacks within the context of an established therapeutic relationship.

Shared and Distinct Therapeutic Perspectives

Although CBT-P and DRT differ in terms of theoretical background and specific methods of intervention, they share several crucial perspectives in their therapeutic approaches to perfectionism.

First, both approaches emphasise the use of *case formulation.* In both CBT-P and DRT, therapists provide a structured collaborative framework to deepen the client's understanding of how his/her perfectionistic striving and interpersonal styles have been shaped and maintained. This shared understanding serves as the foundation for therapeutic change.

Second, both approaches view perfectionism as an *coping strategy for adaptation,* developed in response to specific environmental and emotional contexts. Rather than perceiving perfectionism as a pathological trait, it is seen as something that was once functional or protective—even if it has become maladaptive over time. This perspective allows the therapist and client to cooperatively and non-judgmentally explore the underlying emotional needs and vulnerabilities that the client may be attempting to manage with perfectionism.

Third, both CBT-P and DRT recognise and address the client's *ambivalence about change.* Although clients may wish to let go of their perfectionism, they often fear the consequences of doing so—such as feeling inadequate or being criticiesed by others. Therapy thus involves validating this ambivalence and helping the client move towards change at a sustainable and psychologically safe pace.

A notable distinction between the two approaches lies in the *degree of structure* embedded within the therapeutic process. DRT is a psychodynamic and relatively unstructured approach that allows for flexible, highly individualised interventions. While this flexibility constitutes a strength, it also requires a high level of clinical expertise, which may pose challenges in terms of accessibility and implementation. In contrast, CBT-P is delivered as a structured, manualised programme, consisting of specific modules. The availability of CBT-P in formats conducive to online, self-guided learning may reduce barriers to implementation and broaden its reach.

Another key difference concerns the emphasis on *relational processes.* DRT, along with the SDM, stresses the importance of addressing interpersonal difficulties. In contrast, standard CBT-P protocols do not focus on such relational dimensions. Individuals with perfectionistic tendencies are especially prone to reenacting patterns of social disconnection—even within the therapeutic relationship, such as through ruptures in the alliance or premature termination. Accordingly, establishing a shared framework that facilitates open discussion of patterns of connection and disconnection (as universal challenges that may emerge in therapy) may be critical for effective intervention.

Applying Compassion-Focused Therapy to Perfectionism

As discussed above, therapeutic interventions for perfectionism require the therapist to cooperatively build a case formulation with the client, respectfully recognise perfectionistic behaviours as adaptive strategies for self-protection, and validate ambivalence or fear associated with change. These elements are highly compatible with the core ideas of CFT.

As the case formulation is developed, the client's diverse behaviours and reactions are understood and respected as forms of "wisdom" (Gilbert, 2022c). Moreover, fears, blocks, and resistances (FBRs) to change—especially fear of compassion—are addressed through psychoeducation as well as (both conceptual and experiential) joint exploration (Gilbert, 2022a; Steindl et al., 2023). Another advantage of CFT is that, similarly to CBT, it allows for a degree of structure through the use of specific modules (Irons & Beaumont, 2018; Petrocchi et al., 2025). In addition, because CFT is based on attachment theory and involves working with both compassion and fear of compassion, it naturally facilitates a focus on relational processes of perfectionism. Taken together, these features suggest that CFT may serve as a promising integrative approach for intervening with perfectionism.

As suggested by the SDM, perfectionism is a coping strategy developed to repair attachment-related injuries and unmet emotional needs. Within the CFT framework, perfectionism is seen as a *safety strategy*; this concept is used in CFT case formulation (Kolts, 2016) and encompasses behaviours that have been learned to ensure self-protection in response to key fears shaped by past experiences, such as early life trauma or adversity (Gilbert, 2022c). These fears may include fear of abandonment or feelings of worthlessness. Safety strategies may take the form of avoidance, rumination, substance use, self-harm, and other behaviours. While such strategies may temporarily reduce or suppress the impact of core fears, they often costs in broader life domains such as isolation, depression, exhaustion, or a sense of impostorism. This cycle may cause individuals to become disappointed in themselves for repeating these outcomes, leading to further self-criticism, intensification of core fears, and the perpetuation of a negative feedback loop.

Perfectionistic behaviours often reflect people's efforts to manage distress and vulnerability on their own to secure affection or a sense of worth from others.

However, such behaviours may paradoxically undermine the interpersonal connection that people long for. This understanding is a shared theme between the CFT framework and the SDM.

Case Study of Compassion Focused Therapy

In clinical practice, when using CFT, therapists may frequently encounter perfectionism-related problems. Matos and Steindl (2020) reported on a case in which CFT was effective at addressing shame and perfectionism. The client displayed perfectionistic behaviours in an attempt to gain the attention of a distant father and to ease the anxiety of an overinvolved mother by achieving academic success. Through psychoeducation using the three circles model, the client came to recognise that she was using drive (achievement) system to suppress threat (anxiety) system. She also realised that her soothing system was underdeveloped and something she genuinely needed.

Furthermore, case formulation and functional analysis of self-criticism showed that perfectionism had become a form of submission or appeasement aimed at meeting others' expectations, gaining acceptance, and avoiding criticism—in other words, a strategy for securing psychological safety. Consistent with this fomulation, moments of resistance emerged around the idea of letting go of her perfectionism and self-criticism. The therapist guided her through imagery work in which the "perfect self" was personified and its functional impact was analysed. Through this process, the client and therapist collaboratively discovered that, while the "perfect self" generated anxiety and dissatisfaction, the "compassionate self" offered motivation and support. The client gradually came to appreciate the importance of shifting from self-criticism to compassion.

Mindful Compassion for Perfectionism

Cheli et al. (2021, 2022, 2024) developed a group-based programme called Mindful Compassion for Perfectionism (MCP) that integrates CFT and DRT. MCP consists of nine sessions delivered over eight weeks in a group format, covering topics such as conceptualising perfectionism, mindfulness, compassionate imagery, and understanding cyclical relational patterns.

Cheli et al. (2022) reported on a case in which an integrative intervention that included MCP was used with a woman who had developed perfectionistic tendencies in a highly competitive developmental environment. During the intervention, the client came to recognise that, influenced by her early environment, she held an internalised belief system centred on rigid social comparison, in which people were evaluated in terms of success and failure, and that she tended to view herself as inadequate and lacking worth. Through repeated self-criticism, she maintained a submissive interpersonal style, punishing herself in response to this belief. During the transition from individual therapy to group-based MCP, she repeatedly expressed anxiety and discomfort about sharing her experiences and revealing her imperfections to others. In response, the therapist adopted a nonjudgmental and validating stance, normalised these reactions as common and understandable, and framed direct and open sharing within the group as the best option at this stage, rather than pressing for immediate change. Over time, the client experienced a growing sense of common humanity through mutual sharing and listening within the group. She came to realise that her feelings of anxiety and resistance were not unique to her. As a result, she gradually developed a sense of connection with others and shifted from hiding her imperfections to actively working towards their acceptance.

In a pilot study (Cheli et al., 2021), MCP was implemented with perfectionistic individuals diagnosed with personality disorders, and the programme demonstrated strong feasibility and effectiveness. Qualitative analyses revealed diverse experiences among the participants. For example, participants reported that the group experience enabled insights that had not been achieved in individual therapy, which underlines how self-disclosure and mutual empathy helped reduce self-criticism and foster interpersonal support. More recently, Cheli et al. (2024) reported on the results of a three-arm randomised controlled trial (RCT) in which university students with high levels of perfectionism received MCP either in person or online. Compared to a wait-list control group, both MCP groups showed reductions in perfectionistic thinking and psychological distress. MCP also had low dropout rates, suggesting that it is a promising intervention for reducing perfectionism and associated stress.

Implications for Applying Compassion Focused Therapy to Perfectionism

The studies discussed above imply that CFT may be an effective intervention for perfectionism. As noted previously, an effective intervention requires an approach that includes personalising case formulation, recognising perfectionism as a coping strategy that once served an adaptive function, and understanding clients' ambivalence towards change. In this regard, CFT supports the development of individualised formulation through psychoeducation and reality-testing based on evolutionary theory and neuroscience. This enables clients to perceive their perfectionism with greater clarity and without judgment.

Moreover, when case formulation includes early attachment experiences, it provides a foundation for jointly exploring fear of compassion and other ambivalent feelings or FBRs as they arise. A core principle in working with fear of compassion is simply to talk about and share that fear (Gilbert, 2022a; Steindl et al., 2023); such dialogue is supported by the case formulation itself.

In terms of perfectionism, case formulation often shows that the client has developed perfectionistic behaviours—and accompanying self-criticism—as safety strategies in response to early environments filled with threats. This understanding helps both the therapist and client to appreciate that the fear or resistance that emerges when attempting to change one's perfectionistic strategies is entirely natural. For clients who have adapted to competitive and threat-based social environments by continually proving their worth and maintaining a "perfect self" identity (Matos & Steindl, 2020), letting go of such strategies can feel extremely threatening.

In therapy, it is important to recognise that perfectionism and self-criticism serve as forms of "wisdom" in the client's adaptation to past environments (Steindl et al., 2023). At the same time, it is essential not to attack or argue with the "perfect self". Techniques such as imagery, multiple-self exercises, and chair work (Bell et al., 2021) may be useful in helping personify the "perfect self" as one of the self's many aspects. By first making room for this part of the self, therapy can reduce the dominance of the "perfect self", create space for cultivating a compassionate self, and ultimately foster internal dialogue.

Perfectionism and Culture

The following section considers culturally relevant factors when applying CFT to perfectionism. As noted, much of the existing research on perfectionism has been conducted in Western countries such as Canada, the United Kingdom, Portugal, and Italy. Although there is growing evidence that compassion-based interventions can be effective in non-Western cultural settings (Kariyawasam et al., 2023), it is still crucial to discuss culturally sensitive adaptations in the treatment of perfectionism.

Identity and Cultural Views of the Self

As discussed earlier, perfectionism is not merely a behavioural or emotional issue but is often closely tied to one's sense of identity. Both CBT-P and the SDM assume that perfectionistic behaviours are deeply linked to efforts to maintain or restore a sense of self-worth or identity (Hewitt et al., 2017; Shafran et al., 2018). Resistance to therapeutic change among perfectionists can be understood as a reaction not to the modification of a single behaviour but to the perceived threat of identity transformation or loss.

When perfectionism is viewed as a matter of identity, cultural factors inevitably come into play. Markus and Kitayama (1991) developed the theory of cultural self-construals, which posits that cultural context shapes one's understanding of the self in relation to others and society. The theory distinguishes between two primary self-construals: the independent self and the interdependent self.

Independent self-construal is commonly observed in Western cultures, particularly in the United States and Western Europe (Markus & Kitayama, 1991). Within this framework, the self is perceived as an autonomous entity composed of internal attributes such as personality traits, motives, attitudes, and goals. Actions are guided by internal values and beliefs, and the self is emphasised as an active agent capable of influencing the external world. There is a strong tendency towards self-enhancement, the pursuit of high self-esteem, and a focus on positive emotional experiences (Kitayama et al., 1997).

Interdependent self-construal, originally proposed to characterise East Asian cultural contexts (Markus & Kitayama, 1991), is now seen as prevalent in a broader range of non-Western cultures, including those in South and East Asia, the Middle East, and Latin America (Kitayama & Salvador, 2024). In this framework, the self is defined through relationships with others—roles, social positions, and societal expectations. Rather than being shaped by internal attributes, behaviour is adjusted in response to contextual and relational demands. Emphasis is placed on maintaining harmony through self-restraint, self-modification, and at times, self-criticism (Kitayama et al., 1997).

Perfectionism and Cultural Self-Construal

From the standpoint of cultural self-construal, we can assume that culture also influences how perfectionists build an identity centred on the "perfect self". In particular, the distinction between independent and interdependent self-construal seems multilaterally related to the conceptual difference between self-oriented and socially prescribed perfectionism (Hewitt & Flett, 1991; Hewitt et al., 2017).

Self-Oriented Perfectionism and Self-Construal

Self-oriented perfectionism refers to the tendency to demand absolute perfection from oneself (Hewitt & Flett, 1991; Hewitt et al., 2017). Individuals with this tendency believe that achieving perfection and avoiding imperfection are necessary to preserve their self-worth and consistency. However, because such perfection is often unattainable in reality, they may come to see themselves as "not good enough" or "failures" and experience feelings of shame and self-criticism.

Self-oriented perfectionism can be considered an extreme phenotype of identity construction based on independent self-construal. Individuals with this tendency are strictly committed to the high and rigid standards they set for themselves, even when those standards cause personal distress. The conceptualisation of the perfectionistic individual targeted in CBT-P centres mainly on self-oriented perfectionism (Hewitt et al., 2017), which is characterised by psychological processes that are largely intrapersonal rather than interpersonal.

As Hewitt pointed out, perfectionism functions as a strategy for placing oneself in a state of social disconnection to protect oneself against relational and emotional conflict. It is a way of enhancing and preserving one's value through achievement and effort while emphasising independence and rejecting the need for dependency. Thus, therapeutic transformation of self-oriented perfectionism requires recognising the need for a certain degree of interdependent connection with others—something that can be perceived as a serious threat one's sense of identity.

Socially Prescribed Perfectionism and Self-Construal

In contrast, socially prescribed perfectionism is characterised by the belief that others expect perfection from oneself (Hewitt & Flett, 1991; Hewitt et al., 2017). Individuals with this tendency sense strong expectations and demands directed towards them by family, friends, acquaintances, or society as a whole. Socially prescribed perfectionism is often conceptualised in terms of perceived parental expectations of perfection and criticism of imperfection (Frost et al., 1990).

Socially prescribed perfectionism is thought to be driven by the desire for acceptance, belonging, and love, as well as the desire to avoid rejection and abandonment (Hewitt et al., 2017). While these interpersonal motivations are particularly evident in socially prescribed perfectionism, they are also believed to be present in self-oriented and other-oriented perfectionism (Hewitt et al., 2017).

Socially prescribed perfectionism is a strategy for identity construction based on interdependent self-construal. Specifically, it entails efforts to feel perfect and worthy by fully meeting others' expectations (Hewitt et al., 2017). It is a way of living in which individuals entrust their self-worth to others' evaluations, and their motivation for self-determination is diminished. The wishes and expectations of others become central to self-regulation (Hewitt et al., 2017). Based on these characteristics, socially prescribed perfectionism could be regarded as an extreme phenotype of the interdependent self.

However, in socially prescribed perfectionism, dependency loses the mutual, bidirectional nature implied by "inter-" and becomes a one-sided relationship in which the individual continuously provides resources to others. In other words, it takes on a submissive quality (Cheli et al., 2022; Matos & Steindl, 2020). In such cases, personal value and uniqueness, as part of an independent self, are regarded as noise or even threats to achieving perfect harmony with others. Recognising oneself as a distinct individual, being aware of one's own emotions, setting clear interpersonal boundaries, and holding assertive motives may feel natural, but can simultaneously pose threats to one's sense of identity and social safety.

Cultural Differences in the Level of Perfectionism

As discussed above, socially prescribed perfectionism is expected to be more prevalent in Eastern or non-Western cultural contexts characterised by interdependent self-construal, whereas self-oriented perfectionism is expected to be more prominent in Western contexts that emphasise independent self-construal. Several empirical studies have explored these differences.

DiBartolo and Rendón (2012) reviewed studies comparing perfectionism among Caucasian Americans, Asian Americans, and African Americans. They found no significant differences in achievement striving—reflecting self-oriented perfectionism—but consistently higher levels of evaluative concerns (which include socially prescribed perfectionism) among Asian Americans. Moreover, Asian and African cultural groups scored higher on subscales such as "parental expectations" and "parental criticism".

Asian American university students tend to report greater levels of parental expectations and criticism compared to their European American peers (Chang et al., 2014) and are more likely to perceive high family expectations for achievement and orderliness (Wang, 2010). In a similar vein, a study comparing the United States and the Middle East found that university students from the Middle East scored higher on "parental expectations" (Walton et al., 2020).

Further, Japanese individuals (including university students) tend to report lower levels of self-oriented perfectionism and higher levels of socially prescribed perfectionism compared to their Western counterparts; for example, European American students (Chang et al., 2012) and British individuals (Stoeber et al., 2013). Perera and Chang (2015) examined whose expectations are reflected in socially prescribed perfectionism by comparing Asian American and European American university students. They found that Asian American students tended to strongly perceive culturally embedded expectations for perfection, and that perceived expectations not only from parents but also from friends, peers, and teachers significantly contributed to their socially prescribed perfectionism.

These results suggest that people in non-Western cultures, including in East Asia, tend to adopt interdependent self-construal in which self-worth is defined through relationships with others. As such, they may be more inclined to pursue perfection to meet others' expectations. In particular, many appear to experience strong pressure and high expectations related to parental relationships. The influence of parental behaviour on children's perfectionism has been demonstrated in meta-analytic findings (Smith et al., 2022a); cultural factors may further amplify this effect.

However, the empirical outcomes are not entirely consistent. For instance, Smith et al. (2016) compared Canadian and Chinese university students; they found higher reported levels of perfectionistic striving among the Canadians but no significant difference in perfectionistic concern, a variable that reflects socially prescribed perfectionism. Additionally, studies using cultural self-construal as an individual difference variable have not consistently found significant associations between independent–interdependent self-construal and perfectionism across European and Asian university student samples (Chang, 2013).

These results imply that the relationship between culture and perfectionism cannot be fully captured by simple level-based differences or linear correlations. Instead, a more detailed and multi-layered approach may be required to understand how perfectionism manifests across cultures (Smith et al. 2022b).

Cultural Differences in the Processes of Perfectionism

In exploring the relationship between culture and personality, it is important not only to focus on cultural variation as reflected in individual-level differences, but also to consider the idea that culture generates specific psychological processes (Allik et al., 2023; Triandis & Suh, 2002). For instance, socially prescribed perfectionism may represent different psychological experiences depending on whether it occurs within an interdependent cultural and social environment or within an independent one.

Interdependent or collectivist cultures tend to develop within social contexts characterised by low relational mobility (San Martin et al., 2019; Thomson et al., 2018; Yuki & Schug, 2012, 2020). Relational mobility is "a socio-ecological variable that represents how much freedom and opportunity a society affords individuals to select and replace interpersonal relationships based on personal preference" (Yuki & Schug, 2020, p. 129). In societies with low relational mobility (which are common in non-Western regions), opportunities to freely choose interpersonal relationships are limited, and relationships tend to be relatively stable. However, because individuals cannot easily change or replace these relationships, they must be careful not to damage current ties or gain a bad reputation within their social circles. In these societies, people are essentially "stuck" in irreplaceable relationships. The level of relational mobility influences interpersonal behaviours, self-perception processes, and thinking styles (San Martin et al., 2019; Thomson et al., 2018; Yuki & Schug, 2020). The following sections consider two examples of this influence, both of which are closely linked to perfectionism: the interpersonal behaviour of self-disclosure and the internal process of self-effacement.

Self-Disclosure and Culture

Although people in societies with low relational mobility may appear to have close interpersonal ties, they often avoid disclosing their personal pain or secrets to others (Schug et al., 2010). This tendency was confirmed in a large-scale study conducted across 39 countries (Thomson et al., 2018). In societies with low relational mobility, where individuals have few alternative relationships if others reject or exclude them, maintaining a good reputation and preserving one's existing relationships are crucial.

Therefore, disclosing negative aspects of the self is considered risky and is generally avoided (Schug et al., 2010; Yuki & Schug, 2020).

In contrast, in societies with high relational mobility, interpersonal relationships are not fixed. Individuals must proactively engage with others and present themselves in ways that will lead others to choose them as relationship partners. In such contexts, while showing one's strengths and attractiveness is important, it is also essential to convey internal information to make oneself appear "predictable" to others. Thus, self-disclosure becomes beneficial and is frequently used as a relational strategy (Schug et al., 2010; Yuki & Schug, 2020).

This does not mean that people in societies with low relational mobility never engage in self-disclosure. Rather, the reluctance to disclose may function as a "default strategy" (Yamagishi et al., 2008) and people widely assume the shared norm that individuals may tend to refrain from self-disclosure. In such societies, not disclosing may be seen as natural, while disclosing may be perceived as a risky and exceptional act.

Perfectionistic Self-Presentation and Culture

The above context may also alter the meaning of "not revealing one's imperfections" and "presenting oneself as perfect". Perfectionists tend to engage in behaviours that involve presenting their perfection and concealing their flaws; this is known as perfectionistic self-presentation (Hewitt et al., 2003, 2017), for which the psychological meaning may vary depending on the cultural context.

A comparative study of Chinese and American participants (Wang et al., 2019) found that perfectionistic self-presentation was positively associated with mastery only among the Chinese participants. Though not statistically significant, the same correlation was negative among the Americans. These outcomes suggest that in individualistic cultures like that of the United States, presenting oneself as perfect or concealing imperfections may become a psychological burden. In contrast, in collectivist cultures like that of China, such behaviours may be regarded as helpful strategies that support one's sense of competence and mastery.

Therapeutic Implications of Self-Disclosure

When applying the above results to psychological interventions such as CFT, working on disclosing one's imperfections may carry culturally specific meanings. Perfectionistic individuals already tend to avoid seeking help from others (Abdollahi, 2017; Dang, 2020), and a lack of active engagement in therapy—often observed even after multiple sessions—is common among these clients (Miller et al., 2017; Zuroff et al., 2000). This tendency may be even more pronounced in non-Western cultures. In such contexts, perfectionistic clients may view disclosing their imperfections in therapy as socially and culturally atypical and may experience associated feelings of shame. Thus, special consideration is needed in building the therapeutic alliance.

It may be helpful to explore whether clients' reluctance towards therapy stems from negative evaluations of self-disclosure or feelings of shame. Framing the difficulty in disclosing imperfections as a central aspect of perfectionism, and addressing this explicitly, may be beneficial. In addition, it may be useful to convey to clients that not disclosing imperfections can be a socially adaptive and "wise" behaviour in societies where relational mobility is low and interdependent cultural norms tend to be dominant.

Psychotherapy, as a cultural institution, values self-expression and self-disclosure and encourages these behaviours, which are seen as therapeutic. However, this can feel like a "cross-cultural" experience, especially for clients in non-Western settings, and it is natural for them to feel discomfort or confusion. It is also important for therapists to be aware of these small cultural differences. If the client feels resistance to self-disclosure while the therapist believes self-disclosure "should" occur, the client may sense a critical attitude from the therapist and feel shame in the therapeutic setting. To prevent such mismatches, culturally informed psychoeducation, along with shared discussions and validation of the client's discomfort with self-disclosure, may be especially helpful in the early stages of therapy as the client becomes accustomed to the therapeutic context.

Self-Effacement and Culture

In cultural comparisons between Western and Eastern societies, self-criticism or self-effacement commonly arises (Heine et al., 1999; Kitayama et al., 1997; Yamagishi et al., 2012). The idea that Western cultures tend to be self-enhancing while Eastern cultures tend to be self-effacing or self-criticising is a well-known finding in cultural psychology (Heine et al., 1999; Kitayama et al., 1997). In Eastern contexts, self-effacement functions as a default strategy in interdependent or collectivist societies with low relational mobility (Yamagishi et al., 2012). In such societies, harmony with others is prioritised over self-enhancement, so instead of denying others and demanding that they improve, individuals are more likely to deny or criticise themselves to show their intention to improve themselves (Falk et al., 2009; Yuki & Schug, 2020). This tendency is widely shared as a commonly used strategy, adopted at least temporarily or pragmatically in everyday situations. As a result, self-criticism and self-effacement become routine behaviours.

Perfectionistic Self-Effacement/Criticism and Culture

Self-effacement and self-criticism in Eastern cultures are not necessarily detrimental to one's mental health. In fact, Suh et al. (2023), through a meta-analysis, found that the impact of self-critical perfectionism on depression tends to be relatively weaker in Asian societies; in these cultural settings, self-criticism may be understood as a means of self-cultivation.

Furthermore, self-effacement in Eastern societies is seen as a form of self-presentation aimed at protecting one's social reputation (Yuki & Schug, 2020). For example, university students in East Asia tend to evaluate their own performance as lower than that of an average other (Markus & Kitayama, 1991). However, when they are experimentally driven to assess themselves accurately, they exhibit self-enhancement tendencies similar to those observed in Western participants (Yamagishi et al., 2012). In interdependent contexts, self-criticism and self-effacement are more frequently used, familiar, and socially desirable safety strategies. Whether self-criticism serves as a path to self-improvement or becomes a harmful force is a question often raised both in CFT research and in dialogue with clients. Exploring this distinction together with clients can be an important and necessary part of the therapeutic process (Gilbert, 2022b).

Therapeutic Implications of Perfectionistic Self-Effacement

Based on the above cultural context, the meaning of self-criticism may differ in interdependent cultures. For example, a common CFT exercise involves analysing the function of self-criticism, that is, whether it is truly aimed at helping oneself or promoting one's well-being (Gilbert, 2009; Irons & Beaumont, 2018; Petrocchi et al., 2025). In such exercises, clients are generally encouraged to consider the personal cost or benefit of self-criticism. However, in interdependent societies, self-criticism can have a strong social function directed towards others. Even if clients agree that self-criticism is unhelpful from an individual standpoint, they may still feel anxious if it appears to contradict the value of social harmony.

This meaning may be even more pronounced in individuals with socially prescribed perfectionism rooted in interdependent self-construal. For these clients, abandoning a self-critical stance can threaten the relational identity they hold with others. It is common for clients to express fears such as, "I'd probably just fall apart, do nothing, achieve nothing, and for that matter everyone's opinions of me would be proven right. I am pathetic" (Matos & Steindl, 2020). In interdependent cultural contexts, however, they may fear things such as, "Others might see me as a burden" or "I wouldn't know who I am anymore". These fears reflect a profound entanglement between one's identity and social connections. Rather than perceiving such fears as distortions or immaturity, it may be more accurate to view them as reasonable attempts to navigate cultural expectations.

If therapists push for independence and self-assertion too quickly with perfectionistic clients who are interdependent and self-effacing, they may risk creating therapeutic discord. Self-effacement is not necessarily a personal weakness but a culturally normative (and, in many cases, "wise") strategy used to manage social risk and threat. Pressuring clients to adopt independence or assertiveness too abruptly can come across as imposing foreign values. Clients may then feel judged for their hesitation to change and experience shame. Therapists must recognise that self-effacement can be a culturally rooted, socially adaptive behaviour. When appropriate, this can be acknowledged and validated in psychoeducation. Doing so may help to create a therapeutic space that feels safer and more culturally attuned to the client.

The Three Circles, Multiple Selves, and Cultural Contexts in CFT

A key issue frequently raised in discussions of cultural differences is the contrast between holistic and analytic thinking. Holistic thinking emphasises viewing an object as a whole, paying attention to context, and relationships. In contrast, analytic thinking involves breaking down objects into components and attempting to understand them logically and independently (Nisbett et al., 2001). Research in cultural psychology suggests that holistic thinking is more prevalent in East Asian cultures (Nisbett et al., 2001) and is linked to interdependent self-construal and lower relational mobility (San Martin et al., 2019). In contrast, analytic thinking tends to dominate in Western cultures (Nisbett et al., 2001) and is associated with independent self-construal and higher relational mobility (San Martin et al., 2019).

Throughout this chapter, we have examined the relationship between perfectionism and culture and explored the culturally sensitive application of CFT. Thus far, it seems that CFT holds promise as a cross-cultural therapeutic model.

The Three Circles Model

A representative model within CFT is the three circles model (Gilbert, 2009), which conceptualises emotion in terms of three coexisting and potentially conflicting systems. This model aligns with both Western analytic thinking (which is focused on breaking down complex experiences into logical components) and Eastern holistic thinking (which values context, relationships, and the coexistence of multiple perspectives). CFT incorporates both styles by acknowledging the coexistence and interaction of all three systems, and by encouraging balance and relational integration rather than domination by a single system.

Multiple Selves

A similar conceptual orientation is seen in CFT's idea of multiple selves (Gilbert, 2009). Human beings do not function with a single, unified self-system; instead, individuals contain many coexisting selves (such as an angry self, an anxious self, a sad self, and a compassionate self) that mutually influence one another (Bell et al., 2021; Gilbert, 2010b). CFT's concept of multiple selves integrates both analytic and holistic modes of understanding: Analytically, it allows for the logical differentiation of distinct emotional responses (e.g. anger, fear, sadness), while holistically, it acknowledges the general multiplicity of the self and embraces the internal contradictions that naturally arise among its parts. In this way, CFT draws upon both analytic and holistic approaches to deepen clients' understanding of the self. While Western psychology has often focused on uncovering singular underlying principles, Eastern thought tends to be more accepting of contradiction (Peng & Nisbett, 1999). CFT, by integrating both perspectives, may offer clients a blend of culturally familiar and novel experiences.

Cultural Implications for CFT Practice

This perspective highlights several strengths of CFT in working with perfectionism. One key advantage is its capacity to address ambivalence in a steady and effective manner. As previously discussed, if perfectionism functions as a safety strategy tied to identity, attempts at change may provoke ambivalence. Particularly when moving from social disconnection towards social connection, clients may encounter fear and uncertainty, which pose significant therapeutic challenges (Hewitt et al., 2017).

CFT offers tools for working with this ambivalence through the concept of multiple selves. Clients with perfectionistic features often build a "perfect self" (Matos & Steindl, 2020) to secure acceptance and self-worth. At the same time, they carry imperfect selves burdened by shame, fear of failure, impostorism, or anger at being misunderstood. CFT's multiple selves framework not only recognises this plurality but also permits acceptance of contradictions between selves. Rather than attacking or rejecting perfectionistic parts of the self, CFT encourages therapists and clients to understand all parts as having "wisdom" and adaptive intent (Steindl et al., 2023).

In an illustrative case drawn from the author's clinical experience in Japan, a client with perfectionistic features began embracing compassion and attempted to relinquish her perfectionistic self, which had been shaped by a desire to meet the expectations of those around her. During this process, however, she encountered a therapeutic impasse. She felt as though she were betraying her parents' expectations and feared losing their love. While remaining non-judgmentally aware of this confusion and fear, she continued her work. She gradually developed a more nuanced formulation of herself, recognising that she had long fulfilled various roles within her family, driven by a sincere desire for her parents' attention and love. She also re-accessed memories of compassion expressed by another family member and came to realise that it was acceptable to support people who were experiencing anxiety at a pace that felt right to them. Towards the end of therapy, during a compassionate letter-writing exercise, the client wrote not only to her anxious self but also to her "adult self" who had worked hard under perfectionistic pressures. By directly addressing and speaking to the fears held by her perfectionistic "adult self", she expressed appreciation for its determined efforts and desperate struggle to ensure her safety. As a result, she reported that she was increasingly able to connect with her anxious self, which had previously seemed unreachable.

CFT's respect for the plurality of the self aids clients in accepting their inner diversity. Treating the perfectionistic self not as a problem to be eliminated, but as a form of protective wisdom, can foster internal dialogue and deeper self-integration. By hearing the voices of the individual self along with empathy, clients may experience rich inner processes that promote holistic transformation and growth across cultural contexts.

Conclusion

This paper has examined the psychological mechanisms underlying perfectionism and reviewed two major therapeutic approaches: CBT-P and DRT, highlighting their commonalities and differences. Furthermore, this paper argues that CFT is an effective and integrative approach that encompasses the key elements needed to address perfectionism. In particular, CFT's framework implies that perfectionism is a strategy to secure self-worth and social safety in competitive and threatening social environments. As such, transforming perfectionism may involve fear and ambivalence. However, by conducting case formulations that position perfectionism as a safety strategy, clients can explore the functions of their perfectionism and begin to recognise the need to cultivate compassion.

The investigation of cultural contexts suggests that the expression of perfectionism and client responses to treatment may vary across cultural settings. For instance, in cultures where independent self-construal is dominant, self-oriented perfectionism may be more prominent, whereas in cultures that emphasise interdependent self-construal, socially prescribed perfectionism may be more pronounced (although the empirical findings on this are mixed). In culturally attuned interventions, it is important to consider clients' values and relational styles, and to understand constructs such as self-disclosure and self-criticism within their respective cultural context. Doing so may enhance the formation of the therapeutic alliance and improve clients' sense of safety within the therapeutic context, thereby supporting their motivation and giving them the courage to make a change. Moreover, the CFT framework, which enables both analytic and holistic understanding of the self's multiplicity and inner conflicts, appears to hold promise as a cross-cultural approach.

Future challenges include refining culturally sensitive models of CFT practice and accumulating empirical research to examine their effectiveness. In particular, there is a need for studies that describe in detail how cultural background influences therapeutic processes, and that engage in dialogue with clinical practice on the ground. Regarding the cultural understanding of perfectionism, many current explanations remain at a hypothetical level. Hence, further empirical clarification is warranted.

In this paper, cultural differences have been discussed primarily using dichotomies such as East versus West and interdependence versus independence. However, when considering cultural factors, a more multidimensional perspective would be ideal (Kitayama & Salvador, 2024; Vignoles et al., 2016). Recent discussions, for instance, have pointed to the utility of frameworks such as WIRED (Kotera et al., 2024).

Moreover, the influence of temporal shifts on the development and expression of perfectionism(Curran & Hill, 2019) should not be overlooked. Advancing nuanced theoretical debates along these lines may contribute to a more refined understanding of each individual client who struggles with perfectionism.

Author Contributions Conceptualisation: NK; Investigation: NK; Resources: NK; Writing—original draft: NK; Writing—review & editing: NK; Project administration: NK.

References

Abdollahi, A., Hosseinian, S., Beh-Pajooh, A., & Carlbring, P. (2017). Self-concealment mediates the relationship between perfectionism and attitudes toward seeking psychological help among adolescents. *Psychological Reports, 120*(6), 1019–1036. https://doi.org/10.1177/0033294117713495

Allik, J., Realo, A., & McCrae, R. R. (2023). Conceptual and methodological issues in the study of the personality-and-culture relationship. *Frontiers in Psychology, 14*. https://doi.org/10.3389/fpsyg.2023.1077851

Asano, K., Tsuchiya, M., Ishimura, I., Lin, S., Matsumoto, Y., Miyata, H., Kotera, Y., Shimizu, E., & Gilbert, P. (2017). The development of fears of compassion scale Japanese version. *PLoS ONE, 12*(10), Article e0185574. https://doi.org/10.1371/journal.pone.0185574

Bell, T., Montague, J., Elander, J., & Gilbert, P. (2021). Multiple emotions, multiple selves: Compassion focused therapy chairwork. *The Cognitive Behaviour Therapist, 14*, Article e22. https://doi.org/10.1017/S1754470X21000180

Chang, E. C. (2013). Perfectionism and loneliness as predictors of depressive and anxious symptoms in Asian and European Americans: Do self-construal schemas also matter? *Cognitive Therapy and Research, 37*(6), 1179–1188. https://doi.org/10.1007/s10608-013-9549-9

Chang, E. C., Chang, R., & Sanna, L. J. (2012). A test of the usefulness of perfectionism theory across cultures: Does perfectionism in the US and Japan predict depressive symptoms across time? *Cognitive Therapy and Research, 36*(1), 1–14. https://doi.org/10.1007/s10608-011-9376-9

Chang, E. C., Yu, E. A., & Lin, E. Y. (2014). An examination of ethnic variations in perfectionism and interpersonal influences as predictors of eating disturbances: A look at Asian and European American Females. *Asian American Journal of Psychology, 5*(3), 243–251. https://doi.org/10.1037/A0034621

Cheli, S., Cavalletti, V., Flett, G. L., & Hewitt, P. L. (2021). Mindful compassion for perfectionism in personality disorders: A pilot acceptability and feasibility study. *BPA Applied Psychology Bulletin (Bollettino Di Psicologia Applicata), 68*, 55–65. https://doi.org/10.26387/bpa.287.5

Cheli, S., Cavalletti, V., Flett, G. L., & Hewitt, P. L. (2022). Perfectionism unbound: An integrated individual and group intervention for those hiding imperfections. *Journal of Clinical Psychology, 78*(8), 1624–1636. https://doi.org/10.1002/jclp.23365

Cheli, S., Cavalletti, V., Goldzweig, G., Bui, S., Petrocchi, N., Flett, G. L., & Hewitt, P. L. (2024). A three-arm randomized controlled trial to evaluate the efficacy and feasibility of mindful compassion for perfectionism in reducing perfectionistic cognitions. *Journal of Psychotherapy Integration*. https://doi.org/10.1037/int0000349

Curran, T., & Hill, A. P. (2019). Perfectionism is increasing over time: A meta-analysis of birth cohort differences from 1989 to 2016. *Psychological Bulletin, 145*(4), 410–429. https://doi.org/10.1037/bul0000138

Dang, S. S., Quesnel, D. A., Hewitt, P. L., Flett, G. L., & Deng, X. (2020). Perfectionistic traits and self-presentation are associated with negative attitudes and concerns about seeking professional psychological help. *Clinical Psychology and Psychotherapy,27*(5), 621–629. https://doi.org/10.1002/cpp.2450

DiBartolo, P. M., & Rendón, M. J. (2012). A critical examination of the construct of perfectionism and its relationship to mental health in Asian and African Americans using a cross-cultural framework. *Clinical Psychology Review, 32*(3), 139–152. https://doi.org/10.1016/j.cpr.2011.09.007

Dunkley, D. M., Zuroff, D. C., & Blankstein, K. R. (2006). Specific perfectionism components versus self-criticism in predicting maladjustment. *Personality and Individual Differences, 40*(4), 665–676. https://doi.org/10.1016/j.paid.2005.08.008

Egan, S. J., & Shafran, R. (2017). Cognitive-behavioral treatment for perfectionism. In *The psychology of perfectionism: Theory, research, applications.* https://doi.org/10.4324/9781315536255

Egan, S. J., Wade, T. D., & Shafran, R. (2011). Perfectionism as a transdiagnostic process: A clinical review. *Clinical Psychology Review, 31*(2), 203–212. https://doi.org/10.1016/j.cpr.2010.04.009

Falk, C. F., Heine, S. J., Yuki, M., & Takemurá, K. (2009). Why do Westerners self-enhance more than East Asians? *European Journal of Personality, 23*(3), 183–203. https://doi.org/10.1002/PER.715

Ferrari, M., Yap, K., Scott, N., Einstein, D. A., & Ciarrochi, J. (2018). Self-compassion moderates the perfectionism and depression link in both adolescence and adulthood. *PLoS ONE, 13*(2), Article e0192022. https://doi.org/10.1371/JOURNAL.PONE.0192022

Frost, R. O., Marten, P., Lahart, C., & Rosenblate, R. (1990). The dimensions of perfectionism. *Cognitive Therapy and Research, 14*(5), 449–468. https://doi.org/10.1007/BF01172967

Galloway, R., Watson, H., Greene, D., Shafran, R., & Egan, S. J. (2022). The efficacy of randomised controlled trials of cognitive behaviour therapy for perfectionism: A systematic review and meta-analysis. *Cognitive Behaviour Therapy, 51*(2), 170–184. https://doi.org/10.1080/16506073.2021.1952302

Gilbert, P. (2009). *The compassionate mind: A new approach to life challenges.* New Harbinger Publications Inc.

Gilbert, P. (2010a). *Compassion focused therapy: Distinctive features.* 237.

Gilbert, P. (2010b). *The compassionate mind: A new approach to life's challenges.* New Harbinger Publications.

Gilbert, P. (2022a). Formulation and fears, blocks, and resistances. In P. Gilbert & G. Simos (Eds.), *Compassion focused therapy clinical practice and applications* (pp. 207–242). Taylor and Francis.

Gilbert, P. (2022b). Internal shame and self-disconnection: From hostile self-criticism to compassionate self-correction and guidance. In P. Gilbert & G. Simos (Eds.), *Compassion focused therapy clinical practice and applications* (pp. 164–206). Taylor and Francis.

Gilbert, P. (2022c). The evolved functions of caring connections as a basis for compassion. In P. Gilbert & G. Simos (Eds.), *Compassion focused therapy clinical practice and applications* (pp. 90–121). Taylor and Francis.

Gilbert, P., Durrant, R., & McEwan, K. (2006). Investigating relationships between perfectionism, forms and functions of self-criticism, and sensitivity to put-down. *Personality and Individual Differences, 41*(7), 1299–1308. https://doi.org/10.1016/j.paid.2006.05.004

Gilbert, P., & Simos, G. (2022). *Compassion focused therapy: Clinical practice and applications.* Routledge.

Griner, D., & Smith, T. B. (2006). Culturally adapted mental health intervention: A meta-analytic review. *Psychotherapy: Theory, Research, Practice, Training, 43*(4), 531–548. https://doi.org/10.1037/0033-3204.43.4.531

Heine, S. J., Lehman, D. R., Markus, H. R., & Kitayama, S. (1999). Is there a universal need for positive self-regard? *Psychological Review, 106*(4), 766–794. https://doi.org/10.1037/0033-295X.106.4.766

Hewitt, P. L., & Flett, G. L. (1991). Perfectionism in the self and social contexts: Conceptualization, assessment, and association with psychopathology. *Journal of Personality and Social Psychology, 60*(3), 456–470. https://doi.org/10.1037/0022-3514.60.3.456

Hewitt, P. L., Flett, G. L., & Mikail, S. F. (2017). Perfectionism: A relational approach to conceptualization, assessment, and treatment. In *Perfectionism: A relational approach to conceptualization, assessment, and treatment*. The Guilford Press.

Hewitt, P. L., Flett, G. L., Sherry, S. B., & Caelian, C. (2006). Trait perfectionism dimensions and suicidal behavior. In *Cognition and suicide: Theory, research, and therapy* (pp. 215–235). American Psychological Association. https://doi.org/10.1037/11377-010

Hewitt, P. L., Flett, G. L., Sherry, S. B., Habke, M., Parkin, M., Lam, R. W., McMurtry, B., Ediger, E., Fairlie, P., & Stein, M. B. (2003). The interpersonal expression of perfection: Perfectionistic self-presentation and psychological distress. *Journal of Personality and Social Psychology, 84*(6). https://doi.org/10.1037/0022-3514.84.6.1303

Hewitt, P. L., Kealy, D., Mikail, S. F., Smith, M. M., Ge, S., Chen, C., Sochting, I., Tasca, G. A., Flett, G. L., & Ko, A. (2023). The efficacy of group psychotherapy for adults with perfectionism: A randomized controlled trial of dynamic-relational therapy versus psychodynamic supportive therapy. *Journal of Consulting and Clinical Psychology, 91*(1), 29–42. https://doi.org/10.1037/ccp0000787

Irons, D. C., & Beaumont, E. (2018). *The compassionate mind workbook: A step-by-step guide to developing your compassionate self*. Robinson Press.

James, K., Verplanken, B., & Rimes, K. A. (2015). Self-criticism as a mediator in the relationship between unhealthy perfectionism and distress. *Personality and Individual Differences, 79*, 123–128. https://doi.org/10.1016/j.paid.2015.01.030

Kariyawasam, L., Ononaiye, M., Irons, C., & Kirby, S. E. (2023). Compassion-based interventions in Asian communities: A meta-analysis of randomised controlled trials. In *Psychology and psychotherapy: Theory, research and practice* (Vol. 96, Issue 1, pp. 148–171). Wiley. https://doi.org/10.1111/papt.12431

Kawamoto, A., Sheth, R., Yang, M., Demps, L., & Sevig, T. (2023). The role of self-compassion among adaptive and maladaptive perfectionists in university students. *The Counseling Psychologist, 51*(1), 113–144. https://doi.org/10.1177/00110000221129606

Kawasaki, N., Ishimura, I., Sato, S., Nakatani, T., Oya, K., & Hayama, D. (2023). Processes linking perfectionistic self-presentation and social disconnection: The role of fears of compassion [In Japanese]. In *Proceedings of the 36th annual convention of the Japanese association of health psychology* (pp. 4–16).

Kitayama, S., Markus, H. R., Matsumoto, H., & Norasakkunkit, V. (1997). Individual and collective processes in the construction of the self: Self-enhancement in the United States and self-criticism in Japan. *Journal of Personality and Social Psychology, 72*(6), 1245–1267. https://doi.org/10.1037/0022-3514.72.6.1245

Kitayama, S., & Salvador, C. E. (2024). Cultural psychology: Beyond East and West. *Annual Review of Psychology, 75*(1), 495–526. https://doi.org/10.1146/annurev-psych-021723-063333

Kolts, R. L. (2016). *CFT made simple: A clinician's guide to practicing compassion-focused therapy*. New Harbinger Publications. https://ins.swanlibraries.net/Record/a2605051

Kotera, Y., Martínez-Rives, N. L., Aledeh, M., Colman, R., Veasey, C., Harrington, T., Komori, N., Ozaki, A., Griner, D., Ali, Y., & Taylor, E. C. (2024). Cross-cultural psychology and compassion. *Encyclopedia, 4*(4), 1509–1519. https://doi.org/10.3390/encyclopedia4040098

Limburg, K., Watson, H. J., Hagger, M. S., & Egan, S. J. (2017). The relationship between perfectionism and psychopathology: A meta-analysis. *Journal of Clinical Psychology, 73*(10), 1301–1326. https://doi.org/10.1002/jclp.22435

Linnett, R. J., & Kibowski, F. (2020). A multidimensional approach to perfectionism and self-compassion. *Self and Identity, 19*(7), 757–783. https://doi.org/10.1080/15298868.2019.1669695

Lloyd, S., Schmidt, U., Khondoker, M., & Tchanturia, K. (2015). Can psychological interventions reduce perfectionism? A systematic review and meta-analysis. *Behavioural and Cognitive Psychotherapy, 43*(6), 705–731. https://doi.org/10.1017/S1352465814000162

Markus, H. R., & Kitayama, S. (1991). Culture and the self: Implications for cognition, emotion, and motivation. *Psychological Review, 98*(2), 224–253. https://doi.org/10.1037/0033-295X.98.2.224

Matos, M., & Steindl, S. R. (2020). “You are already all you need to be”: A case illustration of compassion-focused therapy for shame and perfectionism. *Journal of Clinical Psychology, 76*(11), 2079–2096. https://doi.org/10.1002/jclp.23055

Mikail, S. F., Hewitt, P. L., Flett, G. L., & Ge, S. (2022). Group dynamic-relational therapy for perfectionism. *Research in Psychotherapy: Psychopathology, Process and Outcome, 25*, 249–257. https://doi.org/10.4081/ripppo.2022.635

Miller, R., Hilsenroth, M. J., & Hewitt, P. L. (2017). Perfectionism and therapeutic alliance: A review of the clinical research. *Research in Psychotherapy: Psychopathology, Process and Outcome, 20*(1), 19–26. https://doi.org/10.4081/ripppo.2017.264

Nisbett, R. E., Peng, K., Choi, I., & Norenzayan, A. (2001). Culture and systems of thought: Holistic versus analytic cognition. *Psychological Review, 108*(2), 291–310. https://doi.org/10.1037/0033-295X.108.2.291

Patterson, H., Firebaugh, C. M., Zolnikov, T. R., Wardlow, R., Morgan, S. M., & Gordon, B. (2021). A systematic review on the psychological effects of perfectionism and accompanying treatment. *Psychology, 12*(01), 1–24. https://doi.org/10.4236/psych.2021.121001

Peng, K., & Nisbett, R. E. (1999). Culture, dialectics, and reasoning about contradiction. *American Psychologist, 54*(9), 741–754. https://doi.org/10.1037/0003-066X.54.9.741

Perera, M. J., & Chang, E. C. (2015). Ethnic variations between Asian and European Americans in interpersonal sources of socially prescribed perfectionism: It’s not just about parents! *Asian American Journal of Psychology, 6*(1), 31–37. https://doi.org/10.1037/a0036175

Petrocchi, N., Kirby, J., & Baldi, B. (2025). *Essentials of compassion focused therapy: A practice manual for clinicians.* Routledge.

Roxborough, H. M., Hewitt, P. L., Kaldas, J., Flett, G. L., Caelian, C. M., Sherry, S., & Sherry, D. L. (2012). Perfectionistic self-presentation, socially prescribed perfectionism, and suicide in youth: A test of the perfectionism social disconnection model. *Suicide and Life-Threatening Behavior, 42*(2), 217–233. https://doi.org/10.1111/j.1943-278X.2012.00084.x

San Martin, A., Schug, J., & Maddux, W. W. (2019). Relational mobility and cultural differences in analytic and holistic thinking. *Journal of Personality and Social Psychology, 116*(4), 495–518. https://doi.org/10.1037/pspa0000142

Schug, J., Yuki, M., & Maddux, W. (2010). Relational mobility explains between- and within-culture differences in self-disclosure to close friends. *Psychological Science, 21*(10), 1471–1478. https://doi.org/10.1177/0956797610382786

Shafran, R., Egan, S., & Wade, T. (2018). *Overcoming perfectionism: A self-help guide using scientifically supported cognitive behavioural techniques* (2nd ed.). Little Brown Book Group.

Shafran, R., Egan, S. J., & Wade, T. D. (2023). Coming of age: A reflection of the first 21 years of cognitive behaviour therapy for perfectionism. *Behaviour Research and Therapy, 161*, Article 104258. https://doi.org/10.1016/j.brat.2023.104258

Smith, M. M., Hewitt, P. L., Sherry, S. B., Flett, G. L., Kealy, D., Tasca, G. A., Ge, S., Ying, F., & Bakken, K. (2023). A meta-analytic test of the efficacy of cognitive behavioural therapy for perfectionism: A replication and extension. *Canadian Psychology/Psychologie Canadienne.* https://doi.org/10.1037/cap0000360

Smith, M. M., Hewitt, P. L., Sherry, S. B., Flett, G. L., & Ray, C. (2022a). Parenting behaviors and trait perfectionism: A meta-analytic test of the social expectations and social learning models. *Journal of Research in Personality, 96*, Article 104180. https://doi.org/10.1016/j.jrp.2021.104180

Smith, M. M., Sherry, S. B., Ge, S. Y. J., Hewitt, P. L., Flett, G. L., & Baggley, D. L. (2022b). Multidimensional perfectionism turns 30: A review of known knowns and known unknowns. *Canadian Psychology/Psychologie Canadienne, 63*(1), 16–31. https://doi.org/10.1037/cap0000288

Smith, M. M., Saklofske, D. H., Yan, G., & Sherry, S. B. (2016). Cultural similarities in perfectionism: Perfectionistic strivings and concerns generalize across Chinese and Canadian groups. *Measurement and Evaluation in Counseling and Development, 49*(1), 63–76. https://doi.org/10.1177/0748175615596785

Smith, M. M., Sherry, S. B., Vidovic, V., Hewitt, P. L., & Flett, G. L. (2020). Why does perfectionism confer risk for depressive symptoms? A meta-analytic test of the mediating role of stress and social disconnection. *Journal of Research in Personality, 86*, Article 103954. https://doi.org/10.1016/j.jrp.2020.103954

Steindl, S., Bell, T., Dixon, A., & Kirby, J. N. (2023). Therapist perspectives on working with fears, blocks and resistances to compassion in compassion focused therapy. *Counselling and Psychotherapy Research, 23*(3), 850–863. https://doi.org/10.1002/CAPR.12530

Stoeber, J., Kobori, O., & Tanno, Y. (2013). Perfectionism and self–conscious emotions in British and Japanese students: Predicting pride and embarrassment after success and failure. *European Journal of Personality, 27*(1), 59–70. https://doi.org/10.1002/per.1858

Stoeber, J., Lalova, A. V., & Lumley, E. J. (2020). Perfectionism, (self-)compassion, and subjective well-being: A mediation model. *Personality and Individual Differences, 154*, Article 109708. https://doi.org/10.1016/j.paid.2019.109708

Suh, H. N., Pigott, T., Rice, K. G., Davis, D. E., & Andrade, A. C. (2023). Meta-analysis of the relationship between self-critical perfectionism and depressive symptoms: Comparison between Asian American and Asian international college students. *Journal of Counseling Psychology, 70*(2), 203–211. https://doi.org/10.1037/COU0000653

Suh, H., Sohn, H., Kim, T., & Lee, D. G. (2019). A review and meta-analysis of perfectionism interventions: Comparing face-to-face with online modalities. *Journal of Counseling Psychology, 66*(4), 473–486. https://doi.org/10.1037/cou0000355

Thomson, R., Yuki, M., Talhelm, T., Schug, J., Kito, M., Ayanian, A. H., Becker, J. C., Becker, M., Chiu, C-Y, Choi, H. S., Ferreira, C. M., Fülöp, M., Gul, P., Houghton-Illera, A. M., Joasoo, M., Jong, J., Kavanagh, C. M., Khutkyy, D., Manzi, C., … Visserman, M. L. (2018). Relational mobility predicts social behaviors in 39 countries and is tied to historical farming and threat. *Proceedings of the National Academy of Sciences of the United States of America, 115*(29), 7521–7526. https://doi.org/10.1073/pnas.1713191115

Triandis, H. C., & Suh, E. M. (2002). Cultural influences on personality. *Annual Review of Psychology, 53*(1), 133–160. https://doi.org/10.1146/annurev.psych.53.100901.135200

Van Der Kaap-Deeder, J., Smets, J., & Boone, L. (2016). The impeding role of self-critical perfectionism on therapeutic alliance during treatment and eating disorder symptoms at follow-up in patients with an eating disorder. *Psychologica Belgica, 56*(2), 101–110. https://doi.org/10.5334/pb.297

Vignoles, V. L., Owe, E., Becker, M., Smith, P. B., Easterbrook, M. J., Brown, R., González, R., Didier, N., Carrasco, D., Cadena, M. P., Lay, S., Schwartz, S. J., Des Rosiers, S. E., Villamar, J. A., Gavreliuc, A., Zinkeng, M., Kreuzbauer, R., Baguma, P., Martin, M., … Bond, M. H. (2016). Beyond the "East-West" dichotomy: Global variation in cultural models of selfhood. *Journal of Experimental Psychology: General, 145*(8), 966–1000. https://doi.org/10.1037/xge0000175

Walton, G. E., Hibbard, D. R., Coughlin, C., & Coyl-Shepherd, D. D. (2020). Parenting, personality, and culture as predictors of perfectionism. *Current Psychology, 39*(2), 681–693. https://doi.org/10.1007/s12144-018-9793-y

Wang, K. T. (2010). The family almost perfect scale: Development, psychometric properties, and comparing Asian and European Americans. *Asian American Journal of Psychology, 1*(3), 186–199. https://doi.org/10.1037/a0020732

Wang, Y., Li, L. M. W., & Xie, F. (2019). Cultural difference in maladaptive functions of perfectionistic self-presentation. *Asian Journal of Social Psychology, 22*(3), 290–300. https://doi.org/10.1111/AJSP.12371

Yamagishi, T., Hashimoto, H., Cook, K. S., Kiyonari, T., Shinada, M., Mifune, N., Inukai, K., Takagishi, H., Horita, Y., & Li, Y. (2012). Modesty in self-presentation: A comparison between the USA and Japan. *Asian Journal of Social Psychology, 15*(1), 60–68. https://doi.org/10.1111/j.1467-839X.2011.01362.x

Yamagishi, T., Hashimoto, H., & Schug, J. (2008). Preferences versus strategies as explanations for culture-specific behavior. *Psychological Science, 19*(6), 579–584. https://doi.org/10.1111/j.1467-9280.2008.02126.x

Yuki, M., & Schug, J. (2012). Relational mobility: A socioecological approach to personal relationships. In *Relationship science: Integrating evolutionary, neuroscience, and sociocultural approaches* (pp. 137–151). American Psychological Association. https://doi.org/10.1037/13489-007

Yuki, M., & Schug, J. (2020). Psychological consequences of relational mobility. *Current Opinion in Psychology, 32*, 129–132. https://doi.org/10.1016/j.copsyc.2019.07.029

Zuroff, D. C., Sotsky, S. M., Martin, D. J., Sanislow, C. A., Blatt, S. J., Krupnick, J. L., & Simmens, S. (2000). Relation of therapeutic alliance and perfectionism to outcome in brief outpatient treatment of depression. *Journal of Consulting and Clinical Psychology, 68*(1), 114–124. https://doi.org/10.1037/0022-006X.68.1.114

Chapter 6
Cultural Adaptation of Compassion Focused Therapy to East Asian Culture

Kenichi Asano

Introduction

Compassion Focused Therapy (CFT), developed by Paul Gilbert in the United Kingdom (Gilbert, 2010), is utilised for numerous psychiatric disorders and psychological difficulties (Leaviss & Uttley, 2014). Research has demonstrated its effectiveness in improving self-esteem, depression, self-criticism, and various other outcomes (Millard et al., 2023; Petrocchi et al., 2024; Thomason & Moghaddam, 2021; Vidal & Soldevilla, 2023). These findings encourage clinicians and researchers seeking more effective treatments to import theories and programmes from abroad into their own countries. However, when importing psychotherapy across different cultures and countries, it is essential to consider various cultural aspects and identify potential limitations to optimise treatment delivery. To provide successful psychotherapy across diverse cultural backgrounds, the importance of culturally appropriate treatment goals, processes, and content has been emphasised (Lo & Fung, 2003). In psychotherapy, the term 'goal' signifies not only the objective of the therapy itself but also the consensus between the client and therapist regarding the direction they are heading. Furthermore, these Goals vary across different cultural contexts. This variation arises because the environmental demands required for living differ depending on the specific environment an individual inhabits, which in turn means that what constitutes adaptive coping also varies. Cultural influences affect both the individual client level and the level of the groups to which they belong. As these aspects are internalised, whether through cultural transmission or learning, they impact not only how individuals behave towards others and the external world but also how they relate to themselves internally. Consequently, what is considered 'appropriate' or

K. Asano (✉)
Department of Psychology, Institute of Human Sciences, University of Tsukuba, Tsukuba, Japan
e-mail: asano.kenichi.ga@u.tsukuba.ac.jp

Y. Kotera et al. (eds.), *Compassion-Focused Therapy for Mental Health: International Perspectives*, Advances in Mental Health and Addiction,
https://doi.org/10.1007/978-3-032-12438-8_6

'just right' within a particular culture differs with respect to both the external world and the internal self.

'Process' pertains to aspects within the therapeutic relationship, such as the importance of communication style. From the perspective of 'language independence,' the English term 'Compassion' is often translated as '*Jihi*' (慈悲) in Japanese. However, '*Jihi*' encompasses the implication of a superior entity bestowing something upon an inferior one, and it also includes the nuance of an act performed by a transcendent (or superhuman) being. Moreover, because it is a word used very infrequently in daily life, the term '*Jihi*' is likely rarely used in psychotherapy settings (except perhaps when providing CFT). Additionally, from the perspective of 'cultural independence,' the meaning associated with places such as churches, shrines, and temples is likely heavily influenced by the country's religious background. In Japan, where nearly 70% of people identify themselves as non-religious (Hayashi, 2006), the mental representations associated with churches, shrines, and temples—places that are inherently religious—naturally differ from those held in other countries. The words and representations utilised within therapy might only be fully grasped by those with cross-cultural living experience; even then, their understanding may differ from that of individuals born and raised within that specific cultural sphere. Careful assessment and respectful handling of different cultures will be required to bridge these gaps.

'Content' refers to what is specifically addressed within psychotherapy. Of course, Content is influenced by the Goal, and it also likely varies depending on the Process being undertaken. This means that Content is not only directly influenced by culture but also receives cultural influences mediated through the Process and Goal. This interrelationship influences which elements are included within the therapy. Especially from the perspective of therapeutic programmes, defining the Content necessitates considering culturally appropriate Goals and accounting for the Process, particularly regarding the meanings and representations conveyed by the language used.

Cultural Characteristics of CFT-Related Variables in East Asia

CFT was initially developed as an intervention for patient groups exhibiting strong self-criticism. Gilbert et al. focused on the observation that patients with strong self-criticism have a very cold inner voice, which renders the generation of alternative thoughts ineffective and hinders symptom improvement. Subsequently, compassion was employed as a means to warm this inner voice, and various methods were developed to cultivate the compassionate potential within individuals, evolving into therapeutic techniques. These include, for example, exercises involving imagining a compassionate self or others, and writing letters while maintaining a sense of compassion. Since living with compassion and using it to cope with various difficulties are also therapeutic goals, approaches such as intentionally adopting a compassionate stance, engaging in behaviours that foster a sense of compassion, and acting assertively from a compassionate stance have also been proposed. However, it is known that there are clear cultural differences regarding the symptoms, psychological characteristics, and target behaviours that CFT addresses.

Regarding self-compassion, perhaps the most widely researched concept within the broader domain of compassion, a study comparing general adult populations in the United States and Japan was conducted by Arimitsu et al. (2019). The results indicated that Japanese general adults exhibited lower self-compassion scores compared to their American counterparts. Additionally, there are reports indicating that Japanese workers exhibit lower self-compassion than Dutch workers (Kotera et al., 2022). However, this trend does not appear to extend across all of Asia and is likely specific to East Asian regions, including Japan, South Korea, Taiwan, and China. Self-compassion across the United States, Thailand, and Taiwan was compared in a study by Neff et al. (2008), which found that Taiwan showed the lowest scores, while Thailand showed the highest.

Similarly, regarding self-criticism, international comparative studies have revealed notable differences. Dr. Gilbert, the developer of CFT, created a scale to measure self-criticism (Gilbert et al., 2004). This scale conceptualises self-criticism through three factors: the Hated Self, Inadequate Self, and the positive factor, Reassured Self. Hated Self reflects intense anger towards oneself and the desire to inflict self-injury or harm, encompassing destructive self-hatred, contempt, and disgust. In contrast, Inadequate Self is related to the desire to be better or improve, reflecting feelings of personal inadequacy and experiences of failure. Consequently, it is linked to social adaptation and is particularly rooted in feeling insufficient when comparing oneself to desired social standards. Reassured Self represents the ability to soothe, encourage, support, and affirm oneself when facing negative events; unlike the other two factors, it is positive.

Self-critical tendencies were measured in 12 countries (Australia, Canada, Switzerland, Israel, Italy, Japan, the Netherlands, Portugal, Slovakia, Taiwan, the UK, and the USA), and the scale's measurement invariance across these nations was examined in a study by Halamová et al. (2018). Hated Self and Reassured Self demonstrated high measurement invariance, suggesting they represent common aspects across these countries. In contrast, Inadequate Self lacked measurement invariance, indicating it is an aspect of self-criticism susceptible to cultural factors. Furthermore, Japan and Taiwan exhibited the highest scores on Inadequate Self. Additionally, concerning Reassured Self, findings indicate that Japan holds a different understanding or perception compared to other countries, potentially linking back to the previously mentioned disparities in self-compassion. In summary, the results from the self-criticism scale suggest that while Inadequate Self scores are high in East Asia, the construct itself likely holds a different meaning or position compared to other cultures. Furthermore, the actual experience and practice of self-reassurance and self-support ('befriending oneself') are presumed to be substantially different.

Next, we turn to shame, which, similar to self-criticism, is a therapeutic target in CFT. Shame is considered an aspect requiring particular attention when providing counselling or other forms of care to individuals with an Asian background (You, 1997). Indeed, international comparative research indicates that Japanese university students are more prone to feeling shame towards friends compared to British and American university students (Sznycer et al., 2012). On the other hand, no significant differences were found regarding shame felt towards strangers, suggesting that Japanese individuals may be particularly susceptible to experiencing shame within close relationships.

Shame has been assessed using various indicators. Japanese workers report higher levels of mental health problems and feelings of shame compared to British workers (Kotera et al., 2021). Asian Americans may tend to avoid seeking physical medical treatment due to feelings of shame (Kramer et al., 2002).

External and internal shame were compared across Japan, Singapore, Portugal, France, and Australia in a study by Matos et al. (2023). External shame refers to the perception that others view oneself as inferior, bad, inadequate, different, or flawed, accompanied by the fear of potential criticism, rejection, or ostracisation. Therefore, it motivates individuals towards behaviours aimed at securing a positive perception from others. Internal shame relates to how one perceives oneself, reflecting negative self-evaluations such as feeling inferior, flawed, bad, inadequate, unwanted, empty, weak, or lonely. Internal shame can function as a way to protect oneself from potential attack or exclusion by others through self-devaluation or negative self-assessment. Regarding these types of shame, Japan exhibited higher external shame compared to the other four countries and also showed the highest total score when internal and external shame were combined. Furthermore, the finding that external shame scores surpassed internal shame scores points to a specific characteristic of shame within Japanese culture. This tendency might stem from a cultural inclination in Japan to avoid shaming others or causing them to lose face, as suggested by Matos et al. (2023). In other words, there is a tendency not to display one's own superiority or significance (Dessí et al., 2023). This likely connects to the lower levels of self-compassion observed in East Asia and also offers a perspective on how the notion of an 'appropriate self-concept' varies culturally. While possessing self-confidence is generally seen as positive and is often a therapeutic goal, it is crucial to consider, when importing psychotherapies, that the culturally appropriate form or expression of confidence may vary. A demeanour that is confident and compassionate versus one that is confident but arrogant will likely be perceived very differently by others in East Asian contexts.

In addition, research indicates that Japanese university students tend to engage in less self-assertion compared to American university students (Singhal & Nagao, 1993). Similarly, comparisons between Canada and China have shown lower assertiveness among Chinese university students, potentially indicating a greater emphasis on the process and mutual respect in negotiations, rather than focusing solely on monetary outcomes (Ma & Jaeger, 2010). Although assertiveness is sometimes included as a module in CFT (Cattani et al., 2021), the degree to which it is expected or valued varies across cultures. Even in situations where self-assertion might be expected or valued in Western cultures, the same behaviour could potentially be perceived as selfish or self-righteous in East Asian contexts such as Japan and South Korea.

Finally, let us discuss fears of compassion, another important concept within CFT. Cultural differences between East Asia and the West are also anticipated regarding fears of compassion (Asano et al., 2017). Fears of compassion refer to avoidance or fear responses that arise when an individual attempts to be compassionate, occurring in relation to directing compassion towards oneself, directing compassion towards others, and receiving compassion from others (Kirby et al., 2019). Fears of compassion for self and fears of compassion from others, in particular, are factors that threaten mental health and are strongly related to self-criticism. While no studies have directly compared Fear of compassion scores between East Asia and other cultural spheres, Asano et al. (2017) demonstrated differing factor structures for fears of compassion from others and fears of compassion for self in Japan. For fears of compassion from others, two factors were identified: Avoidance and Anxiety, suggesting distinct emotional and behavioural response components. In contrast, fears of compassion for self were divided into Miserable with Self-Compassion (which reflects feelings of sadness, emptiness, loss, or grief when contemplating or trying to feel kind and warm towards oneself) and Demerits of Self-Compassion (which reflects anticipatory anxiety or worry about the perceived negative consequences or disadvantages of being self-compassionate, including fears of losing self-criticism and standards, becoming weak or dependent, becoming someone undesirable, being rejected, or believing bad things will happen). Fears of compassion represent not merely resistance to compassion, but also resistance to stopping self-criticism and the belief that self-correction is necessary. Fears of compassion in East Asia are complexly related to psychological variables such as low self-compassion scores, self-criticism, shame, and assertiveness, and addressing these characteristics sensitively is considered therapeutic. The appropriate degree for various psychological tendencies differs by country and culture, directly implying that the strategies required for survival also differ. These points warrant consideration when introducing Western-developed CFT into Asian cultures, particularly those in East Asia.

Goal, Process, and Content Implications from Research Data

Based on these points, this section considers approaches for applying CFT within East Asian cultures, focusing on Goal, Process, and Content.

First, regarding the Goal, it is necessary to acknowledge that the target 'appropriate' or 'just right' self-image differs. Particularly in East Asian regions, where self-compassion scores are lower than in Western cultures (Arimitsu et al., 2019; Kotera et al., 2022; Neff et al., 2008) and self-criticism is higher, the very psychological variables targeted by CFT present differently. There is a higher cultural tendency to use self-deprecation (Markus & Kitayama, 1991), and avoiding giving others the impression of being superior or excelling functions as a means of social adaptation or survival. While this originates in external interpersonal dynamics, this learned tendency, over time, also impacts the internal sense of self. However, this does not necessarily equate to denying the worthiness of receiving or directing Compassion towards oneself, and it appears to be distinct from fears of compassion (Asano et al., 2017; Gilbert et al., 2011). Even if an individual does not believe they are 'unworthy entities for compassion,' there is a cultural hesitation in East Asia towards externally expressing or internally affirming, 'I am a wonderful person deserving of compassion.' While aiming to hold kindness, compassion, and affection towards oneself and value that feeling, maintaining a humble attitude externally likely enhances social adaptation (Tsuda & Takasawa, 2024). This point should also be kept in mind when providing CFT in a group therapy format.

From the Process perspective, therapists should more consciously and carefully listen to, acknowledge, and validate the client's unique way of experiencing and expressing compassion. From the Content perspective, if a client shows resistance (i.e., fears of compassion) towards engaging with compassionate self or compassionate memory exercises, proposing compassionate others imagery or alternative exercises would be a good approach. Through repeated practice, individuals can develop their own form of compassion and learn to direct it towards themselves and use it flexibly (Asano & Shimizu, 2018). Furthermore, using Case Formulation can make it easier to approach this resistance. Fears of compassion are undoubtedly an important target in CFT, but structured intervention procedures have not yet been clarified. However, Steindl et al. (2023) highlight the importance of utilising Case Formulation and welcoming and respecting fears of compassion. Given that the development of fears of compassion is considered to have high validity within the East Asian cultural sphere, referring to the procedures outlined by Steindl et al. (2023), carefully exploring a deeper understanding through Case Formulation, and respecting the client's thoughts regarding fears of compassion are required.

Next, there are also clinical considerations regarding self-criticism. As mentioned earlier, Japan and Taiwan show high scores on Inadequate Self. This reflects a strong motivation for self-correction and can easily lead to the belief that self-criticism is necessary for oneself. From the Goal perspective, self-correction is considered a virtue in these cultural contexts. Of course, changing behaviours and habits in a compassionate, non-blaming way is possible, and doing so is expected to improve mental health and social adaptation (MacBeth & Gumley, 2012; Marsh et al., 2018; Phillips & Hine, 2021; Zessin et al., 2015). However, it is likely not uncommon for patients in East Asian cultures to show hesitation even when stopping self-criticism is directly proposed. The underlying logic often is: 'Things aren't going well now because my way is bad; I need to change my actions and habits. Therefore, I need self-criticism to achieve that.' Given this background, from a Process standpoint, it is advisable to fully listen to and acknowledge the patient's current coping methods and the functions of their self-criticism before overemphasising the utility of compassion, and then collaboratively explore alternative approaches. While not demonising self-criticism is standard practice in CFT, in East Asian cultures, handling this aspect with even greater care and adopting an approach that respects the patient's established style is particularly crucial. From a Content perspective, similar to addressing fears of compassion, exploring self-criticism after exploring the CFT Case Formulation will likely enable more collaborative engagement with the therapy. Although it may seem like a detour, taking careful, step-by-step, gradual approaches will likely facilitate the acceptance of compassionate methods.

Next, regarding shame and assertiveness. As mentioned in the section on self-compassion, East Asian cultures exhibit high external shame, and particularly in Japan, publicly displaying one's success or achievements to others or the community carries the risk of eliciting social threat (Matos et al., 2023). Therefore, regarding the Goal, a form involving somewhat moderated external expression and assertion may often be more desirable or adaptive. Unfortunately, Japan is also noted as a country with low awareness concerning human rights (Ipsos, 2018), and while this is an area requiring societal improvement, it remains a factor therapists must consider when providing therapy. From a Process perspective, it is advisable to conduct a thorough assessment considering the client's specific social circumstances (e.g., workplace, school) and then collaboratively explore appropriate levels of assertion and self-disclosure with the client. Discussing external behaviour and internal self-treatment as independent aspects, and perhaps sometimes choosing submissive and non-assertive behaviour in social situations, might be explored. While excessive use of such states can hinder internal adaptation (Kuwayama, 2003), balance can be achieved by acknowledging one's internal experiences and emotions with compassion. Compassion is thought to play a crucial role in enabling individuals to internally accept, praise, and view themselves as worthy of affection, even when external behaviour, driven by social adaptation, is incongruent.

Translation and Adaptation of a Group CFT Programme for a Japanese Population

In this section, we will introduce the content and purpose of the modifications undertaken by our research team. To date, our research team has developed two CFT programmes. The first is a group CFT programme developed based on a model originating from the United Kingdom. The second is an individual therapy programme created based on both a standardised international manual and the aforementioned group CFT programme adapted for Japanese individuals.

The group CFT programme tailored for a Japanese population evolved through three stages to reach its final form (Asano et al., 2022). The initial CMT programme (Compassionate Mind Training) was based on unpublished materials provided by Dr. Chris Irons privately. It involved 16 weekly 2-h sessions delivered at a community mental health centre. Based on this programme, we needed to conduct a programme structured into 12 sessions due to therapeutic structural constraints. The implementation setting was a community mental health centre, the same as in the United Kingdom. The contents of both programmes are shown in Table 6.1. At this primary stage, the changes were due to issues with the therapeutic structure, not cultural factors, but we will review the modifications.

First, to create a 12-session programme, we needed to integrate or delete some of the programme's content. Specifically, the 'colour' and 'place' exercises, originally conducted in separate sessions (3 and 4), were combined and introduced within Session 3. Similarly, the compassionate self and other imagery exercises, initially spread across four sessions (5 through 8), were consolidated into two sessions (Sessions 5 and 6). Likewise, the use of imagery in stressful situations, previously addressed over three sessions (10 through 12), was limited to only two sessions (Sessions 7 and 8). Letter writing, initially scheduled for Sessions 13 and 15, was consolidated into Session 10. Despite these edits physically reducing the programme by four sessions, we endeavoured to retain the core content wherever possible.

After implementing the 12-session programme detailed in Table 6.1 for a total of two groups, we introduced further modifications specifically tailored to the Japanese cultural context. This resulted in the structure shown in Table 6.2. A significant change in the Table 6.2 version was moving the Case Formulation component from Session 11, near the end of the programme, to the earlier Session 9. Consequently, the letter writing exercise was moved from Session 9 to Session 11.

These adjustments were primarily driven by participant feedback. Participants reported finding the insights from Case Formulation—understanding how self-criticism and fears of compassion are linked to Key Fears—highly beneficial. Concurrently, they requested more time after this component to reflect on and process these valuable insights. Therefore, the programme was modified to introduce Case Formulation in Session 9, with Session 10 also focusing on this topic, specifically discussing methods for addressing Key Fears and Safety Strategies.

Partly as a consequence of Case Formulation moving earlier, the letter writing was shifted to Session 11. This decision was also supported by participant feedback, such as comments stating, 'I believe it's easier to write the compassionate letter after understanding the importance of compassion through the Case Formulation process.' This particular feedback seems strongly indicative of cultural influence. Specifically, it suggests that understanding why resistance to compassion occurs (viewed through the lens of Key Fears via Case Formulation), recognising that self-criticism or rejecting compassion is ultimately disadvantageous, or adopting the perspective that one's struggles and cycles are 'Understandable,' makes the task of writing a self-compassionate letter more accessible. In other words, this suggests an initial resistance to directing compassion towards oneself, likely reflecting the previously discussed lower baseline levels of self-compassion in this population.

Similarly, in the context of the compassionate self and other imagery exercises, many participants in the Japanese cultural setting report finding it easier to visualise **compassionate others** than a compassionate self. However, it is anticipated that as participants engage with other compassion-focused exercises throughout the programme, their resistance to imagining a compassionate self may gradually diminish. Therefore, a potentially effective approach could be to initially prioritise practice with the imagery exercise the participant finds easier (often **compassionate**

Table 6.1 Primary translation of CMT programme into Japanese cultural setting

No	16 sessions programme in UK	12 sessions programme in Japan
1	Group rules What is compassion Tricky Brain Mindfulness of sounds	Group rules What is compassion Tricky Brain Mindfulness of sounds
2	Three-circle model of emotion regulation (threat, drive, and soothing system) Soothing rhythm breathing	Three-circle model of emotion regulation (threat, drive, and soothing system) Soothing rhythm breathing
3	Psychoeducation of emotions Compassionate behaviour and evolution Image exercise of compassionate color	Psychoeducation of emotions Compassionate behaviour and evolution Image exercise of compassionate color, and compassionate place
4	Three-circle model and self-regulation Image exercise of compassionate place	Compassionate mindset Attributes and skills of compassion Fears of compassion Image exercise of Compassion flowing out
5	Attributes and skills of compassion Recalling compassionate memories Image exercise of compassion flowing out	Image exercise of compassionate self and others
6	Fears of compassion Image exercise of Compassionate Self	Image exercise of Compassionate self and others
7	Image exercise of Compassionate Self and Ideal Compassionate Others	Compassionate thinking towards difficult situations
8	Image exercise of ideal Compassionate Others	Compassionate thinking towards difficult situations
9	Image exercise of Compassionate Self	Compassionate letter writing
10	Using the 'ideal compassionate others' or 'compassionate self imagery' for difficult situations	Compassionate letter writing and fears of compassion
11	Using the 'ideal compassionate others' or 'compassionate self imagery' for difficult situations	Case Formulation of CFT
12	Using the 'ideal compassionate others' or 'compassionate self imagery' for difficult situations Compassionate letter writing	Wrap-up Compassion first-aid kit and relapse-prevention
13	Using the 'ideal compassionate others' or 'compassionate self imagery' for difficult situations Compassionate letter writing	
14	Case Formulation of CFT	

(continued)

Table 6.1 (continued)

No	16 sessions programme in UK	12 sessions programme in Japan
15	Using the 'ideal compassionate others' or 'compassionate self imagery' for difficult situations Compassionate letter writing	
16	Wrap-up Compassion first-aid kit and relapse-prevention	

Table 6.2 Modified CMT programme adapted for a Japanese cultural setting

No	Contents
1	Group rules What is compassion Tricky Brain Mindfulness of sounds
2	Three-circle model of emotion regulation (threat, drive, and soothing system) Soothing rhythm breathing
3	Psychoeducation of emotions Compassionate behaviour and evolution Image exercise of compassionate color, and compassionate place
4	Compassionate mindset Attributes and skills of compassion Fear of compassion Image exercise of Compassion flowing out
5	Image exercise of compassionate self and others
6	Image exercise of Compassionate self and others
7	Compassionate thinking towards difficult situations
8	Compassionate thinking towards difficult situations
9	Case Formulation of CFT
10	Understanding the Case Formulation and understanding key fears and safety strategies
11	Compassionate letter writing
12	Wrap-up Compassion first-aid kit and relapse-prevention

others), and then gradually introduce and encourage practice with the compassionate self imagery as the programme progresses.

Table 6.3 Final version of group programme for treatment-resistant depression

No	Contents
1	Psychoeducation of depression, tricky brain, and mindfulness
2	Three-circle model and soothing rhythm breathing
3	Psychoeducation of emotion, compassionate color or place
4	Psychoeducation for compassion and the compassionate self and memories
5	Images of compassionate self and others
6	Images of compassionate self and others
7	Compassionate thinking
8	Compassionate thinking
9	Case Formulation for shame and self-criticism
10	Key fears and safety behaviours
11	Compassionate letter writing
12	Wrap-up and relapse prevention

Final Version of the Group Programme for Japanese Populations

Finally, we developed the group programme outlined as Table 6.3. Although this programme was developed for patients with treatment-resistant depression, it is applicable to other disorders, excluding the Psychoeducation on depression in the first session. We will introduce the content of each session below.

Session 1 Rationale

In Session 1, there are no major changes from the previous iteration, but as mentioned, psychoeducation about depression has been added. A noted problem in Japanese psychiatric care is the extremely short consultation times with doctors, often meaning patients do not receive adequate explanations about their illness. When symptoms like decline in thinking or concentration occur, beyond the core depressive symptoms of low mood and lack of motivation, patients often become confused or attribute these issues to personal incompetence, leading to increased self-criticism and shame. Considering this, we decided to include illness education in the first session.

Sessions 2 and 3 Rationale

Sessions 2 and 3 are configured similarly to the Table 6.2 version, covering the Three-Circle Model and Soothing Rhythm Breathing. However, in Session 3, Psychoeducation on goal setting was added regarding how to approach homework (HW). Goals like 'I absolutely must do it' or 'Small things are meaningless' were presented as examples of 'Depressive' goal setting. Instead, 'Compassionate Goal Setting' was introduced, emphasising the importance of doing what one can, planning in a way that makes execution easier for oneself, valuing and respecting oneself for trying to build up from small steps, and accepting feelings of reluctance or fear. In Japan, the phrase 'Homework' often implies school assignments, carrying connotations of obligation where only completion is judged, not the effort to try—an unfortunate aspect of the educational culture. As a small countermeasure, we introduced the approach to HW using the phrase 'Compassionate Goal Setting.'

Session 4 Rationale

In Session 4, as a guide for Compassionate Flowing Out, participants were instructed to recall past experiences where they themselves showed compassion. This modification was made as an effort to reduce the resistance stemming from the cultural background towards the 'compassionate self' image, as discussed earlier. The aim was to access the feeling of compassion by recalling actual past actions and evoking the sensations from that time. This adaptation was also expected to serve as a bridge to the Compassionate Self imagery exercise introduced later.

Sessions 5 and 6 Rationale

Sessions 5 and 6 involve practicing the Compassionate Self and Compassionate Others imagery exercises. While both exercises are introduced in the session, participants are encouraged to focus on the one they find easier for HW. This is also a response to the resistance towards Compassionate Self imagery; Japanese participants tend to prefer the Compassionate Others image. Although we haven't collected formal data, the impression is that 80–90% prefer to start with the Compassionate Others image.

Sessions 7 and 8 Rationale

In Sessions 7 and 8, participants practice countering automatic thoughts arising in actual stressful situations with Compassionate Thinking. They are asked to attempt Compassionate Thinking after engaging in the imagery practiced in Sessions 5 and 6. Another incorporated strategy is soliciting Compassionate Thinking ideas from other participants if an individual finds it difficult to generate them on their own. For one person, this is an experience of receiving compassion from others; for another, it is an opportunity to express compassion towards others within the session. Experiencing compassionate attitudes from others and verbalising Compassionate Thinking towards others are expected to stimulate an individual's compassion functions and enhance readiness to direct compassion towards the self.

Sessions 9 and 10 Rationale

Session 9 introduces Case Formulation, and participants apply it to their own experiences. Each person confirms and shares their Key Fears, the Safety Strategies that developed consequently, and the outcomes resulting from these Safety Strategies. Session 10 continues with Case Formulation while proposing replacing previously employed Safety Strategies with alternative ones. Specifically, ideas for replacing self-criticism with Compassionate Thinking (the opposite action of the Safety Strategy) are explored. In Sessions 9 and 10, the therapist can solicit opinions and advice from other participants, allowing individuals to both receive and offer compassionate suggestions. Such compassionate relationships among participants can potentially function more effectively than the therapist-client relationship alone.

Session 11 Rationale

Session 11 is dedicated to Compassionate Letter Writing, which is placed towards the end of the programme compared to the original. The reason is for this letter to serve as the culmination or concluding piece of the programme. Through Session 10, participants have repeatedly practiced enhancing compassion via imagery exercises and Compassionate Thinking, and they have reflected on their past experiences through Case Formulation. The effort involved for clients not only in attending 12 weekly sessions but also in confronting their personal challenges and past adversities with strength and commitment is commendable. Placing Compassionate Letter Writing in Session 11 allows participants to express sincere respect for their own courage and diligence through the letter.

Session 12 Rationale

Finally, Session 12 serves as the programme summary and conclusion.

Programme Effectiveness Summary

This 12-session programme is a group CFT programme developed as support for treatment-resistant depression (Asano et al., 2022). The programme demonstrated high effectiveness in reducing depressive symptoms, with over 70% of patients showing recovery. Considering the prognosis for treatment-resistant depression, this is a groundbreaking result and is thought to reflect the strengths of CFT not found in other psychotherapies. Interestingly, alongside the reduction in depressive symptoms, Fear of Compassion for self decreased, and self-compassion also improved. Although the mechanisms for these changes are not clear, addressing fears of compassion may be key to effective intervention across different cultural contexts. The fact that sufficient effectiveness could be demonstrated by applying culturally adapted modifications and refinements provides strong grounds for aiming to deliver CFT to those suffering from psychological problems and mental disorders.

[...]

Limitations and Future Directions

In this chapter, we have described considerations for adapting the Compassion Focused Therapy programme for other cultures. When importing psychotherapy, it is necessary to sufficiently consider the cultural background and determine the Goal to aim for through psychological support; the Processes and Content must be considered similarly. Research to date indicates that the psychological variables addressed by CFT—such as self-compassion, self-criticism, shame, fears of compassion, and assertiveness—manifest differently in East Asia compared to the West.

These research findings might actually suggest that CFT could be particularly useful in these contexts, but precisely because of the cultural differences, the Goals aimed for in therapy and intervention may differ somewhat, consequently altering the appropriate processes to follow and the Content to introduce. We introduced strategies to address these differences, such as more careful empathy and introduction of concepts, along with several specific adaptations. However, we believe that the spirit and fundamental stance of CFT do not change. Going forward, examining adaptations and procedures for applying CFT in regions beyond East Asia will be necessary, and sharing such knowledge is believed to contribute to the improvement of mental health in our globalised modern society.

However, this chapter also has several limitations. First, the discussion primarily concerns the application of CFT in East Asia, specifically limited regions like Japan and Taiwan. Although perhaps not as pronounced as differences between the West and Asia, cultural variations may exist within the vast Asian continent, even among East Asian countries. Japan and Taiwan, influenced by Confucian culture, may be particularly distinct. The adaptation of CFT to other Asian regions, as well as regions like South America, Oceania, and Africa, requires separate discussion. Sharing knowledge about the process of importing CFT, as introduced in this chapter, is expected to contribute to the development of better programmes globally.

Furthermore, it should be noted that the programme detailed here was developed for treatment-resistant depression. While CFT is a transdiagnostic intervention (Kirby, 2024), and patients with various comorbid conditions participated in the programme described by Asano et al. (2022), different adaptations would likely be required for disorders such as Obsessive Compulsive Disorder or Eating Disorders.

Additionally, this chapter focused on a group programme example; adapting individual CFT would necessitate different considerations. Similarly, beyond programme development, methods for therapist training and strategies for implementing CFT within public health services are points that warrant further discussion. Addressing these challenges seems best approached through collaboration between CFT clinicians and researchers, forming a compassionate community.

Acknowledgements We utilised Google's Gemini for English language editing support.

Author Contributions Conceptualisation: KA; Investigation: KA; Resources: KA; Writing—original draft: KA; Writing—review & editing: KA; Project administration: KA.

References

Arimitsu, K., Hitokoto, H., Kind, S., & Hofmann, S. G. (2019). Differences in compassion, well-being, and social anxiety between Japan and the USA. *Mindfulness, 10*(5), 854–862. https://doi.org/10.1007/s12671-018-1045-6

Asano, K., & Shimizu, E. (2018). A case report of compassion focused therapy (CFT) for a Japanese patient with recurrent depressive disorder: The importance of layered processes in CFT. *Case Reports in Psychiatry, 2018*, 4165434. https://doi.org/10.1155/2018/4165434

Asano, K., Tsuchiya, M., Ishimura, I., Lin, S., Matsumoto, Y., Miyata, H., Kotera, Y., Shimizu, E., & Gilbert, P. (2017). The development of fears of compassion scale Japanese version. *PLoS One, 12*(10), Article e0185574. https://doi.org/10.1371/journal.pone.0185574

Asano, K., Tsuchiya, M., Okamoto, Y., Ohtani, T., Sensui, T., Masuyama, A., Isato, A., Shoji, M., Shiraishi, T., Shimizu, E., Irons, C., & Gilbert, P. (2022). Benefits of group compassion-focused therapy for treatment-resistant depression: A pilot randomized controlled trial. *Frontiers in Psychology, 13*, Article 903842. https://doi.org/10.3389/fpsyg.2022.903842

Cattani, K., Griner, D., Erekson, D. M., Burlingame, G. M., Beecher, M. E., & Alldredge, C. T. (2021). Module 10: Compassionate assertiveness. In M. E. Beecher, D. M. Erekson, D. Griner, & G. M. Burlingame (Eds.), *Compassion focused group therapy for university counseling centers* (pp. 159–171). Routledge. https://doi.org/10.4324/9781003202486-10

Dessí, R., Ren, J., & Zhao, X. (2023). *Shame, guilt, and motivated self-confidence* (CEPR Discussion Paper No. 18629). Centre for Economic Policy Research. https://cepr.org/publications/dp18629

Gilbert, P. (2010). *Compassion focused therapy: Distinctive features*. Routledge. https://doi.org/10.4324/9780203851197

Gilbert, P., Clarke, M., Hempel, S., Miles, J. N. V., & Irons, C. (2004). Criticizing and reassuring oneself: An exploration of forms, styles and reasons in female students. *British Journal of Clinical Psychology, 43*(1), 31–50. https://doi.org/10.1348/014466504772812959

Gilbert, P., McEwan, K., Matos, M., & Rivis, A. (2011). Fears of compassion: Development of three self-report measures. *Psychology and Psychotherapy: Theory, Research and Practice, 84*(3), 239–255. https://doi.org/10.1348/147608310X526511

Halamová, J., Kanovský, M., Gilbert, P., Troop, N. A., Zuroff, D. C., Hermanto, N., Petrocchi, N., Sommers-Spijkerman, M., Kirby, J. N., Shahar, B., Krieger, T., Matos, M., Asano, K., Yu, F., Basran, J., & Kupeli, N. (2018). The factor structure of the Forms of Self-Criticising/Attacking & Self-Reassuring Scale in thirteen distinct populations. *Journal of Psychopathology and Behavioral Assessment, 40*(4), 736–751. https://doi.org/10.1007/s10862-018-9686-2

Hayashi, F. (2006). A study of religious faith and religious feelings. *Kodo Keiryogaku (The Japanese Journal of Behaviourmetrics), 33*(1), 13–24. https://doi.org/10.2333/jbhmk.33.13

Ipsos. (2018). *Human rights in 2018: Global advisor survey graphic report*. Ipsos. https://www.ipsos.com/sites/default/files/ct/news/documents/2018-07/human_rights_in_2018_-_global_advisor_survey_graphic_report_0.pdf

Kirby, J. N. (2024). Compassion as a transdiagnostic target to reduce mental health symptoms and promote well-being. *Nature Reviews Psychology, 3*(6), 359–373. https://www.google.com/search?q=10.1038/s44159-024-00313-y

Kirby, J. N., Day, J., & Sagar, V. (2019). The "Flow" of compassion: A meta-analysis of the fears of compassion scales and psychological functioning. *Clinical Psychology Review, 70*, 26–39. https://doi.org/10.1016/j.cpr.2019.03.001

Kotera, Y., Asano, K., Kotera, H., Ohshima, R., & Rushforth, A. (2022). Mental health of Japanese workers: Amotivation mediates self-compassion on mental health problems. *International Journal of Environmental Research and Public Health, 19*(17), 10497. https://doi.org/10.3390/ijerph191710497

Kotera, Y., Sheffield, D., Green, P., & Asano, K. (2021). Cross-cultural comparison of mental health shame: Negative attitudes and external, internal, and reflected shame about mental health in Japanese and UK workers. In U. Engel, K.-V. L. Truong, & I. R. Wendt (Eds.), *Shame 4.0: Investigating an emotion in digital worlds and the Fourth Industrial Revolution* (pp. 55–71). Springer. https://doi.org/10.1007/978-3-030-59527-2_3

Kramer, E. J., Kwong, K., Lee, E., & Chung, H. (2002). Cultural factors influencing the mental health of Asian Americans. *Western Journal of Medicine, 176*(4), 227–231. https://www.google.com/search?q=10.1136/ewjm.176.4.227

Kuwayama, K. (2003). A study on over-adaptation by means of emotional expressions in the frustrating situations. *Kyoto University Research Studies in Education, 49*, 481–493. https://www.google.com/search?q=10.14989/57218

Leaviss, J., & Uttley, L. (2014). Psychotherapeutic benefits of compassion-focused therapy: An early systematic review. *Psychological Medicine, 45*(5), 927–945. https://doi.org/10.1017/S0033291714002141

Lo, H.-T., & Fung, K. P. (2003). Culturally competent psychotherapy. *Canadian Journal of Psychiatry, 48*(3), 161–170. https://doi.org/10.1177/070674370304800304

MacBeth, A., & Gumley, A. (2012). Exploring compassion: A meta-analysis of the association between self-compassion and psychopathology. *Clinical Psychology Review, 32*(6), 545–552. https://doi.org/10.1016/j.cpr.2012.06.003

Markus, H. R., & Kitayama, S. (1991). Culture and the self: Implications for cognition, emotion, and motivation. *Psychological Review, 98*(2), 224–253. https://doi.org/10.1037/0033-295X.98.2.224

Marsh, I. C., Chan, S. W. Y., & MacBeth, A. (2018). Self-compassion and psychological distress in adolescents-a meta-analysis. *Mindfulness, 9*(4), 1011–1027. https://doi.org/10.1007/s12671-017-0850-7

Matos, M., Galhardo, A., Moura-Ramos, M., Steindl, S. R., Bortolon, C., Hiramatsu, Y., Baumann, T., Yiu, R. X. Q., & Ferreira, C. (2023). Measuring shame across five countries: Dimensionality and measurement invariance of the external and internal shame scale. *Current Psychology, 42*(9), 7161–7170. https://doi.org/10.1007/s12144-021-02019-5

Ma, Z., & Jaeger, A. M. (2010). A comparative study of the influence of assertiveness on negotiation outcomes in Canada and China. *Cross Cultural Management: An International Journal, 17*(4), 333–346. https://doi.org/10.1108/13527601011086568

Millard, L. A., Wan, M. W., Smith, D. M., & Wittkowski, A. (2023). The effectiveness of compassion focused therapy with clinical populations: A systematic review and meta-analysis. *Journal of Affective Disorders, 326*, 168–192. https://doi.org/10.1016/j.jad.2023.01.010

Neff, K. D., Pisitsungkagarn, K., & Hsieh, Y.-P. (2008). Self-compassion and self-construal in the United States, Thailand, and Taiwan. *Journal of Cross-Cultural Psychology, 39*(3), 267–285. https://doi.org/10.1177/0022022108314544

Petrocchi, N., Ottaviani, C., Cheli, S., Matos, M., Baldi, B., Basran, J. K., & Gilbert, P. (2024). The impact of compassion-focused therapy on positive and negative mental health outcomes: Results of a series of meta-analyses. *Clinical Psychology: Science and Practice, 31*(2), 230–247. https://doi.org/10.1037/cps0000193

Phillips, W. J., & Hine, D. W. (2021). Self-compassion, physical health, and health behaviour: A meta-analysis. *Health Psychology Review, 15*(1), 113–139. https://doi.org/10.1080/17437199.2019.1705872

Singhal, A., & Nagao, M. (1993). Assertiveness as communication competence a comparison of the communication styles of American and Japanese students. *Asian Journal of Communication, 3*(1), 1–18. https://doi.org/10.1080/01292989309359570

Steindl, S., Bell, T., Dixon, A., & Kirby, J. N. (2023). Therapist perspectives on working with fears, blocks and resistances to compassion in compassion focused therapy. *Counselling and Psychotherapy Research, 23*(3), 850–863. https://doi.org/10.1002/capr.12530

Sznycer, D., Takemura, K., Delton, A. W., Sato, K., Robertson, T., Cosmides, L., & Tooby, J. (2012). Cross-cultural differences and similarities in proneness to shame: An adaptationist and ecological approach. *Evolutionary Psychology, 10*(2), 352–370. https://doi.org/10.1177/147470491201000213

Thomason, S., & Moghaddam, N. (2021). Compassion-focused therapies for self-esteem: A systematic review and meta-analysis. *Psychology and Psychotherapy: Theory, Research and Practice, 94*(3), 737–759. https://doi.org/10.1111/papt.12319

Tsuda, H., & Takasawa, K. (2024). Humility and life satisfaction in Japan. *Journal of Human Environmental Studies, 22*(1), 61–68. https://doi.org/10.4189/shes.22.61

Vidal, J., & Soldevilla, J. M. (2023). Effect of compassion-focused therapy on self-criticism and self-soothing: A meta-analysis. *British Journal of Clinical Psychology, 62*(1), 70–81. https://doi.org/10.1111/bjc.12394

You, Y. G. (1997). Shame and guilt mechanisms in east Asian culture. *Journal of Pastoral Care, 51*(1), 57–64. https://doi.org/10.1177/002234099705100107

Zessin, U., Dickhäuser, O., & Garbade, S. (2015). The relationship between self-compassion and well-being: A meta-analysis. *Applied Psychology: Health and Well-Being, 7*(3), 340–364. https://doi.org/10.1111/aphw.12051

Chapter 7
Compassion-Focused Therapy in European Latin Cultures

Noelia Lucía Martínez-Rives and Julie Beaumont

Background

Prior to the COVID-19 pandemic anxiety and depression were the most widespread psychological ailments in Europe (5.4% and 4.5% of the total European population respectively), and these worsened in the aftermath (European Council, 2025), especially within healthcare workers (Conti et al., 2021; Ruiz-Fernandez et al., 2022; Ridremont & Boujut, 2023). Efforts have since been made to introduce innovative and more effective therapies over those traditionally used. Previously, Cognitive Behavioral Therapy (CBT) was commonly used to explore why feelings of guilt arise and then apply appropriate techniques based on the cause of those feelings (Young et al., 2021). The mediating role of self-compassion between depressive symptoms and secure affect has been established, highlighting the importance of developing compassion-related competencies when addressing depression and shame in the therapeutic process (Steindl et al., 2021).

Third-generation therapies, such as the Compassion-Focused Therapy (CFT), developed by British psychologist Paul Gilbert (2005), incorporate elements of established therapies, such as CBT, facilitating their acceptance within clinical and non-clinical settings. They do not represent radical change, but rather an evolution based on existing principles, such as the identification and restructuring of dysfunctional thoughts. These evolving therapies provide patients, who have felt CBT was insufficient in addressing their difficulties, a new opportunity to resume treatment from a broader perspective.

N. L. Martínez-Rives (✉)
Department of Psychiatry and Social Psychology, University of Murcia, Murcia, Spain
e-mail: noelialucia.martinezr@um.es

J. Beaumont
School of Psychology, Queen's University Belfast, Belfast, UK
e-mail: jbeaumont01@qub.ac.uk

Y. Kotera et al. (eds.), *Compassion-Focused Therapy for Mental Health: International Perspectives*, Advances in Mental Health and Addiction,
https://doi.org/10.1007/978-3-032-12438-8_7

Unlike CBT or the Dialectical Behavior Therapy (DBT), which have been widely used to treat specific disorders, CFT also focuses on health promotion and the prevention of mental illness. Therapies are often based on a pathology-based intervention model, where the primary goal is to reduce specific symptoms of an existing disorder. In contrast, CFT adopts a developmental model centred on psychological well-being. The emphasis is on strengthening internal emotional resources by promoting resilience, emotional regulation, and self-compassion before symptoms reach clinically significant levels. In European Latin countries, such as Spain, seeking psychological help was traditionally uncommon and often reserved for people with serious mental health conditions, reinforcing the stigma and labelling associated with seeing a psychologist (Civio, 2021). This new approach may generate greater acceptance of psychological support, individuals are not perceived as "sick" or "dysfunctional", but rather as people who are actively taking care of their mental health. The fact that CFT focuses on emotional self-regulation and the promotion of healthy psychological habits rather than labelling the person as a "patient with a disorder" may reduce treatment resistance and decrease the stigma associated with psychological therapy.

CFT or Mindfulness-Based Therapies represent a shift therapeutic perspective, moving away from a pathology-and-diagnosis paradigm toward a focus on strengthening psychological skills and prevention. This makes it more accessible and acceptable to a broader population. The term "self-compassion" is increasingly being introduced in research as a predictor of psychological well-being. For example, Azevedo and Matos (2015) explored its relationship to varying levels of depression in adolescents; Di Fabio and Saklofske (2021) investigated indirect links between self-compassion, emotional intelligence, and personality traits; and Gutiérrez-Hernández et al. (2022) examined how self-compassion influenced emotional distress during the COVID-19 lockdown. Similarly, Di Giuseppe et al. (2023) found increased self-compassion, following neuropsychopedagogical training for adolescents suffering bullying, was associated with improved socioemotional well-being; and self-compassion is found to be a protective factor for radiographers' well-being at work (Jacquet et al., 2024). Self-compassion is also regarded as a mediator between milder and more severe mental health states. For instance, the Portuguese study by Serrao et al. (2023) suggests self-compassion may influence the relationship between stress and depression, as well as between anxiety and depression. These findings support the premise that self-compassion may serve as a protective factor, reducing the negative impact of psychological distress on emotional well-being.

Compassion Focused Therapy (CFT) began gaining recognition in continental Europe shortly after its introduction in the United Kingdom (Gilbert, 2005). In European Latin countries, such as Spain, CFT has progressively increased. For example, national professional groups have been established, including Compassionate Mind España (n.d.) in Valencia—affiliated with the Compassionate Mind Foundation-UK, as well as Compassionate Mind Foundation France (n.d.), The Compassionate Mind Foundation Portugal (2024), and Compassionate Mind Italia (2024). These professional networks are actively involved in scientific research, clinical application of compassion-based practices, and in the organization of training programs and dissemination of resources aimed at fostering compassion development.

The Centre for Mindful Self-Compassion (CMSC) International Teacher Training Partners website features the Official Network of European MSC Teacher Training Centres recognized by the CMSC. It provides access to resources related to self-compassion therapy and includes listings of courses and teacher training programs in Latin European countries such as Spain, Italy, and France. The website also highlights connections with national organizations, providing legitimacy and international support for the MSC courses. Additionally, it serves as a platform for resource sharing and support between MSC teachers. In terms of structure, the provisions include shorter group-based interventions designed to make training more accessible and collaborative (CMSC International Partner, 2020).

Self-Compassion and Related Factors

The self-compassion assessment tools commonly used in European Latin countries were originally developed in the United States, such as Self-Compassion Scale (SCS) (Neff, 2003). This construct is considered relatively universal, and the SCS has been translated and validated in several languages. The Italian version by Veneziani et al. (2017), supports self-compassion as a healthy way to relate to the self; the French version by Kotsou and Leys (2016) links self-compassion to affect and well-being; and Spanish adaptations, such as Elicesa et al. (2017) further support its Latin European validity. Given the individualistic nature of Latin European cultures, fewer cultural nuances may arise as compared to their use in collectivist societies such as many in Asia where self-compassion may be interpreted more in terms of supporting group harmony and collective well-being as opposed to being seen as key to personal growth (Wang & Lou, 2022). Before this widespread use of the SCS there were already adapted instruments in these countries that assessed related constructs. These include the Mindful Attention Awareness Scale (MAAS; Jermann et al., 2009), the Experiences in Close Relationships scale (ECR) (Alonso-Arbiol et al., 2007), and the Acceptance and Action Questionnaire-II (AAQ-II) (Monestès et al., 2009).

In a cross-cultural study comparing American, Asian and European countries, components associated with self-compassion were assessed across cultural dimensions such as individualism, masculinity, power distance, long-term orientation, uncertainty avoidance, and indulgence. The European countries, which included Greece, Spain, and the United Kingdom, showed high and very similar McDonalds's omega coefficients (ranging from 0.70 and 0.94) for the positive components of self-compassion: self-kindness, common humanity, and mindfulness. However, the negative items (e.g., self-judgement, isolation, and over identification) contributed less to the overall construct structure, likely due to the high individualism in these countries (Montero-Marin et al., 2018). Given these cultural tendencies, CFT in such contexts may benefit from a focus on developing self-acceptance and reducing self-punishment, as individuals in highly individualistic societies may be prone to experiencing guilt and shame.

At this point, it is important to reflect on what self-compassion can imply within the context of the Christian religion. In relation to psychological processes that perpetuate harm, even after external causes have disappeared, self-compassion can serve as a key element in overcoming self-punishment and facilitate psychological healing. Emotional pain, trauma or rejection, often stem from external factors such as a childhood marked by criticism or neglect, abusive relationships, academic or professional failures, or other events that generate feelings of inadequacy, shame or guilt. Over time, the original source of pain may no longer be present, yet the internalized patterns of self-relating perpetuate the suffering. This phenomenon is well illustrated by the concept of the internalized critic (Paul, 1970), which explains how individuals exposed to persistent judgment, rejection, or punishment, may unconsciously adopt these same harsh attitudes toward themselves. In such cases, the external environment is no longer necessary for the damage to persist, because the mind itself becomes the harsh judge. Self-compassion, therefore, becomes essential, as it offers a way to break this self-perpetuating cycle of suffering. In cultivating a more understanding, kinder inner dialogue, individuals can commence healing from past trauma and reduce the emotional burden of self-criticism.

Self-punishment is often experienced as a form of redemption or atonement in Christian religion (Ledford, n.d.). Individuals may believe that by punishing themselves, they are paying a "debt" to themselves or others, viewing this additional suffering as a way to validate their original pain or earn forgiveness. However, self-imposed punishment rarely facilitates genuine healing. Instead, it often reinforces feelings of worthlessness, hopelessness, and guilt, therefore entrapping individuals in a cycle of self-generated suffering (Gilbert & Irons, 2005).

In the broader context of Abrahamic religious traditions, including Christianity, guilt and shame are frequently framed as inherent aspects of the individual, with forgiveness and redemption seen as only possible through God, often via repentance and divine grace (Clark, 2012). Within this framework, self-compassion offers a benevolent alternative. Instead of responding to suffering with harshness and punishment, it invites a response grounded in kindness, understanding, and care. This does not imply minimizing one's pain or evading personal responsibility; rather, it acknowledges that healing is not achieved through continued suffering, but through acceptance, self-care and fostering inner self-worth (Gilbert, 2005).

As long as individuals perceive guilt and shame as necessary and useful emotions for correcting mistakes or demonstrating repentance, it can be difficult for them to adopt a more self-compassionate mindset. If they believe that intense guilt is a prerequisite for personal growth or that only forgiveness from an external agent (e.g., a spiritual figure) can alleviate that burden, then self-compassion may be viewed as self-indulgent rather than a legitimate path to well-being. However, self-compassion does not involve excusing or justifying harmful actions. Instead, it offers a balanced approach to confronting guilt and shame, one that encourages accountability and personal change without leading to emotional self-destruction.

In individualistic cultures, which prioritize the individual over the collective, guilt and shame are often viewed as adaptive emotions that help protect people from the social consequences of their actions and maintain social harmony (Lewandowska-Tomaszczyk & Wilson, 2014). Guilt may serve as an internal mechanism for reflecting on one's actions and avoiding harm or discomfort to others, while shame signals a violation of social norms, prompting individuals to avoid behaviors that could harm their social standing. In this way, both emotions can serve to protect the individual from the negative repercussions arising from interpersonal conflict (Clark, 2012).

However, finding a healthy balance with guilt and shame can be very challenging. While these emotions play an important role in guiding our behaviors and maintaining relationships their excessive or chronic presence can become harmful to an individual's mental health. Persistent guilt may lead individuals to feel perpetually inadequate or unforgivable, undermining their self-esteem and hindering their ability to move forward. Similarly, overwhelming shame, can foster feelings of rejection or incompetence, prompting social withdrawal and increasing the risk of anxiety or depression. Achieving balance involves acknowledging guilt and shame when they are appropriate, but also developing the ability to forgive ourselves and avoid over identifying with our perceived flaws.

For example, in a study by Crisan et al. (2023), self-compassion training was compared with unconditional self-acceptance training as psychological interventions, exploring their effects on self-criticism, empathy, guilt-proneness, shame-proneness, and performance. Both interventions showed increases in self-compassion and self-acceptance, along with a reduction in shame proneness. However, no significant differences were observed between the groups in terms of self-blame, empathy, or performance. Notably, only the self-compassion group showed a significant decrease in guilt proneness. These findings suggest that, across cultural contexts, both self-compassion and unconditional self-acceptance can promote reductions in shame and support personal well-being. The reduction in guilt proneness observed in the self-compassion group, however, may indicate that this approach is particularly effective in contexts where guilt serves a central role in social and moral regulation. This study was conducted in Romania, a country that, while not considered Latin European in contemporary geopolitical terms, retains Latin roots in its language and historical heritage. In such a context, self-compassion may be especially tied to social connection and empathy.

Cultural Adaptations of CFT

Adaptations of CFT in European Latin countries have been influenced by distinct cultural and social differences. García-Campayo et al. (2017) conducted a systematic review highlighting differences in how compassion, and mindfulness-based techniques are taught and practiced in Latin countries. Influential factors include the structure of the healthcare system, public healthcare is typically the first point of access, and the attitudes held toward it. Patients often adopt a passive role in the therapeutic process resulting in lower treatment adherence and patient engagement. These tendencies may be linked to shared cultural characteristics across Latin societies (García-Campayo & Alda, 2005; Qureshi et al., 2013), though these studies do not always distinguish between European or American populations. Common traits include the central role of the family as the primary source of social support, which facilitates communication and helps individuals cope with difficulties. There is also a greater willingness to express emotions and share problems with those closest to them along with a higher level of physical contact, which fosters openness and trust. Additionally, there is a strong emphasis placed on personal responsibility for one's illness-related suffering, alongside a tendency for patients to adopt a passive role toward healthcare professionals.

To adapt CFT effectively within these contexts, García-Campayo et al. (2017) recommend modifying therapeutic techniques by incorporating brief daily home practices of approximately 20 min, in place of full-day retreats that require greater commitment from the patient, and which may not align with cultural norms. They also suggest placing greater emphasis on body-based practices and interpersonal mindfulness, as these practices are more easily integrated. Furthermore, when designing interventions, practitioners are encouraged to be mindful of the potential negative religious connotations associated with the concept of compassion within Christian contexts.

While many formal CFT interventions avoid extended retreats due to low adherence, such experiences can nonetheless offer positive individual benefits. Steininger et al. (2023) investigated how the experience of long-distance walking, specifically the Camino Francés of the Camino de Santiago (from Spain), fostered the development of self-compassion in walkers by facilitating psychological processes, such as self-reflection, emotional regulation, and coping with distress. This type of experience can be considered a natural intervention to enhance self-compassion, functioning similarly to a retreat with positive outcomes, but with key differences from structured self-compassion formats. The Camino Francés pilgrimage is a voluntary, immersive, and intrinsically motivated experience, potentially increasing participants' willingness to commit to the process. The combination of physical effort, connection with nature, and opportunities for introspection can foster self-compassion in a more organic, less composed manner than structured retreats. Framed within a recreational and culturally valued activity, participants are afforded the opportunity to experience psychological benefits without the resistance sometimes associated with explicitly therapeutic settings. In this sense, the Camino can be viewed as a naturalistic intervention, illustrating how certain therapeutic practices may be more effectively implemented when integrated into everyday contexts rather than formal clinical environments.

Furthermore, specific adaptations of CFT have been developed in Spain, such as Attachment Styles-Based Compassion Therapy (ABCT), created by García-Campayo et al. (2017). This approach integrates self-compassion and attachment theory within the Spanish healthcare context. The program draws on various psychological concepts including attachment theory, dialectical behavioral therapy, and foundational principles of self-compassion, while deliberately excluding religious elements. ABCT highlights the parallels between the attachment styles developed with others and the treatment we give ourselves. Planned over eight sessions of a couple of hours, it offers a well-structured protocol, including an initial theoretical part of psychoeducation, an essential component of all psychotherapy, followed by formal and informal practices. Formal practices include structured exercises, with a defined time and space, requiring a conscious commitment and informal practices are more flexibly integrated into the patient's daily life, applying what has been learned in therapy to everyday life. Both practices complement each other, making the change sustainable over the long term. This informal part is the one that requires greater involvement and independence of the patient, which emphasizes the role of the patient as agent, more promoted in the psychological model than in the medical one, having an active role in their own therapeutic process, where they must reflect and apply what they have learned without constantly depending on the therapist, implementing strategies on their own.

As can be also seen in an application of this ABCT in the study Navarro-Gil et al. (2020), it provides a session where to integrate components of the Attachment Theory of Bowlby (1980), exploring parenting models and their impact on the capacity to develop compassion for oneself and others; another session to modify dysfunctional relational patterns through self-compassion (reconstruction of a secure attachment through compassion practices), which is not a central focus of well-known CFT; the hindering role of envy and difficult relationships toward self-compassion (emotions less addressed in other compassion therapies); and it introduces the idea of creating a secure base within oneself (internal attachment figure) as a source of compassion, rather than relying exclusively on external figures. Although this is the most differentiated part, it includes aspects common to the well-known CFT, like the emphasis on how insecure attachment can make it difficult to receive and give compassion.

Different Uses of Self-Compassion Therapy

This therapy is being used in Latin European countries in a variety of clinical settings, from private practice to mental health centres. As a complement for conventional therapies for depression and anxiety can help addressing the fear of self-pity, and in the treatment of trauma can help to regulate threat responses and foster a greater sense of security after that experience. In educational settings can contribute to reduce the fear of failure promoting a compassionate attitude toward mistakes, in workplaces reducing stress and fatigue by fostering an organizational climate based on kindness and social support, and in social communities can promote cohesion and resilience in vulnerable populations working of the stigma and discrimination. Through this therapy, patients are helped to cultivate a more compassionate attitude toward themselves, reducing levels of shame and self-criticism, and allowing them to better manage their expectations and mistakes. It has been applied in the treatment of problems such as intellectual disabilities (Clapton et al., 2018; Goad & Parker,

2021), anxiety disorders like OCD (Petrocchi et al., 2021), depression, eating disorders (Marta-Simoes et al., 2016; Horcajo et al., 2019; Bergunde & Dritschel, 2020; Kopland et al., 2023), personality disorders, especially for negative symptoms (Cheli et al., 2023), chronic pain (Carvalho et al., 2022; Torrijos-Zarcero et al., 2021) even in severe mental disorders such as schizophrenia (Kennedy & Ellerby, 2016) or bipolar disorder (Lowens, 2010), reducing shame and perfectionism (Matos & Steindl, 2022; Wakelin et al., 2022), trauma (Lawrence & Lee, 2014), between other psychological disorders, improving overall mental health. It has also been used in psychosomatic illnesses such as inflammatory bowel disease, as a complement to usual treatment (Trindade et al., 2021). Although with more limitations in the results in self-stigma, it has also been used in autism spectrum disorders (Riebel et al., 2024).

Expanding the Application of Self-Compassion Therapy

Traditionally, self-compassion therapy (CFT) has been used clinically to treat psychological disorders. However, its application is evolving toward a more preventative and well-being-promoting approach in non-healthcare settings, such as businesses or schools. This shift in perspective involves recognizing that self-compassion is not only a therapeutic tool but also a protective factor against the development of psychological problems, as preventative strategies are often not given as much priority as therapeutic mental health interventions.

According to this, CFT has been explored in less conventional areas, such as language learning. In this context, it has been used to help students manage self-criticism, anxiety, and fear of making mistakes, which can interfere with the learning process. Many students experience shame or frustration when making mistakes in a foreign language, which can lead to avoidance and blocking. Applying CFT principles, such as compassionate self-talk, accepting mistakes as a natural part of learning, and reducing fear of external judgment, can improve confidence and willingness to practice, as it lessens the negative impact of perfectionism and fosters a more flexible and resilient attitude toward learning challenges (Therapy in Barcelona, 2024).

Like many other therapies, in recent years the online adaptation has allowed a greater number of people to access its benefits, overcoming geographical barriers and facilitating its integration into everyday life. An example of this can be found in the Gracia-Gozalo et al. (2019) study, where CFT was applied in a health institutional context, in an Intensive Care Unit, this time directed at professionals rather than users. This individual training program was designed for a virtual environment via WhatsApp in 8 weeks via audio and text, with very brief practice (5–8 min), achieving effective results decreasing emotional exhaustion. Among the contents included, the body-scan, mindfulness and a meditative practice to cultivate compassion for others, "giving and receiving". Another example of this use in Spain is found in Martinez (2023) most recent thesis trying to evaluate the efficacy of an online attachment-based compassion therapy in chronic medical illness patients showing good results. In 2020, Campos et al. (2020) published the first study to provide preliminary data on the feasibility, acceptance, and efficacy of a web-based compassion and self-compassion training (adapted iABCT) in the Spanish general population.

Despite its benefits, when self-compassion is presented as a preventative strategy in non-clinical settings, it is often viewed as an optional add-on rather than a necessity. This may be due to a lack of awareness about how its practice can improve overall well-being and productivity. The study of Riebel and Weiner (2023) in France, the first in this country trying to evaluate a group-based CFT in a psychiatric care setting, highlights the benefits of using this tool for the treatment of people with psychiatric diagnoses and childhood trauma. In the face of trauma, interventions such as cognitive behavioral therapy or Eye Movement Desensitization and Reprocessing (EMDR) Therapy have always been recommended (APA, 2020), but the CFT focuses on important mediating factors like shame and the results on the patients after a group therapy following this line demonstrated promising effectiveness (Riebel & Weiner, 2023). Another French study showed a different application of the CFT, Leboeuf et al. (2022a, 2022b) not only examined the role of self-criticism in the attentional processing of emotional stimuli but also highlighted the use of the imagery modality through Compassion-Focused Imagery (CFI). This therapeutic technique allows individuals to imagine themselves as compassionate or receive compassion from an ideally compassionate other, which could influence attention toward critical and compassionate emotional stimuli.

In the academic context, we find an example of the application of CFT based on the attachment with university students to improve mental health and reduce psychological distress (Beltrán-Ruiz et al., 2023). This study highlights the usefulness of CFT in a non-clinical, public context, when applied in an educational institution that is not part of the healthcare system, demonstrating its viability in educational settings and opening the door to its use in other non-clinical settings, such as businesses or workplaces. Despite addressing deep topics such as attachment, compassion, and emotional regulation, the program is brief (6 sessions over 6 weeks), making it accessible, practical, and easy to implement without requiring lengthy therapeutic processes.

Another Spanish study applying the CFT in the university academic context is the one of Martínez-Rubio et al. (2022) to reduce stress in the students, brief (6 sessions) but including the main components already mentioned: body scan, mindfulness meditation, breathing exercises, conscious movements, attentive listening, and reinforcement exercises to consolidate what has been learned. Although the component that had the greatest influence on reducing stress levels here was the cognitive process that involves distancing oneself from one's own thoughts, emotions, and internal experiences, observing them objectively instead of completely identifying with them.

We also find other examples of the application of this therapy in non-clinical samples of participants. Leboeuf et al. (2022a, 2022b) made an adaptation of the CFT via a website in a group of students, including two more components, prosocial guided imagery and behavioral activation. Although the CFT has not only been used with students, but also with workers in these fields, like the training program for teachers of Matos et al. (2022), showing good results in reducing burnout and stress.

Accustomed to the structure of the 8-session program based on self-compassion, we found a Spanish research that made a comparison with a shorter 4-session program to reduce the negative consequences of healthcare work in both the family and work environments, since one of the recommendations was to keep it as brief as possible. The main differences between the two interventions lied in the duration, intensity, and daily practice workload. In the 8-session group, the greater depth intervention allowed more time to develop mindfulness and self-compassion skills and in the 4-session group the shorter and less intensive intervention could make it more accessible but with a potentially lower impact on outcomes. This second, abbreviated option managed to have practically the same effectiveness as the longer intervention, which offers advantages for its implementation (Pérula-de Torres et al., 2019).

Longer interventions have also found effective results, such as the 11-week CFT also applied, as has been repeated in numerous studies, to healthcare workers in Portugal (Gaspar et al., 2018). Although this extension was made in an attempt to attract more participants, dedicating these 3 extra sessions, which we do not normally find in 8-session programs, to the practice of those strategies perceived as most useful. This program did not include dedicated sessions to Loving-Kindness Meditations (LKM) and compassion meditations as part of their approach. Instead, it focused more on those mindfulness techniques such as body scan meditation, breathing meditation, sound focus, mindful yoga, sitting meditation, and open awareness practices, introducing mindfulness gradually, beginning with simple and short practices (5–15 min) and increasing complexity over time (extend to 25–30 min in the final weeks). Especially, it focuses on the experience of body and mind and increases flexibility in the final weeks, promoting autonomy and personalized learning.

As can be seen, a large application of CFT has taken place in health institutions aimed at healthcare professionals, which could be one of the groups that would benefit most from the introduction of this type of therapy in the countries mentioned. This is because this group experiences high levels of stress, burnout, and compassion fatigue due to the nature of their work, which involves constant contact with human suffering (De Hert, 2020; Duarte et al., 2020; Gil-Almagro et al., 2025; Perego et al., 2022). A Spanish example of this can be found in the article of Aranda et al. (2018) expanding the benefits of a mindfulness intervention with the self-compassion component, as we could observe in interventions that only included mindfulness from previous years such as that of Martín et al. (2013).

The CFT intervention of Aranda et al. (2018) has similarities with other compassionate-based interventions, but also some differences. Beginning with the common points, self-compassion practices such as the body scan or loving-kindness meditation, strategies for managing stress and burnout (specific challenges in medical practice), and the emphasis on acceptance and reducing self-criticism. Regarding the differences, although there is a focus on self-compassion, the program structure follows a model closer to Mindfulness-Based Stress Reduction (MBSR) than to classic CFT, and it does not explicitly mention the emotion regulation systems theory (threat, impulse, and calming) and it focuses on the doctor-patient relationship or specific ethical dilemmas to foster compassion. To sum up, this program has a closer orientation to mindfulness-based therapies in its structure and theoretical foundation, rather than treating clinical problems of severe self-criticism or shame as traditional CFT would.

Author Contributions Conceptualisation: N.L.M.-R. and J.B.; Investigation: N.L.M.-R.; Resources: N.L.M.-R. and J.B.; Writing—original draft: N.L.M.-R.; Writing—review & editing: N.L.M.-R. and J.B.; Project administration: N.L.M.-R. and J.B.

References

Alonso-Arbiol, I., Balluerka, N., & Shaver, P. R. (2007). A Spanish version of the Experiences in Close Relationships (ECR) adult attachment questionnaire. *Personal Relationships, 14*(1), 45–63. https://doi.org/10.1111/j.1475-6811.2006.00141.x

American Psychological Association. (2020). Clinical practice guideline for the treatment of Posttraumatic Stress Disorder. PTSD Treatments. https://www.apa.org/ptsd-guideline/treatments. Retrieved from February 21, 2025.

Aranda, G., Elcuaz, M. R., Fuertes, C., Güeto, V., Pascual, P., & Sainz de Murieta, E. (2018). Evaluation of the effectiveness of a mindfulness and self-compassion program to reduce stress and prevent burnout in primary care health professionals. *Atención Primaria, 50*(3), 141–150. https://doi.org/10.1016/j.aprim.2017.03.009

Azevedo, A., & Matos, A. (2015). Psychological flexibility and self-compassion: Contributions of gender and its association with adolescent depression. *Psychology*. https://api.semanticscholar.org/CorpusID:148938460

Beltrán-Ruiz, M., Fernández, S., García-Campayo, J., Puebla-Guedea, M., López-del-, Y., Navarro-Gil, M., & Montero-Marin, J. (2023). Effectiveness of attachment-based compassion therapy to reduce psychological distress in university students: A randomised controlled trial protocol. *Frontiers in Psychology, 14*, 1185445. https://doi.org/10.3389/fpsyg.2023.1185445

Bergunde, L., & Dritschel, B. (2020). The shield of self-compassion: A buffer against disordered eating risk from physical appearance perfectionism. *PLoS One, 15*(1), e0227564. https://doi.org/10.1371/journal.pone.0227564

Bowlby, J. (1980). *Attachment and loss: Vol. 3. Sadness and depression*. 2. Basic Books.

Campos, D., Navarro-Gil, M., Herrera-Mercadal, P., Martínez-García, L., Cebolla, A., Borao, L., López-Del-Hoyo, Y., Castilla, D., del Río, E., García-Campayo, J., & Quero, S. (2020). Feasibility of the internet attachment–based compassion therapy in the general population: Protocol for an open-label uncontrolled pilot trial. *JMIR Research Protocols, 9*(8), e16717. https://www.researchprotocols.org/2020/8/e16717

Carvalho, S. A., Gillanders, D., Forte, T., Trindade, I. A., Pinto-Gouveia, J., Lapa, T., Valentim, A., Santos, E., Paciência, J., Guiomar, R., & Castilho, P. (2022). Self-compassion in acceptance and commitment therapy for chronic pain: A pilot study. *Scandinavian Journal of Pain, 22*(3), 631–638. https://doi.org/10.1515/sjpain-2021-0214

Cheli, S., Chiarello, F., & Cavalletti, V. (2023). A psychotherapy oriented by compassion and metacognition for schizoid personality disorder: A two cases series. *Journal of Contemporary Psychotherapy: On the Cutting Edge of Modern Developments in Psychotherapy, 53*(1), 61–70. https://doi.org/10.1007/s10879-022-09566-3

Civio. (2021, marzo 9). *Pay up or put it off: How Europe treats depression and anxiety*. Civio. https://civio.es/sanidad/2021/03/09/access-to-mental-health-in-europe/

Clapton, N. E., Williams, J., Griffith, G. M., & Jones, R. S. (2018). 'Finding the person you really are… on the inside': Compassion focused therapy for adults with intellectual disabilities. *Journal of Intellectual Disabilities, 22*(2), 135–153. https://doi.org/10.1177/1744629516688581

Clark, A. (2012). Working with guilt and shame. *Advances in Psychiatric Treatment, 18*(2), 137–143. https://doi.org/10.1192/apt.bp.110.008326

CMSC International Partner. (2020). *CMSC international teacher training partners; MSC in Europe.* https://www.mindfulnessyautocompasion.com/msc-europa

Compassionate Mind España. (s.f.). *Compassionate mind España.* https://compassionatemind.es/

Compassionate Mind Foundation France. (s.f.). *Compassionate mind foundation France.* http://www.compassionatemindfoundationfrance.com/

Compassionate Mind Italia. (2024). *Compassionate mind Italia.* https://compassionatemind.it/

Conti, C., Fontanesi, L., Lanzara, R., Rosa, I., Doyle, R. L., & Porcelli, P. (2021). Burnout status of Italian healthcare workers during the first COVID-19 pandemic peak period. *Healthcare (Basel), 9*(5), 510. https://doi.org/10.3390/healthcare9050510

Crisan, S., Canache, M., Buksa, D., & Nechita, D. (2023). A comparison between self-compassion and unconditional self-acceptance: Interventions on self-blame, empathy, shame-, guilt-proneness, and performance. *Journal of Rational-Emotive & Cognitive-Behavior Therapy, 41*(1), 64–80. https://doi.org/10.1007/s10942-022-00451-5

De Hert, S. (2020). Burnout in healthcare workers: Prevalence, impact and preventative strategies. *Local and Regional Anesthesia, 13*, 171–183. https://doi.org/10.2147/LRA.S240564

Di Fabio, A., & Saklofske, D. H. (2021). The relationship of compassion and self-compassion with personality and emotional intelligence. *Personality and Individual Differences, 169*, Article 110109. https://doi.org/10.1016/j.paid.2020.110109

Di Giuseppe, T., Perasso, G., Serantoni, G., Lillo, C., Anella, S., Maculan, A., Vianello, F., & Paoletti, P. (2023). A Neuro-psychopedagogical training for adolescents: An exploratory study on self-compassion and detection of bullying episodes. *Journal of Psychological and Educational Research, 31*(2), 59–70. https://www.researchgate.net/publication/375671531_A_NEUROPSYCHOPEDAGOGICAL_TRAINING_FOR_ADOLESCENTS_AN_EXPLORATORY_STUDY_ON_SELF-_COMPASSION_AND_DETECTION_OF_BULLYING_EPISODES

Duarte, I., Teixeira, A., Castro, L., et al. (2020). Burnout among Portuguese healthcare workers during the COVID-19 pandemic. *BMC Public Health, 20*, 1885. https://doi.org/10.1186/s12889-020-09980-z

Elicesa, M., Carmona, C., Pascuala, J. C., Feliu-Solerd, A., Martin-Blancoa, A., & Soler, J. (2017). Compassion and self-compassion: Construct and measurement. *Mindfulness & Compassion, 2*, 34–40. https://doi.org/10.1016/j.mincom.2016.11.003

European Council. (2025). *Mental health. European Council.* https://www.consilium.europa.eu/en/policies/mental-health/. Retrieved from February 3, 2025.

García-Campayo, J., & Alda, M. (2005). *Salud Mental e Inmigración (mental health and immigration)* (Vol. 17, no. 4). Edikamed.Salud mental e inmigración. Monografías de psiquiatría.

García-Campayo, J., Demarzo, M., Shonin, E., & Van Gordon, W. (2017). How do cultural factors influence the teaching and practice of mindfulness and compassion in Latin countries? *Frontiers in Psychology, 8*, 1161. https://doi.org/10.3389/fpsyg.2017.01161. PMID: 28744247; PMCID: PMC5504142.

Gaspar, I., Martinho, A., & Lima, M. (2018). Exploring the benefits of a mindfulness program for Portuguese public healthcare workers. *Current Psychology*, 1–10. https://doi.org/10.1007/s12144-018-9987-3

Gil-Almagro, F., Carmona-Monge, F. J., García-Hedrera, F. J., & Peñacoba-Puente, C. (2025). Evolution of burnout syndrome in Spanish healthcare professionals during and after the COVID-19 pandemic: Psychosocial variables involved. *Frontiers in Medicine, 12*. https://doi.org/10.3389/fmed.2025.1522134

Gilbert, P. (Ed.). (2005). *Compassion: Conceptualisations, research and use in psychotherapy.* Routledge. https://doi.org/10.4324/9780203003459

Gilbert, P., & Irons, C. (2005). Focused therapies and compassionate mind training for shame and self-attacking. In P. Gilbert (Ed.), *Compassion: Conceptualisations, research and use in psychotherapy* (pp. 263–325). Routledge.

Goad, E. J., & Parker, K. (2021). Compassion-focused therapy groups for people with intellectual disabilities: An extended pilot study. *Journal of Intellectual Disabilities, 25*(4), 661–679. https://doi.org/10.1177/1744629520925953

Gracia-Gozalo, R. M., Ferrer-Tarrés, J. M., Ayora, A. A, Alonso-Herrero, M., Amutio-Kareaga, A., & Ferrer Roca, R. (2019). Aplicación de un programa de mindfulness en profesionales de un servicio de medicina intensiva. Efecto sobre el burnout, la empatía y la autocompasión. *Medicina Intensiva, 43*(4), 207–216. https://doi.org/10.1016/j.medin.2018.02.005

Gutiérrez-Hernández, M. E., Fanjul Rodríguez, L. F., Díaz, A., Oyanadel, C., & Peñate, W. (2022). Analysis of the predictive role of self-compassion on emotional distress during COVID-19 lockdown. *Social Sciences, 11*, 151. https://doi.org/10.3390/socsci11040151

Horcajo, L., Quiles, Y., & Quiles, M. J. (2019). Aplicación de la terapia centrada en la compasión en pacientes con un trastorno de la conducta alimentaria: un estudio piloto. *Behavioral Psychology, 27*(2), 295–309. https://dialnet.unirioja.es/servlet/articulo?codigo=7057542

Jacquet, L., Paucsik, M., Guy, J. B., Eve, K., Ben-Taarit, I., & Lantheaume, S. (2024). Self-compassion and psychological well-being of radiographers at work. *International Journal of Qualitative Studies on Health and Well-being, 19*(1), 2287621. https://doi.org/10.1080/17482631.2023.2287621

Jermann, F., Billieux, J., Larøi, F., d'Argembeau, A., Bondolfi, G., Zermatten, A., et al. (2009). Mindful Attention Awareness Scale (MAAS): Psychometric properties of the French translation and exploration of its relations with emotion regulation strategies. *Psychological Assessment, 21*, 506–514. https://doi.org/10.1037/a0017032

Kennedy, A., & Ellerby, M. (2016). A Compassion-Focused approach to working with someone diagnosed with Schizophrenia. *Journal of Clinical Psychology, 72*(2), 123–131. https://doi.org/10.1002/jclp.22251

Kopland, M. C. G., Vrabel, K., Melsom, L., Hoffart, A., & Johnson, S. U. (2023). Self-compassion in eating disorders and childhood trauma: A study of within-person effects in a randomized controlled trial. *Psychotherapy Research, 33*(5), 640–653. https://doi.org/10.1080/10503307.2022.2149363

Kotsou, I., & Leys, C. (2016). Self-Compassion Scale (SCS): Psychometric properties of the French translation and its relations with psychological well-being, affect and depression. *PLoS One, 11*(4), e0152880. https://doi.org/10.1371/journal.pone.0152880

Lawrence, V. A., & Lee, D. (2014). An exploration of people's experiences of compassion-focused therapy for Trauma, using interpretative phenomenological analysis. *Clinical Psychology Psychotherapy, 21*(6), 495–507. https://doi.org/10.1002/cpp.1854

Leboeuf, I., Andreotti, E., Irons, C., Beaumont, E., & Antoine, P. (2022). A randomized controlled study of a French compassionate mind training. *Mindfulness, 13*(3). https://doi.org/10.1007/s12671-022-01987-4

Leboeuf, I., McEwan, K., Rusinek, S., Andreotti, E., & Antoine, P. (2022b). Can compassion-focused imagery be used as an attention bias modification treatment? *Current Psychology: A Journal for Diverse Perspectives on Diverse Psychological Issues, 41*(11), 8021–8031. https://doi.org/10.1007/s12144-020-01241-x

Ledford, T. (n.d.). *Confusing humility with self-punishment*. Terry Ledford, Ph.D. https://www.terryledford.com/confusing-humility-with-self-punishment/

Lewandowska-Tomaszczyk, B., & Wilson, P. A. (2014). Self-conscious emotions in collectivistic and individualistic cultures: A contrastive linguistic perspective. In J. Romero-Trillo (Ed.), *Yearbook of Corpus Linguistics and Pragmatics 2014: New empirical and theoretical paradigms* (pp. 123–148). Springer. https://doi.org/10.1007/978-3-319-06007-1_7

Lowens, I. (2010). Compassion focused therapy for people with bipolar disorder. *The International Journal of Cognitive Therapy, 3*(2), 172–185. https://doi.org/10.1521/ijct.2010.3.2.172

Marta-Simões, J., Ferreira, C., & Mendes, A. L. (2016). Exploring the effect of external shame on body appreciation among Portuguese young adults: The role of self-compassion. *Eating Behaviors, 23*, 174–179. https://doi.org/10.1016/j.eatbeh.2016.10.006

Martín, A., Rodríguez, T., Pujol-Ribera, E., Berenguera, A., & Moix, J. (2013). Evaluación de la efectividad de un programa de mindfulness en profesionales de atención primaria. *Gaceta Sanitaria, 27*(6), 521–528. https://doi.org/10.1016/j.gaceta.2013.04.007

Martínez, M (2023). *Efficacy of an online self-applied intervention for improving quality of life and wellbeing in a chronic medical illness population* (Doctoral Thesis, Universidad de Valencia). https://dialnet.unirioja.es/servlet/tesis?codigo=323887

Martínez-Rubio, D., Navarrete, J., & Montero-Marin, J. (2022). Feasibility, effectiveness, and mechanisms of a brief mindfulness- and compassion-based program to reduce stress in university students: A pilot randomized controlled trial. *International Journal of Environmental Research and Public Health, 19*(1), 154. https://doi.org/10.3390/ijerph19010154

Matos, M., Albuquerque, I., Galhardo, A., Cunha, M., Pedroso Lima, M., Palmeira, L., et al. (2022). Nurturing compassion in schools: A randomized controlled trial of the effectiveness of a Compassionate Mind Training program for teachers. *PLoS One, 17*(3), Article e0263480. https://doi.org/10.1371/journal.pone.0263480

Matos, M., & Steindl, S. R. (2020). "You are already all you need to be": A case illustration of compassion-focused therapy for shame and perfectionism. *Journal of Clinical Psychology, 76*(11), 2079–2096. https://doi.org/10.1002/jclp.23055

Monestès, J. L., Villatte, M., Mouras, H., Loas, G., & Bond, F. W. (2009). Traduction et validation française du questionnaire d'acceptation et d'action (AAQ-II). [French translation and validation of the Acceptance et Action Questionnaire (AAQ-II).] *European Review of Applied Psychology/ Revue européenne de psychologie appliquée, 59*(4), 301–308. https://doi.org/10.1016/j.erap.2009.09.001

Montero-Marin, J., Kuyken, W., Crane, C., Gu, J., Baer, R., Al-Awamleh, A. A., Akutsu, S., Araya-Véliz, C., Ghorbani, N., Chen, Z. J., Kim, M. S., Mantzios, M., Rolim Dos Santos, D. N., Serramo, L. C., Teleb, A. A., Watson, P. J., Yamaguchi, A., Yang, E., & García-Campayo, J. (2018). Self-compassion and cultural values: A cross-cultural study of self-compassion using a Multitrait-Multimethod (MTMM) analytical procedure. *Frontiers in Psychology, 9*, 2638. https://doi.org/10.3389/fpsyg.2018.02638

Navarro-Gil, M., Lopez-del-Hoyo, Y., Modrego-Alarcón, M., et al. (2020). Effects of Attachment-Based Compassion Therapy (ABCT) on self-compassion and attachment style in healthy people. *Mindfulness, 11*, 51–62. https://doi.org/10.1007/s12671-018-0896-1

Neff, K. D. (2003). The development and validation of a scale to measure self-compassion. *Self and Identity, 2*(3), 223–250. https://doi.org/10.1080/15298860309027

Paul, L. (1970). The cruel inner critic. *Psychotherapy: Theory, Research & Practice, 7*(3), 178–180. https://doi.org/10.1037/h0086583

Perego, G., Cugnata, F., Brombin, C., Milano, F., Preti, E., Di Pierro, R., De Panfilis, C., Madeddu, F., & Di Mattei, V. E. (2022). The "healthcare workers' wellbeing [Benessere Operatori]" project: A longitudinal evaluation of psychological responses of Italian healthcare workers during the COVID-19 pandemic. *Journal of Clinical Medicine, 11*(9), 2317. https://doi.org/10.3390/jcm11092317

Pérula-de Torres, L. A, Atalaya, J. C. V., García-Campayo, J., Roldán-Villalobos, A., Magallón-Botaya, R., Bartolomé-Moreno, C., Moreno-Martos, H., Melús-Palazón, E., Liétor-Villajos, N., Valverde-Bolívar, F. J., Hachem-Salas, N., Rodríguez, L. A., Navarro-Gil, M., Epstein, R., Cabezón-Crespo, A., Moreno, C. M., & Collaborative group of the MINDUUDD study. (2019). Controlled clinical trial comparing the effectiveness of a mindfulness and self-compassion 4-session programme versus an 8-session programme to reduce work stress and burnout in family and community medicine physicians and nurses: MINDUUDD study protocol. *BMC Family Practice, 20*(1), 24. https://doi.org/10.1186/s12875-019-0913-z

Petrocchi, N., Cosentino, T., Pellegrini, V., Femia, G., D'Innocenzo, A., & Mancini, F. (2021). Compassion-focused group therapy for treatment-resistant OCD: Initial evaluation using a multiple baseline design. *Frontiers in Psychology, 11*, Article 594277. https://doi.org/10.3389/fpsyg.2020.594277

Qureshi, A., Collazos, F., Sobradiel, N., Eiroa-Orosa, F. J., Febrel, M., Revollo-Escudero, H. W., et al. (2013). Epidemiology of psychiatric morbidity among migrants compared to native born population in Spain: A controlled study. *General Hospital Psychiatry, 35*, 93–99. https://doi.org/10.1016/j.genhosppsych.2012.09.010

Ridremont, D., & Boujut, E. (2023). Burnout among French pediatric healthcare workers during the COVID-19 pandemic. *Psychology, Health & Medicine, 28*(7), 1901–1915. https://doi.org/10.1080/13548506.2023.2216465

Riebel, M., Krasny-Pacini, A., Manolov, R., Rohmer, O., & Weiner, L. (2024). Compassion focused therapy for self-stigma and shame in autism: A single case pre-experimental study. *Frontiers in Psychiatry, 14*, 1281428. https://doi.org/10.3389/fpsyt.2023.1281428

Riebel, M., & Weiner, L. (2023). Feasibility and acceptability of group compassion-focused therapy to treat the consequences of childhood maltreatment in people with psychiatric disorders in France. *The Journal of Nervous and Mental Disease, 211*(5), 393–401. https://doi.org/10.1097/nmd.0000000000001603

Ruiz-Fernández, M. D., Alarcón-Ortega, C., Ventura-Miranda, M. I., Ortega-Galán, Á. M., Alcaráz-Córdoba, A., Berenguel-Marínez, A., Lirola-Manzano, M. J. (2022). Burnout in specialized care nurses during the first COVID-19 outbreak in Spain. *Healthcare, 10*, 1282. https://doi.org/10.3390/healthcare10071282

Serrão, C., Valquaresma, A., Rodrigues, A. R., & Duarte, I. (2023). Mediation of self-compassion on pathways from stress and anxiety to depression among Portuguese Higher Education Students. *Healthcare (Basel), 11*(18), 2494. https://doi.org/10.3390/healthcare11182494

Steindl, S. R., Matos, M., & Creed, A. K. (2021). Early shame and safeness memories, and later depressive symptoms and safe affect: The mediating role of self-compassion. *Current Psychology, 40*, 761–771. https://doi.org/10.1007/s12144-018-9990-8

Steininger, Y., Braun, A., & Morgenroth, O. (2023). Becoming self-compassionate step by step — a field study on the effect of long-distance walking on self-compassion in hikers traveling the Camino Francés. *Mindfulness, 14*(1), 101–112. https://doi.org/10.1007/s12671-022-02056-6

The Compassionate Mind Foundation Portugal. (2024). The Compassionate Mind Foundation. https://www.compassionatemind.co.uk/resource/portugal

Therapy in Barcelona. (2024). *Self-talk, self-compassion, and success in language learning*. https://www.therapyinbarcelona.com/self-talk-self-compassion-and-success-in-language-learning/

Torrijos-Zarcero, M., Mediavilla, R., Rodríguez, B., Río, M., López-Álvarez, I., Rocamora-González, C., & Palao, A. I. (2021). Mindful self-compassion program for chronic pain patients: A randomized controlled trial. *European Journal of Pain, 25*(4), 930–944. https://doi.org/10.1002/ejp.1734

Trindade, I. A., Pereira, J., Galhardo, A., Ferreira, N. B., Lucena-Santos, P., Carvalho, S. A., Oliveira, S., Skvarc, D., Rocha, B. S., Portela, F., & Ferreira, C. (2021). The LIFE with IBD intervention: Study protocol for a randomized controlled trial of a face-to-face acceptance and commitment therapy and compassion-based intervention tailored to people with inflammatory bowel disease. *Frontiers in Psychiatry, 12*, Article 699367. https://doi.org/10.3389/fpsyt.2021.699367

Veneziani, C. A., Fuochi, G., & Voci, A. (2017). Self-compassion as a healthy attitude toward the self: Factorial and construct validity in an Italian sample. *Personality and Individual Differences, 119*, 60–68. https://doi.org/10.1016/j.paid.2017.06.028

Wakelin, K. E., Perman, G., & Simonds, L. M. (2022). Feasibility and efficacy of an online compassion-focused imagery intervention for veterinarian self-reassurance, self-criticism and perfectionism. *Vet Record, 192*(2), Article e2177. https://doi.org/10.1002/vetr.2177

Wang, H., & Lou, X. (2022). The correlation between self-compassion and life satisfaction varies across societal individualism-collectivism: A three-level meta-analysis. *Journal of Cross-Cultural Psychology, 53*(9), 1097–1116. https://doi.org/10.1177/00220221221109547

Young, K., Chessell, Z. J., Chisholm, A., et al. (2021). A cognitive behavioural therapy (CBT) approach for working with strong feelings of guilt after traumatic events. *The Cognitive Behaviour Therapist., 14*, Article e26. https://doi.org/10.1017/S1754470X21000192

Chapter 8
Culturally Adapted CFT Group Psychotherapy: A US Perspective

Derek Griner, David M. Erekson, Kristina Hansen, Mark E. Beecher, and Hiu Wai Yoko Caldwell

From the inception of the US with the declaration that "all men are created equal" (Declaration of Independence, 1776, para. 2), the history of multiculturalism in the country has been both promising and fraught. While a full history is beyond the scope of this paper, early settlements of immigrants from Europe, with the accompanying genocide of North America's indigenous people, forced migration of African individuals in the early slave trade, and tensions between cultures and ethnicities throughout the early settlement of the US and its more recent history have shaped the current culture (Spickard et al., 2022). The culture has also been shaped by an early experiment in democracy, with declarations of freedom, equality, and certain inalienable human rights (where, in the early US, each of these promises applied only to White, land-owning men). These ideals, however, helped fuel the eradication of slavery in the US and the civil rights movement, the women's rights movement, and more recent social justice movements, while backlash to these movements have consistently occurred (Neal-Stanley et al., 2024). The shifting metaphor of the US as a melting pot (i.e., individuals assimilate towards a single culture) to a salad bowl (where cultures remain distinct while mutually interactive and beneficial) celebrates multiculturalism, while a recent presidential administration's worry around using the words "race" and "culturally appropriate" in federal documents (Stolberg, 2025) indicates significant resistance to the idea.

It is within this context that psychological science and practise in the US has developed. While psychology has been focused on the reduction of human suffering, it has historically, like the broader US, used a narrow definition of human experience. Although it has improved over time, recent reviews of the literature have indicated a continued centring on Whiteness (e.g. "most participants were White") with poor representation of race, socioeconomic status, and sexual orientation within

D. Griner (✉) · D. M. Erekson · K. Hansen · M. E. Beecher · H. W. Y. Caldwell
Brigham Young University, Provo, UT, USA
e-mail: derek_griner@byu.edu

Y. Kotera et al. (eds.), *Compassion-Focused Therapy for Mental Health: International Perspectives*, Advances in Mental Health and Addiction,
https://doi.org/10.1007/978-3-032-12438-8_8

the psychological literature (McGorray et al., 2023; Roberts et al., 2020). In the most recently available report of individuals participating in mental health research in the US, however, 62–64% identified as White (US Department of Health and Human Services, 2023), coming closer to the reported national percentage of non-Hispanic White individuals (58%, U.S. Census Bureau, 2024).

Given the complex, tumultuous history and a historical blindness to minoritised groups, multicultural competence and cultural humility are not givens in our field. There are, however, decades of research and practise guidelines that support these, and this book is salient evidence that it is considered an important part of ethical practise across theoretical orientations. The evolutionary and biopsychosocial roots of Compassion Focused Therapy (CFT) suggest it as an ideal theory and approach by which to explore the crossroads between multicultural competence; the emergence of culturally shaped mental states, values, and beliefs; and psychotherapy. One of the reasons for this is because it sets a context for the therapeutic encounter in basic evolved strategies of interpersonal relating through *caring and sharing*. These strategies are known to have multiple beneficial biopsychosocial effects (Gilbert, 1995, 2021; Slavich et al., 2023). However, in line with basic evolutionary approaches to the nature of mind (Buss, 2024), we have multiple motives and potentials that also include more primitive strategies of self-focused competition, or interpersonal relating through *holding and controlling*. Gilbert (2021) highlights these two approaches and notes that competition is the basic evolved strategy for resource distribution in multiple species, where the more dominant, powerful individuals get more control over and work to hold onto a greater share of resources. For this reason, considerable time and attention of most primates is rank focused. In contrast to sharing and caring societies, operating in hierarchies of competitive interactions can be extremely stressful (Clark et al., 2019).

At some point in our ancestral history, however, females and subordinate males began to form coalitions against dominant males, deposing them and sharing resources in cooperative teams (Boehm, 1999). This shift is linked to the evolution of friendliness and prosocial behaviour and is sometimes referred as the domestication hypothesis for human nature (Hare, 2017; Hare & Woods, 2020). Over time, caring and sharing relationship building had profound impacts on both resource acquisition and human physiology, where multiple physiological systems are regulated through friendly and caring relationships (including the immune system, threat system, and the central nervous system (Slavich et al, 2023).

Crucially, however, caring and sharing strategies evolved within relatively small hunter gatherer, low resource, mutually dependent groups that facilitated reciprocal relating (Dunbar, 2022; Hare & Woods, 2020). When groups become very large and begin interacting with strangers, and when the availability of resources (wealth) increases, cooperation can begin to breakdown and is subsequently replaced with self- and kin-focused competition.

The field of multiculturalism faces the challenge of in-group and out-group dynamics, in which competition is not only within groups but between groups as well. These cross-group competitive strategies follow the hold and control mentality, where groups seek to dominate, exploit, and inferiorise other groups (Clark et al.,

2019). Compared to other primates, humans differ in that we have historically desired to control the minds, beliefs, and ways of life of others, particularly in political or religious ideologies. This hold and control mentality is often enforced with violence, threat of violence, threat of punishment, and desires to "cleanse or eradicate" alternative belief systems (Gilbert, 2005; Hobfoll, 2019). Hold and control strategies applied to an outgroup have been responsible for some of the worst atrocities humanity has seen, including torture, terrorism, slavery, and genocide. In contrast, the emergence of multiculturalism, (rooted in the caring and sharing mentalities of mutual respect and cooperation) promotes potential cross fertilisation of ideas across a variety of experiences, cultures, and fields, and has been the road to some of the greatest human achievements.

Psychotherapists can mindfully bring these evolutionary contexts to bear as they intentionally create sharing and caring environments, particularly within group psychotherapy. Stimulating these strategies can facilitate a sense of social safeness (rather than social danger), open attention (rather than narrow attention), and feeling valued and cared for by the group (rather than feeling at risk of being kicked out). All this leads to an increased capacity for emotion regulation through prosocial compassionate motivation.

Fostering environments that encourage a sense of safeness and belonging is clearly aligned with the healing values of psychotherapy and the environments psychotherapists hope to create. It is also aligned with the values of multicultural competence. Indeed, the extraordinary range of physiological, psychological, and social impacts that these contexts have enable us to move towards psychological and social healing (Slavich et al., 2023).

In that vein, and by way of introduction, the five of us are professional faculty members at a large, private university in the US who are all invested in CFT, multiculturalism, and group psychotherapy. We are all licensed psychologists who consider ourselves scientist practitioners, as the clinical work we do influences our research and the research we engage in influences our clinical work. In this chapter we will explore the theoretical underpinnings of CFT, group psychotherapy, and multicultural competency. We will further describe ways we have incorporated CFT into group psychotherapy and have further attempted to adapt this therapy to best meet the needs of the clients with whom we work. We will also discuss a potential structure for group CFT and provide a clinical vignette illustrating ways we have worked to culturally adapt the treatment in our US-based college counselling centre. We hope this perspective will add to the international conversation present in this book and support a multicultural approach particularly in group psychotherapy.

CFT Theoretical Underpinnings

CFT is a biopsychosocial model of psychotherapy that incorporates evolutionary theory, neuroscience, Buddhist principles, and attachment theory. From its inception, it has been a continuously evolving theory, incorporating new elements as the science of psychology continues to develop. While several other volumes present comprehensive explanations of the theory (e.g., see Gilbert & Simon, 2022), we wish to focus on two elements that are specifically relevant to group psychotherapy—social mentality theory and the flows of compassion.

Social mentality theory states that humans have innate patterns that assist us in interacting with each other in evolutionarily advantageous ways (e.g., care-seeking, reproduction, competition, etc.) that are characterised by specific affect, cognitions, behaviour, and physiology (Gilbert, 2014). These social mentalities are connected to our three motivational systems, clusters of emotion that help keep us safe (threat); help us gather resources and compete (drive); and help us rest and digest, connect with others, and feel peaceful and playful (soothing). When these systems are balanced, a compassionate social mentality is more likely to be able to be present, characterised by a sensitivity to suffering, a willingness to enter it, and a caring motivation to alleviate it.

These evolved social mentalities have a significant effect on mental and physical health, and are connected to our early life experiences of feeling connected to a caregiver as a safe haven and a secure base (Bowlby, 1978). Our interactions, then, where we reciprocally prompt these social mentalities, are of utmost importance in CFT.

Additionally, these social mentalities are the same systems that individuals use to relate to themselves. When encountering suffering, individuals may have reassuring, compassionate self-interactions, or they may have a harsh, critical internal voice. CFT posits that we can intentionally enter a compassionate mind in order to increase the likelihood of mutually beneficial interactions rather than mutually harmful interactions or patterns of hierarchy or dominance. (These reciprocal patterns are common enough to enter popular art and culture, from The Beatles "The love you take is equal to the love you make" [1969, 1:36] to Joni Mitchell's "Do you see how you hurt me, baby? So I hurt you too, then we both get so blue" [1971, 1:53]). A compassionate mind turned inward activates the affiliative system in the face of threats and allows the individual to move forward in ways that wisely and courageously alleviate suffering.

More simply put, compassion has three flows—offering it to others, receiving it from others, and engaging in self-compassion. Because these are all based on the same affiliative system, they are reciprocally reinforcing. For example, in a study examining these flows, research has found that high levels of caregiving and care seeking were associated with high levels of self-compassion, while high levels of caregiving and low levels of care seeking were associated with low levels of self-compassion (Hermanto & Zuroff, 2016; Hermanto et al., 2017). It is unsurprising, then, that CFT would be particularly efficacious in a group setting that allows for immediate practise with all three flows.

Multicultural Competency and Cultural Adaptations

While CFT theory is particularly amenable to both group and multicultural work, as noted above, psychotherapy has traditionally focused on the therapeutic needs of individuals who are White (European), straight, educated, cisgender, and middle-class. As such, the needs of culturally diverse clientele have often been minimised or ignored (e.g., Henrich et al., 2010; Norcross & Wampold, 2019). Fortunately, over the past five decades, the field of psychology has made major advances in acknowledging the role that cultural factors play in psychotherapy (Norcross & Wampold, 2019). Even so, there is still much work to be done. Culture is everywhere (both in and out of the therapy room) and it is critical that clinicians attend to the complex cultural processes that occur within psychotherapy. Paying attention to culture has the potential to broaden the reach of psychotherapy and provide effective services to those who have commonly been excluded (Sue et al., 2009).

Evidence shows that the cultural experiences and background of clients impact the types of therapy they choose, the manner in which a client-therapist relationship (alliance) is established, and ultimately the outcomes of psychotherapy (e.g., Casas et al., 2016; Vasquez, 2007). While therapists must account for client culture, it should not be to the exclusion of examining how a therapists' cultural characteristics, worldview, and biases impact treatment. Ignoring therapists' cultural characteristics runs the risk of oversimplifying, and potentially blaming, clientele for therapeutic difficulties and treatment failures that may occur.

Meta-analytic research shows that the multicultural competence (or lack thereof) of the therapist providing psychotherapy services impacts treatment outcome (e.g., Soto et al., 2018; Tao et al., 2015). Furthermore, the clients' view of their therapists' multicultural competence is what truly matters. That is, while a therapist may believe themselves to be multiculturally competent (as many of us do), if the client does not view their therapist as such, treatment outcomes deteriorate. It is therefore imperative that therapists continually engage in becoming increasingly multiculturally competent and work to adapt therapy to better meet the needs of their clients.

While it is far beyond the scope of this chapter to describe the nuance associated with engaging in multiculturally competent care, we provide some basic definitions regarding therapist multicultural competence and cultural adaptation of psychotherapy. Any therapist engaging in CFT should continually keep these ideas in mind.

A therapist's level of multicultural competence refers to their ability to actively engage and work effectively with clients from diverse backgrounds. Multicultural competencies have often been operationalised using a tripartite model that includes awareness, knowledge, and skills (e.g., Arredondo et al., 1996). A therapist's multicultural *awareness* refers to their ability to acknowledge and recognise the cultural experiences and background of their clients and themselves. This awareness extends to therapists understanding how their own privilege, assumptions, biases, and worldview impact the therapeutic process. As there will always be more to learn about ourselves and others, increasing cultural awareness is a lifelong effort.

A therapist's multicultural *knowledge* refers to their understanding and familiarity of cultural groups and norms associated with particular groups. While cultural norms are potentially helpful heuristics, they should not be the basis for therapeutic intervention, as each individual within a group is unique. Furthermore, multicultural knowledge extends to therapists being able to nondefensively recognise ways that historical oppression has impacted and continues to impact assumptions inherent in much of psychotherapy. A therapist's journey to increase multicultural knowledge will ideally be a lifelong endeavour as well.

Finally, a therapist's multicultural *skill* refers to their ability to engage diverse clientele in treatment. While skills were originally conceptualised as how a therapist may work specifically with a particular group of individuals, the field has moved towards describing a multiculturally skilled therapist as one who is flexible enough to adapt therapy to best meet the needs of their clients. Such therapists are humble, curious, flexible, and open to learning from their clientele (e.g., Hook et al., 2013; Mosher et al., 2017).

Psychotherapy interventions that are *culturally adapted* involve modifying evidence-based treatments according to the culture of the people being treated. While there are innumerable ways to adapt therapy, one comprehensive model (Bernal et al., 1995) includes eight dimensions of intervention (language, persons, metaphors, content, concepts, goals, methods, and context). Systematic reviews and meta-analytic research have shown that culturally adapting psychotherapy is indeed effective, particularly when the treatment is adapted to better match a client's worldview (e.g., Benish et al., 2011; Griner & Smith, 2006; Hall et al., 2016; Smith & Trimble, 2016).

CFT aligns well with the aims of multicultural therapy in that both take a biopsychosocial approach and examine ways that genetics, life experiences, and different cultural identities (e.g., race, gender, abilities, SES, sexual orientation, religion, national origin, power, etc.) influence a person's attention, thoughts, feelings, motivations, behaviours, and even physiology. CFT and multicultural psychology encourage flexibility in working with individuals and recognise that clients are the experts of their own reality. Attempting to manualise multicultural psychology or CFT would ultimately eliminate the flexibility necessary to meet clients where they are and subsequently tailor treatment accordingly.

Group Psychotherapy

Parallel to the complexities of multicultural psychology, group psychotherapy is a complex mental health treatment modality especially well-suited to addressing many different issues for which people often seek treatment. As humans, we move about the world influencing and being influenced by our biologies, histories, cultures, relationships, experiences, and internal phenomena—all while participating throughout our lives in varied groups of others. Kaklauskas (2020) encapsulates the omnipresence of these groups stating that "the entire world is a group, and we are merely group members in the various communities of our lives" (p. xviii). These communities are peopled with folks who are similar to and different from ourselves and our fellow group members in myriad ways. Group therapy aims to explore the relationships between and among group members, the group leaders, and the group as a whole as a social microcosm of real-world experiences that help group members move towards change and healing.

But just because humans exist in naturalistic and formulated groups does not automatically make group psychotherapy effective. So how do we know that it works? An ever-growing body of outcome studies (especially since the 2000s), as well as multiple meta-analyses provide strong empirical evidence that group therapy is effective compared to nonactive treatments such as waitlist control groups or other minimal-contact interventions (Burlingame & Strauss, 2021; Burlingame et al., 2013), equivalent to other active treatments such as individual psychotherapy (Burlingame et al., 2016; Rosendahl et al, 2021), and generally efficient in terms of financial and time costs (Tucker & Oei, 2006; Weatherford, 2017; Whittingham et al., 2023). In addition, Rosendahl et al. (2021) summarised recent developments in group psychotherapy research suggesting that group therapy can be recommended for treating a wide range of issues (e.g., mood disorders, anxiety disorders, thought disorders, SPMI concerns, eating disorders, etc.).

What is it about group psychotherapy that makes it effective? Different group theoretical orientations may answer this question differently, but all seem to have a few things in common. Yalom and Leszcz (2020) delineate and describe 11 elemental component processes occurring in the "intricate interplay of human experiences" in group therapy which they refer to as "therapeutic factors" (p. 10). These therapeutic factors were distilled from therapist views of what seems helpful to group members, members' reports of their own group experiences, and systematic research usually correlating therapy outcomes with in-therapy variables. The therapeutic factors include instillation of hope, universality, imparting information, altruism, the corrective recapitulation of the primary family group, development of socialising techniques, imitative behaviour, group cohesiveness, catharsis, and existential factors.

In addition, Day (2014) posits that *learning*—"a change in behaviour resulting from experience" (p. 25)—is a key component of group therapy that unites various group theories. The author cites social learning theory (Bandura, 1986) combined with Lewin's (1948) *groupdynamics*, or all that goes on in a group, both obvious and subtle, to highlight learning that can occur in the social microcosm of the group (Yalom & Leszcz, 2020). Essentially, learning in the group grows from patterns in the world being mirrored in transactions within the group and worked through for more favourable and adaptive outcomes and healing. When we think about impactful experiences in our various life groups, it is the presence of important others that create the conditions for the impacts. Learning gleaned through group therapy may be especially fitting for addressing issues related to painful social systems, interpersonal struggles, beliefs about the self, behaviour patterns, and symptoms specific to many different diagnoses (and no diagnoses). As it turns out, humans are social creatures (even those of us who prefer to be alone), and our relationships contribute to the hurt and healing that result in our learning. Group therapy is an especially suitable treatment modality for improving that learning.

Some key components contribute to successful group psychotherapy. As with individual and other forms of talk therapy, the therapeutic relationship matters quite a lot, and the degree to which it predicts patient outcomes is related to client factors, leader factors, and group structural factors (Burlingame et al., 2014, 2021). But the therapeutic relationship of a group is multidimensional and complex in ways that an individual client-therapist relationship (alliance) is not. Specifically, relationships are also present and likely influential between and among the group members (cohesion) and each member with the group as a whole (climate). These structural factors can be crossed with relational constructs (plus empathy) and conceptualised as positive bond, positive work, and negative relationship (Burlingame et al., 2017). Positive bond attempts to capture a group member's emotional attachment with the group, members, and leader. Positive work reflects the collaborative working engagement towards treatment tasks and goals of the member, leader, and group. And negative relationship explores a group member's tolerance of conflict, group ruptures, and empathic failure that may adversely affect member attachments or therapeutic work (Burlingame et al., 2017). Because the group therapeutic relationship includes so many different components of group dynamics and the unique constellation of people involved in the therapy, leader interventions and presence that contribute positively to the bonds, work, and tolerable conflict of the group are likely to activate the therapeutic factors shown to contribute to learning and successful group psychotherapy.

Applying CFT to Group Therapy

Now that we have discussed the fundamental components of CFT, the importance of multicultural competencies, and the power of group therapy, we can begin to see how combining all three provides a powerful framework for promoting client healing and growth. Group therapy provides an ideal environment for clients to experientially engage in the three flows of compassion; experiment with different ways of relating to themselves and others; be supportively challenged as they face their fears, blocks, and resistances (FBRs); and utilise the examples of others as they develop their compassionate self. Our work with CFT groups has primarily been in a university counselling centre in the US. We believe that the principles and structure for the group that we will discuss are applicable or adaptable to most settings. In fact, since practicing in multiculturally competent ways requires adaptation to each unique group (and, really, every individual in that group), the framework we will discuss requires a focus on flexibility and here-and-now process over adherence to any manualised form of treatment.

Before we lay out the basic structure of the guide we co-created with Paul Gilbert (the founder of CFT) that we use in our CFT groups for university students, it is important to discuss some initial concepts and practises that lay the foundations of a successful, multiculturally attuned, CFT group. The goal of such a group is to establish an environment where every individual feels welcome and able to vulnerably work on their concerns.

Attending group therapy is a highly courageous act for most people that tends to activate the threat system, sometimes in intense ways. CFT theory posits that humans in a state of threat tend to struggle with novel or higher-order tasks. Therefore, attending to safety and safeness early and often in the group is of prime importance.

One traditional way to begin group psychotherapy is to set the frame with rules of attendance, participation, and other group norms. Unfortunately, individuals often have tricky relationships with *rules*. From an evolutionary perspective, a list of rules may indicate ways that a group member may be expelled from the group. In a CFT-oriented group, we use the word *guidelines* and have the group members generate these in an effort to share power and authority (this may be the first time group members experience a leader sharing power). We remind group members that because of their unique biologies and life histories, they may each have different guidelines that will help them feel safe and secure. We encourage discussion about setting the frame for *their* group through a collaborative discussion of safety (protection from harm) and safeness (a sense that others are supportive and that there is caring and concern from others that will allow for vulnerable exploration and play), with the intention of creating feelings of friendliness, acceptance, openness, and playfulness in the group.

Though such a discussion may generate many of the same points as traditional group rule lists (i.e., confidentiality and the limits thereof, attendance expectations, ways to interact with each other in and out of the group, how to address group members who are quiet or who monopolise the group, etc.), having the group members work together to feel out what will help them create safety and safeness seems to move them more quickly into a condition where there is cohesion among members and a desire to work vulnerably together. It also allows more room for varied multicultural perspectives on what safety and safeness might mean for each individual group member.

Another important consideration for enhancing the working of the group is understanding how to balance psychoeducation and process in the group. Helping group members learn and understand CFT requires psychoeducation. However, the need to convey material can easily lead group leaders to focus so much on the content/information of the group that the process (what is happening for members in the here-and-now) is neglected or lost altogether.

Prioritising the principle over the process in this way leads to a loss of the potential power of the group. The most important work of CFT is addressing FBRs. This is unlikely (or potentially impossible) to happen if group leaders are not attending to what is happening in the moment and intentionally slowing down to help group members explore their reactions to the content and each other.

We have intentionally transitioned to using the word *guide* instead of *manual* to help ourselves and others see the importance of moving away from script-based approaches and towards knowing the CFT material well enough that we can agilely move between concepts according to the momentary needs of the group. This flexibility allows for greater multicultural sensitivity and a move away from more rigid, hierarchical, therapeutic structures.

CFT Group Therapy Content, Structure, and Process

In the past we have used a guide (Cattani et al., 2022) and accompanying workbook (Arnold et al., 2022) to help group leaders direct CFT group psychotherapy in our centre. More recently, we have used an updated guide that Paul Gilbert and Derek Griner are developing for publication. We now give a brief description of each module from this newer guide. Again, these modules are meant to be applied in whatever time frame and structure is clinically appropriate for each specific group. That is, *module* is not synonymous with *session,* and therapists are not expected to follow these modules in a lock-step manner.

Module 1

Therapists help the group establish a sense of safety and safeness, introduces brain state theory, and helps clients understand that we can work to intentionally shift our brain states.

Module 2

The group works to deepen an understanding of compassion and recognise compassion as an algorithm. The therapists introduce the three flows of compassion, the tricky brain, and soothing rhythm breathing (SRB).

Module 3

The group learns about the three life tasks and how these are linked to the threat, drive, and soothing motivational systems. Clients begin to explore the threat system, and the concept of "not your fault" is emphasised.

Module 4

The group explores ways to balance the three motivational systems and engage in a safe place imagery exercise. This practice helps group members begin to intentionally engage the soothing system, while beginning to develop an internal sense of safeness.

Module 5

Therapists help the group explore the flow of receiving compassion from another and engage in an ideal compassionate other visualisation, activating and practicing a sense of safeness in the presence of another.

Module 6

Clients are introduced to social mentality theory and self-to-self relating. The group explores the disappointment gap between the ideal self and the actual self, the six steps to enact compassion, and a functional analysis of the critical self and the compassionate self.

Module 7

Therapists lead the group in a deeper exploration of the critical self and use the compassionate self to see behind the critic. In this module, clients embody their compassionate-self, particularly in regards to how they respond to the disappointment gap. We remind clients that we are not trying to reform the self-critic but rather understand its motivations.

Module 8

We explore if/why group members want to develop compassion and explore the fears, blocks, and resistances to this development. Clients begin practising moving about the world as their compassionate self.

Module 9

We continue to deepen self-compassion and engage in writing a compassionate letter to past or present self.

Module 10

Clients now begin to consolidate the skills they have learned and explore compassionate assertiveness as engaging with both self-compassion and compassion for others in difficult interpersonal interactions. We begin practising compassionate assertiveness and the variations of how this may manifest according to context.

Module 11

We discuss warning signs (when compassion may be needed most), explore maintenance strategies (how to keep practising the acquired skills and learning), wish one another well (in preparation for the group's end), and say goodbye.

Extending CFT Group Treatment

After group members have completed an initial CFT group covering the concepts in the modules above, we have offered a follow up process-oriented group that enables group members to continue practicing and applying these concepts. The group typically begins with SRB, then a check-in with each group member about their experiences over the past week, then allows for unstructured process. At various times throughout the group, members may request specific exercises from the first CFT group to buttress their efforts to develop their compassionate selves. This second group can be particularly useful as members share a common CFT language that enables them to confront complex life difficulties and their FBRs. Additionally, the "social laboratory" of the group allows members to experiment with the three flows of compassion in the here-and-now as they explore their life experiences and relationships within and outside the group.

Clinical Vignette

The following vignette is based on real experiences from several group members attending a semester-long (about 16 weeks), process-oriented CFT-1 psychotherapy group in a university counselling centre. To protect the anonymity of group members, we have intentionally changed names and identifying information. This particular group had eight members with the following demographics:

Bernila 21-year-old, single, cisgender, straight, Filipina, woman, first-generation college student
Rachel 20-year-old, committed relationship (boyfriend), cisgender, straight, White, woman
Will 18-year-old, single, cisgender, gay, White, man
Emilio 19-year-old, single, cisgender, straight, Latino, man
Max 22-year-old, married, cisgender, straight, White, woman
Meilani 24-year-old, single, cisgender, straight, Polynesian, woman, doctoral student
Sophie 20-year-old, partnered (girlfriend), cisgender, pansexual, White, woman
Sarah 21-year-old, single, cisgender, straight, White, woman

The vignette we describe below happened during the seventh session and the group had covered materials found up through module four. (Quick reminder that process is more important than psychoeducation and, as such, each module will not necessarily correspond with session number; please remember to modify your materials to the needs of your groups). During the seventh session, we had plans to begin covering the materials found in module five which focuses on the flow of compassion from another and the ideal compassionate other visualisation.

As had become customary for this group, the leader began by passing around the basket of fidget toys for those interested. Once everyone had what they needed, the leader helped members engage in SRB. By this point, group members were accustomed to beginning each group with slowing their body and mind; imagining a friend or loved one to help shift their brain towards compassion; and noticing their compassionate body posture, friendly facial expression, and internal voice tone.

Leader Thanks for taking the time to slow your body and mind. Why don't we begin with some check-ins and see what's been going on for people this past week—are you all okay with that?

The group collectively expressed that they were.

Leader (in a playful tone) Alright, I bet you can't guess what I'm going to ask next. [Group members smiled.] Who wants to go first today?
Rachel (who had smiled immediately responded): Yeah, I think we all kinda knew you were going to say that. [The group laughed.] This week was pretty good for me. I've been thinking a lot about the safe place thing we did last week (safe place imagery) and I even listened to the recording you sent a few times. There was something kinda nice about thinking about my

childhood home being a place that feels really safe for me. You asked us to think about whether we'd want people there with us and I definitely would want my parents there. This (safe place imagery) came at the perfect time for me since we have a long weekend coming up. I'm going back to my parent's home for five days and I'm just going to relax and eat good food. I'm really looking forward to it!

Several in the group began talking about the comfort that they, too, felt at their childhood homes and about connections that they had with family members. Some expressed wishing that they could have the same weekend that Rachel had planned. As the conversation continued, Bernila eventually entered.

Bernila I'm having a different experience as we talk about going to our family homes. I hope that's okay. [Group members nodded yes and smiled.] You know that I'm Filipina and there's a pretty big population of us in L.A. (Los Angeles). I'm going home this weekend, but I feel like I have to because my family is doing some celebrations. I really love my family and my culture, and it will be cool in some ways because we'll dress up in our traditional Baro't Saya (traditional Filipino clothing) and eat good food. But I'll be expected to put aside everything and help my family out the entire time. My family doesn't quite get me. I want to be more independent, but we have this saying, *utang na loob,* which basically means that there is a life-long debt that we owe our parents for raising us. If I don't have *utang na loob* then I'll be seen as less than or ungrateful. [Bernila began to tear up and while laughing through the tears continued.] I never cry…I just want to do things that matter to me, but I don't want to let my family down.

Leader I notice that I'm having reactions, and it looks like others in the room are too. What do you think about having people respond to what you just shared?

Bernila I'd actually really like that. I feel like I'm talking bad about my family, but I really do love them. It's just really confusing and frustrating.

Rachel I'm so glad to hear your experience. If I made you feel bad talking about my family, I'm sorry [Bernila shook her head 'no' and expressed that she did not feel this way at all.] I guess I also want to say that I don't hear you talking bad about your family. It's really clear, at least to me, that you love them so much. You've talked about how much you love them since we began our group.

Emilio I also didn't hear you talking bad about your family. I like how you talked about real stuff in here—that makes it easier for me to talk about real stuff too. My family is fine, but I just don't feel really super connected to them. So, when you said that going home felt difficult, I think it made me feel a little better about my situation. I hope that doesn't sound bad.

Bernila Not at all.

Sarah It makes a lot of sense to me that going home would be tricky. I want to join the chorus that you're not a bad person for having mixed feelings about going home.

The group continued to talk about ways that they felt about their own family situations and connections they did and did not have with their family of origins. As the conversations slowed down, the leader intervened.

Leader Bernila, what was it like to hear feedback from the group?
Bernila That actually felt *so* good. I think I hold all of this stuff inside and it feels really connecting to say it out loud and have others tell me I'm okay. Thanks so much.
Max Oh, you're better than okay, Bernila. I'm so happy you're in our group!

The group responded with several affirming statements of one another and expressed gratitude that they could speak openly with each other in spite of different circumstances.

Leader Isn't it interesting how we can have such varied reactions to a question about what it is like to go back to our childhood homes? I think this is such a brilliant example of just how much our genetics, families, and life experiences shape who we are and ways we view the world.

The group continued with check-ins and the theme of connection seemed to be a unifying thread. During our teatime, Bernila and others talked about their plans to go home over the longer weekend, and they seemed to be well-connected as they laughed and joked with one another. Following the break, the leader provided psychoeducation about the flow of receiving compassion from others and asked the group if they would be willing to engage in the ideal compassionate other visualisation—they all agreed. Following this visualisation, the leader asked group members about their experience. Some members described their ideal compassionate others as animals, others described humans, and some described more abstract shapes and textures.

Bernila I know I spent the first half of the group talking about how I have conflicted feelings about my family, but my ideal compassionate other was a mix of my grandmother and, weirdly, a professor here who is so nice to me.
Max What is your professor like?
Bernila She's just really supportive of me and interested in helping me pursue my goals. She keeps encouraging me to apply to grad school and is helping me connect with some of her colleagues. She's really great.

Bernila went on to describe her grandmother and professor in more detail. The group collectively expressed happiness about Bernila having both of these individuals in her life and shared that her ideal compassionate other felt like the perfect combination of her family and her desires to move in directions different than family expectation. As the conversation progressed another member entered.

Will Yeah, I don't know about this one. You all know I have a hard time with visualizations anyway, but this one—I just couldn't really do it.

Group members expressed sympathy for Will and wishes that he would be able to engage in visualisations more easily.

Leader Visualizations can absolutely be tricky. I'm really glad that you're bringing this up. Last week we talked about thinking in terms of preferences rather than having a clear picture in our mind. So maybe you could try thinking about, "Would I rather have an ideal other who is rude and dismissive or one who listens intently with the hope of understanding me?" or "Would I rather have an ideal other who checks their watch every few seconds or one who sits patiently with me as I figure things out?" [Will smiled.]

Will I think that helps. I remember you talking about that before, and I bet that could help some with this one too.

Leader Another thing that can work sometimes is to borrow ideas from one another. What do you all think about the idea of "borrowing" from each other if you feel like you're getting stuck?

Group members expressed that they were happy to share with one another.

Bernila Will, you can borrow my grandmother. She's really great! I bet she'd like you too. [The group laughed.]

Will I was actually really enjoying your description of her. She sounds so nice and patient. Seriously, thank you guys for helping me out with this. I think it's just going to take some more practise.

Leader I've said this kind of thing before, but it's so nice to see the way you're all working to help each other. Also, what you just shared is such good insight, Will. [He smiled.] The more we practise any of these skills we're talking about, the better we get. Remember how tough it was at the beginning to do soothing rhythm breathing? Now look at us...we're pros.

Group members laughed as they discussed the difficulties they had practising SRB early on. They then spent time talking about how they had seen one another improve in various ways and talked about how nice it felt to be together each week.

Leader I'm so happy that, as a group, we're talking about the difficulties associated with some of these practises. We've talked about this before, but if developing compassion were a really simple process, none of us would be here. I hope you'll take time to continue noticing ways you're improving. I know we're close on time. Does this feel like an okay place to end?

The group expressed that this felt like a good place to end, and several stayed in the room talking with one another before leaving their separate ways.

As one can see from the example above, multicultural considerations are omnipresent in group work and can arise organically and through direct intervention by leaders or group members. In this example, the initial check-in with group members about the safe space imagery exercise led to several individuals agreeing about their happy experiences of home. This application of the safe space imagery to their external world helped connect members of the group; as this moment of connection unfolded, however, the group had previously established enough safeness for a group member with a different experience to speak up. This safeness is the first step in allowing for multicultural differences to arise, where group members feel secure in their differences and in the belief that the group can tolerate and support different experiences.

As one group member expressed a different experience (i.e., home does not feel relaxing), it allowed for other group members to feel more comfortable sharing their different experiences, increasing the sense of vulnerability and support in the group. It also allowed members to hear feedback from their peers regarding potential judgments of their thoughts or actions (i.e., "I hope that doesn't sound bad"). As group members are able to authentically engage in compassionate feedback, these messages can support an internalised sense of self-compassion that may be more likely to arise in future difficult circumstances.

After the group member was able to express her experience of going home, the other group members were later able to connect her ideal compassionate other to the complex multicultural factors she experiences (i.e., duty to family versus academic ambition). This then became a moment where, rather than being alone in her circumstances (as she initially feared), she was supported by the group in noticing and exploring the complexity. She was then able to lend some of her connection to her family (i.e., her grandmother) to another group member who expressed difficulty with the ideal compassionate other visualisation, allowing her initial vulnerability to support another group member in their difficulty. The ability of the group to identify and care for these kinds of differences in experience is profound, and the group leader can point out these processes to amplify the power of the group as they work together to alleviate suffering.

Conclusions

The nature of group therapy includes multiple cultural perspectives, where individuals with different experiences, struggles, and lenses are given a space to work together towards amelioration of their suffering. Given CFT's emphasis on genetics and environments that shape our current selves, this approach demands that therapists pay attention to the unique cultural experiences, backgrounds, and worldviews that each member will bring to the group. CFT group psychotherapy offers individuals from all walks of life opportunities to heal from life difficulties and pain by fostering a deeper sense of connection with self and others, reducing shame, and strengthening emotional resilience in the face of self-criticism. A CFT group is ideal for fostering group cohesion (positive bond), working towards common goals (positive work), and creating an environment where ruptures (negative relationship) can be addressed in compassionate and caring ways.

Further, a CFT framework provides group members with psychoeducation and experiential activities that promote compassionate skills and qualities. All of these skills are provided in the service of cultivating connection among group members. As group members address their FBRs in the presence of others, they learn that such responses are part of common humanity and can be a source of connection and healing.

As noted above, social mentality theory and the three flows of compassion support this work, where group members experience and experiment with the flows in real time, and then broaden their interpersonal repertoire in ways that increase the likelihood of an internalised, self-compassionate response. These processes are also supported by the intersectional identities and experiences of diverse group members, where developing an early sense of safeness in the group allows for these differences to be discussed—the differences then expand the group's (and the group members') ability to engage compassionately.

In our earlier presentation of a potential structure for group CFT, we want to emphasise three aspects. First, the structured elements of CFT treatment can provide a shared understanding and language for clients to make sense of their experiences. Second, these elements can support group process, where group members' thoughts and experiences will be important to bring into the group. Finally, any structured elements should be flexibly applied, with the main goal of helping clients experience, through interpersonal processes, the power of engaging a compassionate brain state as they encounter suffering (both their own and the suffering of others).

As noted in our introduction, the history of multiculturalism in the US has been fraught, with early acts of cruelty and callousness imprinted in our institutions and echoing across time. As is clear in CFT theory, engaging a compassionate mind in the face of threat is challenging, and particularly challenging as the tides of society are pulled towards hold and control mentalities. It is within this context that our clients are attempting to navigate their own identities, experiences, and suffering. Group therapy as a social microcosm allows clients to make this journey a shared one and has inward- and outward-facing ramifications. Inward-facing in that the group gives the client the opportunity to examine and respond to their own suffering; and outward-facing in that the client becomes more able to engage with others in sharing and caring ways. Outside of therapy, we all navigate a world of groups, of various compositions and sizes. As we employ CFT principles, we are more able to connect through our similarities *and* our differences and are more likely to move towards a compassionate world.

Author Contributions Conceptualisation: DG, DME, KH, MEB, and HWYC. Investigation: DG, DME, KH, MEB, and HWYC. Resources: DG, DME, KH, MEB, and HWYC. Writing—original draft: DG, DME, KH, MEB, and HWYC. Writing—review and editing: DG, DME, KH, MEB, and HWYC. Project administration: DG, DME, KH, MEB, and HWYC.

References

Arnold, R., Alldredge, C. T., Cattani, K., Griner, D., Erekson, D. M., Burlingame, G. M., & Beecher, M. E. (2022). *Compassion focused therapy participant workbook*. Routledge.

Arredondo, P., Toporek, R., Brown, S. P., Jones, J., Locke, D. C., Sanchez, J., & Stadler, H. (1996). Operationalization of the multicultural counseling competencies. *Journal of Multicultural Counseling and Development, 24*(1), 42–78.

Bandura, A. (1986). *Social foundations of thought and action*. Prentice-Hall.

Benish, S. G., Quintana, S., & Wampold, B. E. (2011). Culturally adapted psychotherapy and the legitimacy of myth: A direct-comparison meta-analysis. *Journal of Counseling Psychology, 58*(3), 279.

Bernal, G., Bonilla, J., & Bellido, C. (1995). Ecological validity and cultural sensitivity for outcome research: Issues for the cultural adaptation and development of psychosocial treatments with Hispanics. *Journal of Abnormal Child Psychology, 23*, 67–82.

Boehm, C. (1999). The natural selection of altruistic traits. *Human Nature, 10*(3), 205–252.

Bowlby, J. (1978). Attachment theory and its therapeutic implications. *Adolescent Psychiatry, 6*, 5–33.

Burlingame, G. M., Alldredge, C. T., & Arnold, R. A. (2021). Alliance rupture detection and repair in group therapy: Using the Group Questionnaire–GQ. *International Journal of Group Psychotherapy, 71*(2), 338–370. https://doi.org/10.1080/00207284.2020.1844010

Burlingame, G. M., Gleave, R., Beecher, M., Griner, D., Hansen, K., Jensen, J., Worthen, V., & Svien, H. (2017). *Administration and scoring manual for the Group Questionnaire.* OQ Measures, LLC.

Burlingame, G. M., Seebeck, J. D., Janis, R. A., Whitcomb, K. E., Barkowski, S., Rosendahl, J., & Strauss, B. (2016). Outcome differences between individual and group formats when identical and nonidentical treatments, patients, and doses are compared: A 25-year meta-analytic perspective. *Psychotherapy, 53*(4), 446–461. https://doi.org/10.1037/pst0000090

Burlingame, G. M., & Strauss, B. (2021). Efficacy of small group treatments: Foundation for evidence-based practise. In M. Barkham, W. Lutz, & L. G. Castonguay (Eds.), *Bergin & Garfield's handbook of psychotherapy and behavior change: 50th anniversary edition* (7th ed., pp. 583–624) John Wiley & Sons, Inc.

Burlingame, G. M., Strauss, B., & Joyce, A. S. (2013). Change mechanisms and effectiveness of small group treatments. In M. J. Lambert (Ed.), *Bergin & Garfield's handbook of psychotherapy and behavior change* (6th ed., pp. 640–689). John Wiley & Sons, Inc.

Burlingame, G. M., Whitcomb, K., & Woodland, S. (2014). Process and outcome in group counseling and psychotherapy: A perspective. In J. L. Delucia-Waack, C. Kalodner, & M. T. Riva, *Handbook of group counseling and psychotherapy* (2nd ed., pp. 55–67), Sage.

Buss, D. M. (2024). *Evolutionary psychology: The new science of the mind.* Routledge.

Casas, J. M., Suzuki, L. A., Alexander, C. M., & Jackson, M. A. (Eds.). (2016). *Handbook of multicultural counseling.* Sage Publications.

Cattani, K., Griner, D., Erekson, D. M., Burlingame, G. M., Beecher, M. E., & Alldredge, C. T. (2022). *Compassion focused group therapy for University counseling centers: A clinician's guide.* Routledge.

Clark, C. J., Liu, B. S., Winegard, B. M., & Ditto, P. H. (2019). Tribalism is human nature. *Current Directions in Psychological Science, 28*(6), 587–592.

Day, S. X. (2014). A unifying theory for group counseling and psychotherapy. In J. L. DeLucia-Waack, C. R. Kalodner, & M. T. Riva (Eds.), *Handbook of group counseling and psychotherapy* (2nd ed., pp. 24–33). Sage.

Dunbar, R. I. M. (2022). Structural and cognitive solutions to prevent group fragmentation in group-living species. *BioRxiv*, 2022–12.

Gilbert, P. (1995). Attachment, cooperation and rank: the evolution of need for status and social support. *Social support and psychiatric disorder: Research findings and guidelines for clinical practice*, 117–144.

Gilbert, P. (Ed.). (2005). *Compassion: Conceptualisations, research and use in psychotherapy.* Routledge.

Gilbert, P. (2014). The origins and nature of compassion focused therapy. *British Journal of Clinical Psychology, 53*(1), 6–41.

Gilbert, P. (2021). Creating a compassionate world: Addressing the conflicts between sharing and caring versus controlling and holding evolved strategies. *Frontiers in Psychology, 11*. https://doi.org/10.3389/fpsyg.2020.582090

Gilbert, P., & Simos, G. (Eds.). (2022). *Compassion focused therapy: Clinical practise and applications.* Routledge.

Griner, D., & Smith, T. B. (2006). Culturally adapted mental health intervention: A meta-analytic review. *Psychotherapy: Theory, research, practise, training, 43*(4), 531.
Hall, G. C. N., Ibaraki, A. Y., Huang, E. R., Marti, C. N., & Stice, E. (2016). A meta-analysis of cultural adaptations of psychological interventions. *Behavior therapy, 47*(6), 993–1014.
Hare, B. (2017). Survival of the friendliest: Homo sapiens evolved via selection for prosociality. *Annual Review of Psychology, 68*(1), 155–186.
Hare, B., & Woods, V. (2020). *Survival of the friendliest. Understanding our origins and rediscovering our common humanity*. One World Books
Henrich, J., Heine, S. J., & Norenzayan, A. (2010). The weirdest people in the world? *Behavioral and Brain Sciences, 33*(2–3), 61–83.
Hermanto, N., & Zuroff, D. C. (2016). The social mentality theory of self-compassion and self-reassurance: The interactive effect of care-seeking and caregiving. *The Journal of Social Psychology, 156*(5), 523–535.
Hermanto, N., Zuroff, D. C., Kelly, A. C., & Leybman, M. J. (2017). Receiving support, giving support, and self-reassurance: A daily diary test of social mentality theory. *Personality and Individual Differences, 107*, 37–42.
Hobfoll, S. E. (2019). Threat and the rise of fear politics and tribalism. *Stress and anxiety-contributions of the STAR award winners, 3*.
Hook, J. N., Davis, D. E., Owen, J., Worthington, E. L., Jr., & Utsey, S. O. (2013). Cultural humility: Measuring openness to culturally diverse clients. *Journal of Counseling Psychology, 60*(3), 353.
Kaklauskas, F. (2020). Preface. In F. J. Kaklauskas & L. R. Greene (Eds.), *Core principles in group psychotherapy: An integrated theory, research, and practise training manual* (pp. xvii–xviii). Routledge.
Lewin, K. (1948). *Resolving social conflicts: Selected papers on group dynamics*. Harper.
McGorray, E. L., Emery, L. F., Garr-Schultz, A., & Finkel, E. J. (2023). "Mostly White, heterosexual couples": Examining demographic diversity and reporting practises in relationship science research samples. *Journal of Personality and Social Psychology, 125*(2), 316.
Mitchell, J. (1971). All I want. In On *Blue* [Song]. Reprise Records.
Mosher, D. K., Hook, J. N., Captari, L. E., Davis, D. E., DeBlaere, C., & Owen, J. (2017). Cultural humility: A therapeutic framework for engaging diverse clients. *Practise Innovations, 2*(4), 221.
Neal-Stanley, A., Duncan, K., & Love, B. (2024). "A brief moment in the sun": Mapping white backlash in the history of K-12 black education in the United States. *International Journal of Multicultural Education, 26*(1), 31–56.
Norcross, J. C., & Wampold, B. E. (2019). *Psychotherapy relationships that work: Evidence-based therapist responsiveness* (Vol. 2).
Roberts, S. O., Bareket-Shavit, C., Dollins, F. A., Goldie, P. D., & Mortenson, E. (2020). Racial inequality in psychological research: Trends of the past and recommendations for the future. *Perspectives on Psychological Science, 15*(6), 1295–1309.
Rosendahl, J., Alldredge, C. T., Burlingame, G. M., & Strauss, B. (2021). Recent developments in group psychotherapy research. *American Journal of Psychotherapy, 74*(2), 52–59. https://doi.org/10.1176/appi.psychotherapy.20200031
Soto, A., Smith, T. B., Griner, D., Domenech Rodríguez, M., & Bernal, G. (2018). Cultural adaptations and therapist multicultural competence: Two meta-analytic reviews. *Journal of Clinical Psychology, 74*(11), 1907–1923.
Slavich, G. M., Roos, L. G., Mengelkoch, S., Webb, C. A., Shattuck, E. C., Moriarity, D. P., & Alley, J. C. (2023). Social safety theory: Conceptual foundation, underlying mechanisms, and future directions. *Health Psychology Review, 17*(1), 5–59.
Smith, T. B., & Trimble, J. E. (2016). *Culturally adapted mental health services: An updated meta-analysis of client outcomes*.
Spickard, P., Beltrán, F., & Hooton, L. (2022). *Almost all aliens: Immigration, race, and colonialism in American history and identity*. Routledge.
Stolberg, S. G. (2025, February 26). C.D.C suggests terms like 'race' and 'health equity' are off-limits, then backtracks. *The New York Times*, 13.

Sue, S., Zane, N., Nagayama Hall, G. C., & Berger, L. K. (2009). The case for cultural competency in psychotherapeutic interventions. *Annual Review of Psychology, 60*(1), 525–548.

Tao, K. W., Owen, J., Pace, B. T., & Imel, Z. E. (2015). A meta-analysis of multicultural competencies and psychotherapy process and outcome. *Journal of Counseling Psychology, 62*(3), 337.

The Beatles. (1969). The end. On *Abbey Road* [Song]. Apple Records.

Tucker, M., & Oei, T. P. S. (2006). Is group more cost effective than individual cognitive behavioral therapy? The evidence is not solid yet. *Behavioural and Cognitive Psychotherapy, 35*, 77–91. https://doi.org/10.1017/S1352465806003134

US Department of Health and Human Services. (2023). *NIH RCDC inclusion statistics report*.

U.S. Census Bureau. (2024). QuickFacts: United States. U.S. Department of Commerce. Retrieved October 14, 2025, from https://www.census.gov/quickfacts/fact/table/US/PST045221

Vasquez, M. J. (2007). Cultural difference and the therapeutic alliance: An evidence-based analysis. *American Psychologist, 62*(8), 878.

Weatherford, R. D. (2017). Estimating the efficiency of therapy groups in a college counseling center. *Journal of College Student Psychotherapy, 31*(3), 231–237. https://doi.org/10.1080/87568225.2016.1277815

Whittingham, M., Marmarosh, C. L., Mallow, P., & Scherer, M. (2023). Mental health care equity and access: A group therapy solution. *American Psychologist, 78*(2), 119–133. https://doi.org/10.1037/amp0001078

Yalom, I. D., & Leszcz, M. (2020). *The theory and practise of group psychotherapy* (6th ed.). Basic Books.

Chapter 9
Compassion-Focused Therapy in Ireland: Cultural, Clinical, and Systemic Perspectives Across the Island of Ireland

Julie Beaumont

Introduction

This chapter examines Compassion Focused Therapy (CFT) in the island of Ireland (Republic of Ireland and Northern Ireland), situating the current approach within the region's unique mental health landscape, political and religious environments, and emerging evidence of CFT application. Applicability of CFT in relation to both generational trauma and violence towards women and girls is discussed.

What is Compassion-Focused Therapy?

CFT is an evolutionary psychological intervention that addresses the difficulties many individuals experience, shame, self-criticism, and with receiving care from others, by supporting individuals to develop a motivation and skillset for compassion (Gilbert, 2014). Gilbert's model of CFT uses the Buddhist definition of compassion '*a sensitivity to suffering in self and others, with a commitment to try to alleviate and prevent it*' (Gilbert, 2014, p. 19). Compassion can be viewed as tri-directional, the compassion one has for oneself, the compassion one feels for others, and the compassion one receives from others (Gilbert et al., 2017).

CFT has its foundations in the functional analysis of social motivational and emotional systems that evolved to preserve life, such as to live within groups and exhibit behaviours supporting procreation, and to stimulate protective responses to

J. Beaumont (✉)
School of Psychology, Queen's University Belfast, Belfast, Northern Ireland
e-mail: jbeaumont01@qub.ac.uk

Y. Kotera et al. (eds.), *Compassion-Focused Therapy for Mental Health: International Perspectives*, Advances in Mental Health and Addiction,
https://doi.org/10.1007/978-3-032-12438-8_9

threat and to seek safety or resources (Gilbert, 2014). More recently developed cognitive competencies, including for reasoning and contextualising a sense of self, potentially create a conflict with these older systems leading to self-destructive behaviours and mental health challenges (Gilbert, 2014). These are sometimes referred to as the 'Old Brain' (social, emotional, and behavioural), and 'New Brain' (Reasoning, imagining, and sense of self), with the disrupted interaction between the two earning the title of the 'tricky brain' (see Fig. 9.1.)

Essentially, humans are equipped with threat (stimulating protectiveness), drive (motivating resource-seeking), and soothing (affiliate feelings and safeness) systems (Gilbert, 2009b). In circumstances that arouse high shame or self-criticism, the threat systems tend to dominate while the soothing system responds with less vigour and strength (Gilbert, 2005). CFT aims to train skills that help individuals self-regulate and re-balance with a focus on developing soothing, affiliation, and sense of safety (Gilbert, 2009a).

Gilbert and Procter (2006) explored group-based Compassionate Mind Training (CMT) which, over a period of 12 weekly session, integrated several steps including psychoeducation, exploration of self-criticism, and compassionate imagery exercises, addressing fears and integrating the activities into daily life; participants

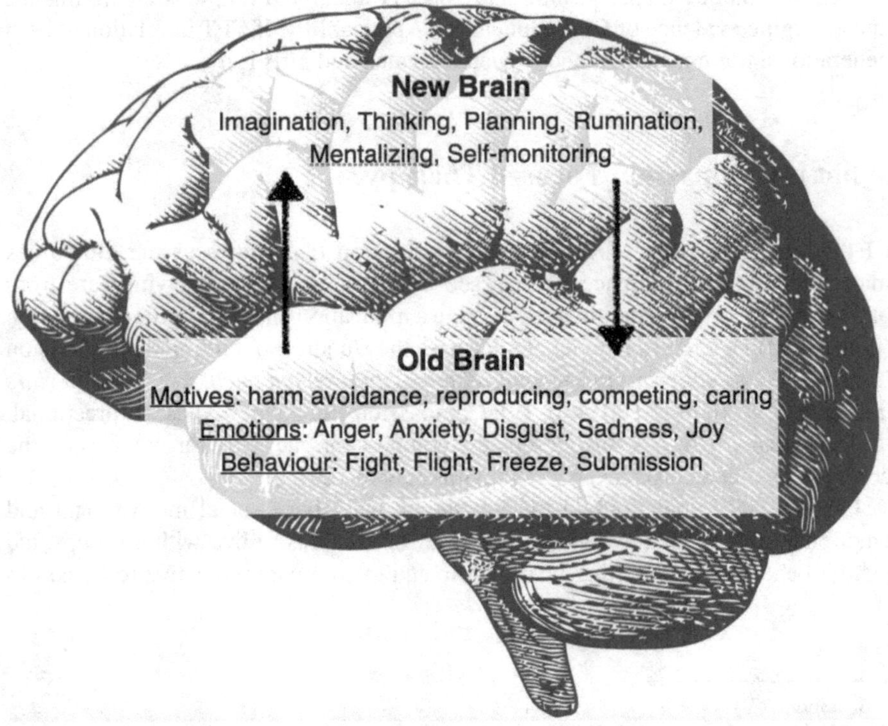

Fig. 9.1 Tricky brain (Balanced Minds, n.d.)

showed significant increases in self-soothing ability along with improvement in self-reassurance. Matos et al. (2021) found that individuals may experience fears, blocks, or resistance to offering compassion to others, accepting compassion from others or exercising compassion towards themselves. These fears were associated with higher self-criticism and shame, linked to insecure attachment styles, reduced psychological well-being and those who exhibited fear of self-compassion had more hostile inner dialogues (Matos et al., 2021). Importantly this highlights the need to address barriers to compassion in tandem with teaching skills in compassion to improve effectiveness of future CFT interventions (Matos et al., 2021).

Compassion is more than an emotion, it is a motivational orientation which requires input from specific skills and attributes (Gilbert, 2009a). These components include the ability to recognise distress in oneself and others, distress tolerance whereby the individual can remain present with suffering without becoming overwhelmed or avoidant, sympathy and empathy, remaining non-judgemental without harsh self-criticism or condemnation of others, and a motivation to alleviate the suffering through helpful action (Gilbert, 2009a). CFT techniques to foster these competencies may include mindfulness and attention exercises, psychoeducation, rhythmic breath work or possibly compassionate imagery or letter writing (Gilbert, 2009a). Improved regulation of the threat, drive, and soothing systems is the goal following these targeted intervention tools.

An important element in CFT is establishing how an individual frames a set of circumstances. The Compassionate Engagement and Action Scales (CEAS) were developed to not only measure strength in compassion but also to differentiate between engagement, empathy, distress tolerance and attention to suffering, and action, taking intentional steps to ameliorate distress (Gilbert et al., 2017). This provides the CFT clinician with insights into compassion competencies that may be underdeveloped or blocked, for example low scores in action may indicate a difficulty in the active translation of compassionate intent into behaviour, and the compassion from others scale may reveal blocks in receiving compassion often stemming from mistrust, fear, or negative experiences of care. This information is crucial for providing CFT intervention plans tailored to the individual and their needs (Gilbert et al., 2017).

It is important to emphasise that, in CFT, the therapeutic aim is not simply to think differently. Rather, the goal is to cultivate an affiliative motivational system, the social safeness-soothing system, that down-regulates threat and allows alternative, compassionate appraisals to feel credible at parasympathetically mediated, felt level as well as cognitively (Gilbert, 2014; Rockliff et al., 2008). In summary, CFT seeks an embodied shift from threat dominance to affiliative regulation, so that compassionate meanings are not only understood but felt (Gilbert, 2014).

Why is CFT Pertinent in Ireland (All island)?

An "all Island approach" is taken in the context of Northern Ireland (NI) and the Republic of Ireland (ROI) to account for the shared challenges and opportunities available due to cross-border collaboration and initiatives in both healthcare and research (Heenan, 2021; Lawler et al., 2023).

Current evidence shows a substantial level of psychological distress across the island of Ireland. In the ROI, the Healthy Ireland Survey (2023) reports that 12% of adults score ≤56 on the MHI-5 (indicative of a mental health problem), with the lowest mean MHI-5 among 15–24-year-olds. A surge in demand for mental health services in ROI has resulted in lengthy waiting lists, particularly for adolescent services (OECD, 2023). In NI, the Department of Health Survey (2023) indicates that 20% of respondents have a high GHQ-12 score suggestive of possible mental ill-health, with evidence of a higher burden in areas of deprivation.

In NI the legacy left by the troubles extends to several mental health concerns including higher rates of post-traumatic stress disorder (PTSD), depression, and suicide. Bunting et al. (2013), found that 39% of the population in NI had experienced conflict-related trauma, that PTSD lifetime prevalence was 8.8% one of the world's highest population figures; almost half of these PTSD cases were attributed to troubles related trauma. Over 60% of NI residents had experienced a conflict-related traumatic event with this exposure linked to higher rates of depression, anxiety, and substance misuse, indicating a higher mental health burden stemming from the troubles than in other regions (Ferry et al., 2014).

Suicide ideation and patterns in NI indicate an association with conflict trauma, where those directly exposed to troubles-related violence experienced significantly higher risks and intergenerational transmission with parental exposure increasing risk in their children's generation (O'Neill et al., 2014). The effects of the troubles permeate beyond the active period with post-peace suicide rates increasing sharply following the 1998 Good Friday Agreement with proposed explanations including unresolved conflict trauma, ongoing paramilitary and community pressures and enduring social and economic inequalities (Tomlinson, 2012). It would be reductive to cite the troubles for the entirety of the elevated suicide rates in NI, O'Neill and O'Connor (2020) emphasise that conflict legacy and intergenerational stress form part of the underlying problem with additional factors including socioeconomic deprivation, alcohol misuse, poor access to mental health support, and gender differences making contributions.

Cummings et al. (2011) longitudinal study found that a child's exposure to community-based violence, threat, had a detrimental impact on their emotional security and adjustment. Exposure to community conflict violence, at a young age, can intensify childhood adversity with parental adverse childhood event (ACE) exposure predicting higher prevalence of ACEs in their children (Walsh et al., 2025). ACEs negatively predict self-regulation by impacting its development and sustainability (Rollins & Crandall, 2021), underscoring an enduring threat context in which affiliative regulation may be constrained. CFT's goal of fostering self-regulation appears to be a good match for this population. Percolation of the effects of the troubles down through future generations presents a long-term problem that requires a mitigating solution potentially found in CFT.

In the ROI, state inquiries underscore how some religiously governed settings have shaped help-seeking and threat-shame dynamics relevant to CFT. The investigations into the Mother and Baby Homes (Department of Children, 2021) revealed institutional regimes marked by emotional degradation with minimal or no counselling prior to the 1970s. The Scoping Inquiry's survivor-engagement material records harrowing accounts with enduring impacts into adulthood, notes that many participants found it difficult to talk about what happened, and explicitly recommends trauma-informed, non-adversarial processes to avoid re-traumatisation (Department of Education, 2023); all of which signal persistent threat responses and barriers to disclosure that are directly relevant to CFT's focus on cultivating safeness and compassion.

Across the Island of Ireland, violence against women and girls (VAWG) represents a significant public health, mental health, and social justice concern, intersecting with many of the trauma and threat-based contexts already described. Recent evidence highlights the scale of the problem: In NI, Lagdon et al. (2023) report that 98% of women surveyed had experience at least one form of violence or abuse in their lifetime with 70% disclosing a recent experience of abuse within the previous year. In the ROI, the Garda Síochána recorded 46,765 disclosures of domestic abuse in 2024, an almost 38% increase in comparison to 2022 (Womens Aid, 2024). Cross-border initiatives are under way to aid prevention and collaboration between services with the British Psychological Society (BPS) welcoming NI Executive funding to tackle this area of public concern (BPS, 2025a). In their response, they highlight the need to work with perpetrators addressing trauma and attachment issues (BPS, 2025b), which could potentially respond to appropriate CFT interventions.

Priority is being given to this area in both NI, where Woman's Aid NI are campaigning for a Domestic Abuse Commissioner (O'Carroll, 2024), and Senator Fiona O'Loughlin pushes for a Domestic Abuse Register Bill to aid potential partners and employers (Fianna Fáil, 2024). The landscape is one that is currently open to active and effective change laying a foundation for both concerted research with CFT and potential intervention across the island of Ireland.

Taken together, an all-island picture of psychological distress (ROI 12% MHI-5; NI 20% GHQ-12), the Troubles' enduring and intergenerational mental health burden, developmental impacts of community violence and ACEs on self-regulation, institution-related harms that entrench shame and barriers to disclosure, alongside the scale of VAWG, defines a clear need for mechanism-based care. CFT, by reducing threat and shame whilst cultivating safeness, compassion, and self-regulation, offers a coherent, cross-border compatible approach for survivor support, and where appropriately safeguarded, exploratory work with perpetrators within cross-border North–South initiatives.

Mental Health Service Landscape and Delivery Channels

ROI

Ireland's national mental health policy "Sharing the Vision", sets out an ambitious collection of objectives to improve mental health in ROI through education, prevention and early intervention with delivery mechanisms focusing on a four-tier approach from social and peer support in tier one through to specialist residential care at tier four (Department of Health, 2020). Emphasis on scalable psychological interventions is apparent including access to digital-health interventions (Department of Health, 2020). The implementation plan sets out several recommendations including ensuring women's mental health is adequately addressed, enhancing service delivery via digital health solutions, and to learn from innovations that have brought about improvements for children and young people including cross-border initiatives (Department of Health, 2025b).

Current delivery modes in ROI include counselling in primary care, which is time limited for those with a health card (Ward et al., 2022), and for those who have experienced childhood abuse, or were previous residents of mother and baby homes there is a national counselling service that offers survivor-focused, trauma-informed work (Health Service Executive, 2025). Child and Adolescent Mental Health Service (CAHMS) provide multidisciplinary assessment and treatment for under-18 s however the demand outweighs current provisions resulting in lengthy waiting lists underscoring the need for evidence-based, group deliverable interventions (OECD, 2023).

NI

A decade-long pathway is outlined in the Mental Health Strategy 2021–2031 (Department of Health (NI), 2021), with an emphasis on prevention and early-intervention and a goal to expand psychological therapies. In practice, primary care talking therapies teams (NIdirect, 2025) and Trust-based psychological therapy services provide consultation, individual therapy and group-based workshops (Northern Health & Social Care Trust, 2025), while community and specialist pathways sit within the Health and Social Care system (NIdirect, 2025). Plans to implement a regional trauma network require structures that are compatible with brief, mechanism-targeted group programmes (Carville, 2023).

Cross-Border

The Co-operation and Working Together (CAWT) partnership established a cross-border Mental Health Recovery College Network, Innovation Recovery, to co-produce and deliver education for mental well-being across the island of Ireland (CAWT, 2022). This, and other associated projects may serve as an existing infrastructure that could support shared training and evaluation of approaches such as CFT.

From a scoping perspective CFT could provide solutions to several of the challenges faced within the health care systems spanning all of Ireland. Primary and community care mental health points of access could provide brief group CFT with standardised outcome measures within general mental health patients, trauma survivors, and within youth pathways such as CAMHS.

Empirical Evidence of CFT in the Island of Ireland

NI

Empirical work considering CFT is limited but is growing. O'driscoll & Mcaleese (2021) explored the feasibility of Compassionate Mind Training (CMT), a psychoeducational skills package within the CFT umbrella, within a cohort of sixth-form pupils n = 47 which resulted in a reduction in test anxiety and trait anxiety and increased self-compassion, in comparison to usual school support. Related research further identified self-compassion as a protective factor for test anxiety in adolescents studying beyond compulsory education (O'Driscoll & McAleese, 2023). Within the grey literature, feasibility of CFT and CMT delivery across populations is beginning to be explored (Gilsenan, 2023). At a system level, the Regional Trauma Network, was established to address Troubles-related mental health needs across HSC Trusts and community providers, underscoring a service context in which compassion-based approaches are pertinent (Department of Health, 2025a).

In research considering the application in alternative education settings, CFT for pupils, and it's the acceptability by teachers, found that group-based CFT for alternative education provision pupils appeared to foster relating compassionately to others and to themselves, with teachers finding CMT techniques acceptable within their teaching for this cohort (Sutton, 2022).

Within the healthcare setting, research indicated that intensive care nurses engaging in a four-week online CFT intervention showed improved compassion, indicating higher soothing and reduced threat, along with reductions in burnout (Corrigan et al., 2024). Whilst this evidence relies upon mainly grey literature, studies with small samples and without control groups, an active NI research pipeline in CFT indicates a growing attention to CFT as a feasible option within the NI cultural setting.

ROI

Routine outcomes from St Patricks Mental Health Services (SPMHS) indicate that group-based CFT is associated with clinically meaningful change across several programmes. In the core CFT Programme, pre-post analyses in 2024 showed medium-large effect on depression, anxiety and stress and reliable gains in compassion, measured with the Compassionate Engagement and Action Scales (CEAS), with accompanying reductions in fears of compassion and self-criticism (SPMHS, 2024).

Specialist adaptions of CFT for older adults, individuals with eating disorders, and psychosis also showed promise in improvements in depression anxiety stress scales, improvements in well-being, and self-compassion respectively (SPMHS, 2024).

Peer-reviewed data from ROI exploring CFT is limited, however, Mernagh et al. (2020) found that CFT may benefit individuals experiencing psychological distress through improvement in disrupted mind–body attunement, by fostering a more self-compassionate mindset through reflective practice and meditation centred on compassion. It is prudent to note that the sample sizes within these clinical pre-post reports were small and lacked a control group.

Cultural Adaptations for Delivering CFT Across the Island of Ireland

The all-island context includes a high burden of conflict and community-related adversity in NI, with intergenerational pathways from sectarian violence to children's emotional insecurity, and state-acknowledged harms in religiously governed settings in ROI with documented shame, silence, and barriers to disclosure. These contextual considerations sit alongside elevated exposure to domestic and sexual violence on both sides of the border. CFT implementation should therefore be explicitly trauma-informed, shame sensitive, and culturally and faith-aware. Empirically, NI population studies link conflict exposure to poorer mental health and child adjustment, emphasising the need to stabilise threat and build affiliative regulation at individual and community levels (Bunting et al., 2013; Cummings et al., 2011). In ROI, Government inquiries highlight enduring threat-shame dynamics and recommend non-adversarial, trauma-informed responses, consistent with CFT's emphasis on cultivating safeness (Department of Children, 2021; Department of Education, 2023). As both NI and ROI become increasingly multicultural sensitivity towards language use and understanding should extend to additional cultural needs (HSE, 2009).

Language, Framing, and Faith-Sensitivity

Given the legacies outlined above, initial CFT psychoeducation should aim to normalise threat responses and carefully differentiate compassion from self-indulgence or self-pity using Gilbert's (2014) evolutionary model to explain why affiliative systems regulate threat physiology, e.g., vagal pathways, while avoiding moralising language that could activate a shame response. Delivery should also adhere to health guidelines on culturally responsive practice, including sensitivity to religious beliefs and to those harmed in religious contexts. In practice this would support offering secular, value-based framings and choice of imagery or practice that reference religious symbolism (HSE, 2009).

Working with Fears, Blocks, and Resistance to Compassion

Fear of compassion is associated with shame, self-criticism, and poorer mental health, so Irish implementations should routinely assess and adjust interventions to both measure and adjust accordingly (Kirby et al., 2019). Recommendations for therapists to persist with CFT, through an initial resistance from the service user, were made following a qualitative study where trauma survivors disclosed initial fears of compassion early in the CFT therapeutic process (Lawrence & Lee, 2014). Participants subsequently experienced positive outcomes to self-compassion highlighting the therapeutic relationship as a key component of this progress (Lawrence & Lee, 2014). Within the all-island context, where the shame-threat systems may be typically activated, this is an important consideration in CFT implementation.

Trauma-Informed Approach for Conflict Affected and High-ACE Contexts

The first all-age NI ACEs study indicates high prevalence of childhood adversity, with a distinctive layer of conflict-specific adversities; intergenerational patterns reinforce the need to prioritise stabilisation, emotional regulation and social safeness before deep work can be attempted (Walsh et al., 2025). Longitudinal NI data suggest sectarian community violence predicts poorer child emotional security, supporting CFT's focus on cultivating inner and interpersonal safeness as a buffer (Cummings et al., 2011). These considerations, along with post-traumatic stress disorder intervention protocols (Darby et al., 2023), justify a phased CFT including skill development through breath work, compassionate imagery, and safe-other practices, prior to trauma processing (Gilbert, 2014).

For Survivors of Violence Against Women and Girls

Figures for both ROI and NI indicate a high prevalence of VAWG across the island of Ireland. CFT with this cohort should integrate appropriate safeguarding, choice and multi-agency links. Internationally, randomised trials with women who have PTSD following intimate partner violence (IPV) show that group CFT reduces experiential avoidance, improves meaning in life, and reduced suicide ideation, all of which are steps towards risk reduction and recovery (Daneshvar et al., 2022). Learnings from studies such as this could support cautious, survivor-led adaptation across the island of Ireland.

Delivery Mechanisms and Dosage

Given the resource constraints across both health care systems on the island of Ireland, cost-efficient approaches are essential. Group-based compassion-focused interventions offer such an option (D'amico et al., 2020). Evidence from Irish cohorts shows that group CFT significantly decreases fear of receiving compassion and increases perceived compassion from others (SPMHS, 2024). Annual service reviews further support its feasibility, providing practice-based evidence through standardised pre-post measures and qualitative feedback within the existing ROI infrastructure (SPMHS, 2024).

Building on this, Innovation Recovery (CAWT, 2022) demonstrates the potential to expand digital compassion interventions delivered through local trust recovery college networks in both NI and ROI. Tailoring these interventions to the specific needs and capacities of identified cohorts could strengthen both reach and relevance. These existing delivery and evaluation platforms provide a strong foundation for a broader understanding and refinement of current and future CFT programmes.

Meta-analytical findings indicate that CFT reliably reduces self-criticism and increases soothing activation, supporting these as primary outcomes. However, further randomised controlled trials are required, and services should continue to monitor acceptability, particularly in populations with high levels of shame or religious trauma exposure (Kirby et al., 2019; Vidal & Soldevilla, 2023).

To ensure trauma-informed, non-adversarial delivery, CFT programmes should prioritise informed consent, careful pacing, attention to power dynamics, and collaborative formulation. These steps help reduce shame and mitigate threat reactivation among survivors engaging with care providers (Department of Children, 2021; Department of Education, 2023).

All-island health service guidance recommends cultural competence training, access to interpreters, and sensitivity to diverse religious and identity contexts (HSE, 2009; Singh et al., 2018). CFT teams should integrate these recommendations—for example, providing language-appropriate materials and screening for minority stress or migration-related threats to ensure compassion practices remain inclusive and do not inadvertently reinforce shame.

Overall, the all-island context demonstrates a clear population need, supportive policy environment, and expanding delivery infrastructure. Together, these factors position CFT as a timely, mechanism-based intervention for careful, evaluation-led implementation across services in both Northern Ireland and the Republic of Ireland.

Challenges and Enablement of Implementation

There are a few key challenges to CFT across the island of Ireland. Lengthy waiting lists present a supply and demand issue which supports group and online solutions, however, these may not be suitable for all cohorts. Consideration should be given to the environment around those accessing digital interventions, e.g. those experiencing domestic violence (Lattie et al., 2022), for the appropriateness of the group setting for acute risk or in crisis (Ezhumalai et al., 2018).

CFT research within both NI and ROI populations is at an embryonic stage; current evidence stemming from uncontrolled practice-based evaluation (SPMHS, 2024) and early-stage academic research (Sutton, 2022). This calls for embedded evaluation throughout any scale up of current provision and future interventions.

The contextual sensitivities presented from the Troubles legacy, intergenerational trauma, ACEs, and religious institution abuse indicate a clear need for shame and threat aware delivery through clear consent, pacing and opt-out options to be offered. These circumstances require a healthcare workforce that are appropriately trained in both CFT and trauma which will require funding and time.

Promisingly, policy supports brief stepped-care psychological interventions such as CFT (Department of Health, 2020; Department of Health (NI), 2021) and VAWG frameworks in both jurisdictions call for survivor-focused psychosocial support (Womens Aid, 2024).

Networks within which CFT and compassion-based approaches currently exist, e.g. Innovation Recovery (CAWT, 2022) providing an established starting point to expand CFT services from. The measurement culture within these services provides a template for future evaluation both for intervention efficacy and efficiency along with identifying any required adjustments.

Conclusions

On an all-island basis, current policy frameworks, ROI's Sharing the Vision and NI's Mental Health Strategy, along with the existing delivery infrastructure for both jurisdictions provide immediate channels to trial group and digital delivery of CFT and CMT pilots. Existing Irish practice data already provide feasible group implementation with pre-post improvements in distress, self-criticism, fears of compassion and compassion skills; NI education data show short-term CMT benefits in adolescents. Stepping forward with evaluation-led implementation within additional cohorts such as survivors of domestic violence or religious institutional abuse may provide a more robust evidence base for CFT within the all-island population.

Author Contributions Conceptualisation: JB; Investigation: JB; Resources: JB; Writing—original draft: JB; Writing—review & editing: JB; Project administration: JB.

References

Balanced Minds. (n.d.). *Old brain new brain model - CFT - balanced minds #1*. https://Balancedminds.Com/Old-Brain-New-Brain-4/#:~:Text=Compassion%20Focused%20Therapy%20(CFT)%2C,Sometimes%20get%20in%20a%20tussle. Retrieved August 13, 2025, from https://balancedminds.com/old-brain-new-brain-4/

BPS. (2025a). *BPS responds to launch of northern Ireland fund to help tackle violence against women and girls | BPS*. https://www.bps.org.uk/news/bps-responds-launch-northern-ireland-fund-help-tackle-violence-against-women-and-girls?utm_source

BPS. (2025b). *BPS response to consultation on a strategic framework to end violence against women and girls & foundational action plan*. https://doi.org/10.1177/15248380221147558

Bunting, B. P., Ferry, F. R., Murphy, S. D., O'Neill, S. M., & Bolton, D. (2013). Trauma associated with civil conflict and posttraumatic stress disorder: Evidence from the northern Ireland study of health and stress. *Journal of Traumatic Stress, 26*(1), 134–141. https://doi.org/10.1002/jts.21766

Carville, D. (2023). *Report by the comptroller and auditor general mental health services in Northern Ireland*. www.niauditoffice.gov.uk

CAWT. (2022). *Mental health innovation recovery 'i-Recovery.'* https://cawt.hscni.net/projects/eu-interreg-va-programme-2014-2020/mental-health-innovation-recovery-i-recover/?utm

Corrigan, J. P., Browne, D., Gilsenan, J., & Irons, C. (2024). Evaluating a brief online compassion-focused intervention for intensive care nurses. *Nursing in Critical Care, 29*(2), 303–306. https://doi.org/10.1111/NICC.12860

Cummings, E. M., Merrilees, C. E., Schermerhorn, A. C., Goeke-Morey, M. C., Shirlow, P., & Cairns, E. (2011). Longitudinal pathways between political violence and child adjustment: The role of emotional security about the community in Northern Ireland. *Journal of Abnormal Child Psychology, 39*(2), 213–224. https://doi.org/10.1007/s10802-010-9457-3

D'amico, F., Feliu-Soler, A., Montero-Marín, J., Peñarrubía-María, M. T., Navarro-Gil, M., Van Gordon, W., García-Campayo, J., & Luciano, J. V. (2020). Cost-utility of attachment-based compassion therapy (ABCT) for fibromyalgia compared to relaxation: A pilot randomized controlled trial. *Journal of Clinical Medicine, 9*(3). https://doi.org/10.3390/JCM9030726

Daneshvar, S., Shafiei, M., & Basharpoor, S. (2022). Group-based compassion-focused therapy on experiential avoidance, meaning-in-life, and sense of coherence in female survivors of intimate partner violence with PTSD: A randomized controlled trial. *Journal of Interpersonal Violence, 37*(7–8), NP4187–NP4211. https://doi.org/10.1177/0886260520958660

Darby, R. J., Taylor, E. P., & Cadavid, M. S. (2023). Phase-based psychological interventions for complex post-traumatic stress disorder: A systematic review. *Journal of Affective Disorders Reports, 14*, Article 100628. https://doi.org/10.1016/J.JADR.2023.100628

Department of Children, D. and E. (2021). *Final report of the commission of investigation into mother and baby homes*. https://www.gov.ie/en/department-of-children-disability-and-equality/publications/final-report-of-the-commission-of-investigation-into-mother-and-baby-homes/

Department of Education. (2023). *Scoping inquiry into historical sexual abuse in schools run by religious orders.* https://www.gov.ie/en/education-scoping-inquiry/publications/scoping-inquiry-into-historical-sexual-abuse-in-schools-run-by-religious-orders/

Department of Health. (2020). *Sharing the vision: A mental health policy for everyone.* https://www.gov.ie/en/department-of-health/publications/sharing-the-vision-a-mental-health-policy-for-everyone/?utm_source

Department of Health. (2025a). *Regional trauma network - DOH/HSCNI strategic planning and performance group (SPPG).* https://online.hscni.net/partnerships/regionaltraumanetwork/

Department of Health. (2025b). *Sharing the vision a mental health policy for everyone implementation plan a mental health policy for everyone.*

Department of Health (NI). (2021). *Mental health strategy 2021–2031.* https://www.health-ni.gov.uk/sites/default/files/publications/health/doh-mhs-strategy-2021-2031.pdf

Department of Health (NI). (2023, November 29). *Health survey (NI).* https://www.health-ni.gov.uk/news/health-survey-ni-first-results-202223?utm_source

Ezhumalai, S., Muralidhar, D., Dhanasekarapandian, R., & Nikketha, B. S. (2018). Group interventions. *Indian Journal of Psychiatry, 60*(Suppl 4), S514–S521. https://doi.org/10.4103/PSYCHIATRY.INDIANJPSYCHIATRY_42_18

Ferry, F., Bunting, B., Murphy, S., O'Neill, S., Stein, D., & Koenen, K. (2014). Traumatic events and their relative PTSD burden in Northern Ireland: A consideration of the impact of the 'Troubles.' *Social Psychiatry and Psychiatric Epidemiology, 49*(3), 435–446. https://doi.org/10.1007/s00127-013-0757-0

Fianna Fáil. (2024, July 4). *"Vital"that bill to establish a domestic violence register proceeds as quickly as possible - O'Loughlin.* https://www.fiannafail.ie/news/vital-that-bill-to-establish-a-domestic-violence-register-proceeds-as-quickly-as-possible-oloughlin

Gilbert, P. (2005). Compassion: Conceptualisations, research and use in psychotherapy. In P. Gilbert (Ed.), *Compassion: Conceptualisations, research and use in psychotherapy* (First). Taylor and Francis. https://doi.org/10.4324/9780203003459

Gilbert, P. (2009a). Introducing compassion-focussed therapy. *Advances in Psychiatric Treatment, 15,* 199–208. https://doi.org/10.1192/apt.bp.107.005264

Gilbert, P. (2009b). *The compassionate mind : A new approach to life's challenges.* Constable. https://books.google.com/books/about/The_Compassionate_Mind.html?id=krNPL6xCVL0C

Gilbert, P. (2014). The origins and nature of compassion focused therapy. *British Journal of Clinical Psychology, 53,* 6–41. https://doi.org/10.1111/bjc.12043

Gilbert, P., Catarino, F., Duarte, C., Matos, M., Kolts, R., Stubbs, J., Ceresatto, L., Duarte, J., Pinto-Gouveia, J., & Basran, J. (2017). The development of compassionate engagement and action scales for self and others. *Journal of Compassionate Health Care 2017 4:1, 4*(1), 1–24. https://doi.org/10.1186/S40639-017-0033-3

Gilbert, P., & Procter, S. (2006). Compassionate mind training for people with high shame and self-criticism: Overview and pilot study of a group therapy approach. *Clinical Psychology and Psychotherapy, 13,* 353–379.https://doi.org/10.1002/cpp.507

Gilsenan, J. (2023). *Developing an evidence base for compassion focused therapy and compassionate mind training - Queen's University Belfast* [Thesis - Doctorate in Clinical Psychology, Queen's University Belfast]. https://pure.qub.ac.uk/en/studentTheses/developing-an-evidence-base-for-compassion-focused-therapy-and-co

Health Service Executive. (2025). *About the national counselling service.* https://www2.hse.ie/mental-health/services-support/ncs/about/

Healthy Ireland. (2023, November 22). *Healthy Ireland survey 2023.* https://www.gov.ie/en/healthy-ireland/publications/healthy-ireland-survey-2023/?utm_source

Heenan. (2021). Collaborating on healthcare on an all-island basis: A scoping study. *Irish Studies in International Affairs, 32*(2), 413. https://doi.org/10.3318/isia.2021.32b.43

HSE. (2009). *Health services intercultural guide : responding to the needs of diverse religious communities and cultures in healthcare settings.* Health Service Executive.

Kirby, J. N., Day, J., & Sagar, V. (2019). The 'Flow' of compassion: A meta-analysis of the fears of compassion scales and psychological functioning. *Clinical Psychology Review, 70*, 26–39. https://doi.org/10.1016/j.cpr.2019.03.001

Lagdon, S., Owczarek, M., Mccartan, C., Anyadike-Danes, N., Shevlin, M., & Jordan, J. -A. (2023). *Every voice matters! Violence against women in Northern Ireland.*

Lattie, E. G., Stiles-Shields, C., & Graham, A. K. (2022). An overview of and recommendations for more accessible digital mental health services. *Nature Reviews Psychology 2022 1:2, 1*(2), 87–100. https://doi.org/10.1038/s44159-021-00003-1

Lawler, M., Sullivan, R., Abou-Alfa, G. K., McCloskey, K., Keatley, D., Feighan, J., Dahut, W., Mulroe, E., Ladner, R., Genead, M., Lowery, M., Gulley, J. L., Scott, C. J., Longley, D. B., Culhane, A., Gallagher, W. M., Orr, N., Chanock, S. J., & Gopal, S. (2023). Health diplomacy in action: The cancer legacy of the good Friday agreement. *Journal of Cancer Policy, 38*, Article 100448. https://doi.org/10.1016/j.jcpo.2023.100448

Lawrence, V. A., & Lee, D. (2014). An exploration of people's experiences of compassion-focused therapy for trauma, using interpretative phenomenological analysis. *Clinical Psychology & Psychotherapy, 21*(6), 495–507. https://doi.org/10.1002/cpp.1854

Matos, M., McEwan, K., Basran, J., & Gilbert, P. (2021). *Fears of compassion magnify the harmful effects of threat of COVID-19 on mental health and social safeness across 21 countries.*

Mernagh, M., Baird, K., & Guerin, S. (2020). Subjective changes in mind-body attunement associated with transdiagnostic group–based compassion-focused therapy. *Mindfulness, 11*(8), 2016–2026. https://doi.org/10.1007/S12671-020-01417-3/METRICS

NIdirect. (2025). *Mental health services.* https://www.nidirect.gov.uk/articles/mental-health-services?utm_source

Northern Health and Social Care Trust. (2025). *Psychological therapies service (PTS) - Northern health and social care trust.* https://www.northerntrust.hscni.net/services/psychological-therapies-service-pts/?utm_source

O'Carroll, L. (2024, November 10). Domestic abuse commissioner needed to tackle femicide in Northern Ireland, charity says. *The Guardian.* https://www.theguardian.com/society/2024/nov/10/domestic-abuse-commissioner-needed-to-tackle-femicide-in-northern-ireland-charity-says?utm_source

O'driscoll, D., & Mcaleese, M. (2021). *Counselling and psychotherapy research the feasibility and effectiveness of compassionate mind training as a test anxiety intervention for adolescents: A preliminary investigation.* https://doi.org/10.1002/capr.12447

O'Driscoll, D., & McAleese, M. (2023). The protective role of self-compassion on test anxiety among adolescents. *Pastoral Care in Education, 41*(2), 211–224. https://doi.org/10.1080/02643944.2022.2054021

OECD. (2023). *Ireland: Country health profile 2023, State of health in the EU.* https://eurohealthobservatory.who.int/publications/m/ireland-country-health-profile-2023?utm_source

O'Neill, S., Ferry, F., Murphy, S., Corry, C., Bolton, D., Devine, B., Ennis, E., & Bunting, B. (2014). Patterns of suicidal ideation and behavior in Northern Ireland and associations with conflict related trauma. *PLoS ONE, 9*(3), Article e91532. https://doi.org/10.1371/journal.pone.0091532

O'Neill, S., & O'Connor, R. C. (2020). Suicide in Northern Ireland: Epidemiology, risk factors, and prevention. *The Lancet Psychiatry, 7*(6), 538–546. https://doi.org/10.1016/S2215-0366(19)30525-5

Rockliff, H., Gilbert, P., McEwan, K., Lightman, S., Glover, D., Stafford Lightman, P., Royal Infirmary, M., & Corresponding Author Professor Paul Gilbert, U. (2008). A pilot exploration of heart rate variability and salivary cortisol responses to compassion-focused imagery. *Clinical Neuropsychiatry, 5.*

Rollins, E. M., & Crandall, A. (2021). Self-regulation and shame as mediators between childhood experiences and young adult health. *Frontiers in Psychiatry, 12.* https://doi.org/10.3389/fpsyt.2021.649911

Singh, P., King-Shier, K., & Sinclair, S. (2018). The colours and contours of compassion: A systematic review of the perspectives of compassion among ethnically diverse patients and healthcare providers. *PLoS ONE, 13*(5), Article e0197261. https://doi.org/10.1371/journal.pone.0197261

SPMHS. (2024). *Outcomes report 2024 annual review of St Patrick's mental health services' outcomes.*

Sutton, A. (2022). An exploration of staff and student perspectives on the use of compassion focused therapy within an alternative education provision in Northern Ireland - Queen's University Belfast [Doctorate in Educational, Child and Adolescent Psychology, Queen's University Belfast]. In *Queen's University.* https://pure.qub.ac.uk/en/studentTheses/an-exploration-of-staff-and-student-perspectives-on-the-use-of-co

Tomlinson, M. W. (2012). War, peace and suicide: The case of Northern Ireland. *International Sociology, 27*(4), 464–482. https://doi.org/10.1177/0268580912443579

Vidal, J., & Soldevilla, J. M. (2023). Effect of compassion-focused therapy on self-criticism and self-soothing: A meta-analysis. *British Journal of Clinical Psychology, 62*(1), 70–81. https://doi.org/10.1111/bjc.12394

Walsh, L., Bunting, G., Davidson, N., Doherty, C., McCartan, C., Mulholland, M., & Shevlin, C. (2025). The prevalence and impact of adverse childhood experiences in Northern Ireland. In *The executive programme on paramilitarism and organised crime.* https://pureadmin.qub.ac.uk/ws/portalfiles/portal/631630700/Impact_of_Adverse_Childhood_Experiences_-_Tagged.pdf

Ward, F., Brand, D. C., Cunningham, S., & MacDonagh, N. (2022). *Changing lives for the better: A national evaluation of the counselling in primary care (CIPC) service.*

Womens Aid. (2024). *Annual s.* https://www.womensaid.ie/app/uploads/2025/06/Womens-Aid-Annual-Impact-Report-2024.pdf?utm_source

Chapter 10
Future Directions and Recommendations

Yasuhiro Kotera, Julie Beaumont, Rory Colman, Annabel Rushforth, and Kenichi Asano

Emerging Landscape of CFT

Compassion Focused Therapy (CFT), developed by Paul Gilbert (2009), has become an influential therapeutic approach aimed at addressing shame, self-criticism, and difficulties in emotional regulation. It draws from evolutionary psychology, attachment theory, affective neuroscience, and cognitive behavioural therapy, offering a distinctive framework that focuses on the cultivation of compassion for self and others. Over the past decade, research on CFT has grown rapidly, providing a strong evidence base for its use across a wide range of mental health conditions including depression, anxiety, trauma, and personality disorders (Gilbert, 2014; Kolts et al., 2016; Leaviss & Uttley, 2015).

The expansion of CFT has been marked by its successful implementation in various contexts, including clinical settings, education, workplaces, and communities. Researchers such as Chris Irons, Deborah Lee, Russell Kolts, and James Kirby

Y. Kotera (✉)
Faculty of Medicine and Health Sciences, University of Nottingham, Nottingham, UK
e-mail: yasuhiro.kotera@nottingham.ac.uk

Center for Infectious Disease Education and Research, University of Osaka, Suita, Japan

Department of Social Sciences, Azerbaijan University, Baku, Azerbaijan

J. Beaumont
School of Psychology, Queen's University Belfast, Belfast, UK

R. Colman
College of Health, Psychology and Social Care, University of Derby, Derby, UK

A. Rushforth
Clinical and Applied Psychology Department, University of Sheffield, Sheffield, UK

K. Asano
Institute of Human Sciences, University of Tsukuba, Tsukuba, Japan

Y. Kotera et al. (eds.), *Compassion-Focused Therapy for Mental Health: International Perspectives*, Advances in Mental Health and Addiction,
https://doi.org/10.1007/978-3-032-12438-8_10

have advanced the theoretical and empirical understanding of CFT's processes and outcomes. Their work has contributed to refining interventions, exploring compassion's neurobiological mechanisms, and adapting CFT for specific populations such as individuals with PTSD, eating disorders, or high levels of self-criticism (Kirby et al., 2017; Kolts et al., 2016).

Alongside these CFT movements, research targeting self-criticism and shame has also advanced as they are the primary outcomes of CFT (Gilbert, 2010). For example, The Forms of Self-Criticising/Attacking & Self-Reassuring Scale (FSCRS) was developed to measure self-criticism (Gilbert et al., 2016; Sommers-Spijkerman et al., 2018). Using FSCRS, the relationships among the two constructs of self-criticism—self-hated and self-inadequacy—and self-reassurance have been evaluated in various populations (Kotera et al., 2018, 2021b; Petrocchi et al., 2019; Stevenson & Akram, 2022). To apply to different contexts, different versions of FSCRS including the shorter version were developed and validated (Cunha et al., 2024; Kishimoto et al., 2024; Kotera & Sheffield, 2020). Likewise, a measure to assess shame associated with mental health problems—The Attitudes Towards Mental Health Problems Scale (ATMHPS)—was developed (Gilbert et al., 2007). ATMHPS categorises mental health shame into seven subscales, enabling multi-dimensional assessment of mental health shame: Community attitudes, family attitudes, internal shame, external community shame, external family shame, family-reflected shame and self-reflected shame. The applications of ATMHPS varied, and different versions have been developed and validated (Kotera et al., 2022f, 2023a). These tools and findings fostered wider research about self-criticism and shame, highly relevant outcomes of CFT.

As the field moves forward, future developments in CFT will benefit from both foundational work and contemporary contributions. Priorities include conducting rigorous trials, refining theoretical frameworks, expanding digital and blended delivery models, and deepening cultural adaptations. The landscape of compassion-based therapy is increasingly shaped by collaborative, interdisciplinary efforts that integrate clinical insight, cultural sensitivity, and empirical research to promote mental wellbeing in diverse populations.

Digital Futures: Online and Remote Delivery of CFT

The COVID-19 pandemic dramatically accelerated the transition of mental health services to online and digital platforms, prompting clinicians and researchers alike to explore the efficacy and accessibility of remote psychological interventions. In this evolving digital mental health landscape, CFT has also begun to be delivered through various online modalities, including self-guided programmes, video conferencing sessions, and mobile applications (de Krijger et al., 2023; Marques et al., 2024). The future of CFT increasingly depends on our ability to harness digital technologies to reach underserved populations, reduce stigma, and expand the accessibility of compassion-based care.

In addition to therapeutic applications, CFT has found fertile ground in digital education and training. Online courses have been developed for both mental health professionals and broader populations, enabling learners to engage with compassion-based practices in flexible and accessible ways. For instance, the Compassionate Mind Training programme has been adapted for online formats, offering modules that include guided practices, reflective exercises, and peer support features (https://www.compassionatemind.co.uk/training). Teaching about compassion was helpful for university lecturers and students participating in online learning from around the world (Kotera et al., 2021e). While these interventions show clear benefits, challenges persist—particularly regarding engagement, digital fatigue, and the absence of real-time therapist support in self-guided programmes. Research, practice and education of CFT still have further potential for improvement.

Cultural Adaptation and Global Relevance

As CFT expands beyond its Western origins, cultural adaptation has emerged as an essential consideration in ensuring its relevance and efficacy across global contexts. While the foundational principles of CFT—such as cultivating compassion, reducing shame, and regulating emotion (Gilbert, 2009)—are broadly applicable, their expression and acceptance vary significantly depending on cultural norms, values, and social expectations (Kotera et al., 2024b). In particular, societies that emphasise collectivism, modesty, or emotional restraint may interpret self-compassion differently from those that value individual autonomy and emotional expressiveness (Uneno et al., 2024).

A growing body of cross-cultural research demonstrates that psychological interventions developed in individualistic societies may not fully align with the worldviews of clients from collectivist or traditional cultures unless modifications are made (Kotera et al, 2023c). For example, self-compassion may be misunderstood as self-indulgent or self-centred in cultures that prioritise self-sacrifice and group harmony (Kotera et al., 2025; Neff, 2022). To address this, CFT practitioners are encouraged to reframe compassion not only as an individual healing process but also as a socially constructive and relational strength. In such contexts, compassion practices may be more readily accepted when linked to concepts such as duty, responsibility to others, or spiritual wellbeing.

Effective cultural adaptation of CFT requires more than surface-level adjustments (Morales & Burnett-Zeigler, 2024). It involves integrating culturally resonant language, metaphors, and modes of practice—such as storytelling, proverbs, or community-based rituals—into the therapeutic process. These modifications allow clients to connect more deeply with the therapy's core messages and reduce resistance arising from cultural dissonance. Importantly, this process does not dilute the essence of CFT, but rather enriches it by ensuring the delivery remains meaningful and accessible to diverse populations.

Equipping practitioners with cultural competence is equally critical. Training should incorporate cultural humility, awareness of cultural narratives around suffering and help-seeking, and familiarity with diverse emotional expression styles (Kotera et al., 2022c). This includes adapting assessments, therapeutic goals, and outcome measures to reflect culturally relevant markers of progress and wellbeing. As CFT continues to be implemented internationally, its global relevance will depend on the extent to which it can honour cultural differences while maintaining its core commitment to compassion and human flourishing.

CFT Across the Lifespan and Populations

CFT demonstrates a versatile applicability across a wide range of populations and age groups, from children and adolescents to older adults and individuals with neurodiverse conditions or chronic health issues (Craig et al., 2020). While traditionally employed in clinical mental health settings, recent developments suggest that CFT's core strategies—cultivating emotional regulation, building resilience, and reducing self-criticism—can support wellbeing across the entire lifespan.

Notably, CFT has shown strong potential in occupational settings, especially among adults in high-stress professions such as healthcare, education, and social care (Beaumont et al., 2021). Research indicates that compassion training in these fields can mitigate symptoms of burnout and secondary trauma, while also enhancing work engagement and job satisfaction (Kotera & Van Gordon, 2021). These benefits are particularly pertinent in the aftermath of the COVID-19 pandemic, which intensified emotional demands on essential workers (Kotera et al., 2023b). Such findings support the integration of CFT into workplace wellbeing programmes, offering a proactive approach to sustaining mental health in demanding environments.

In educational contexts, studies on university students have highlighted the role of self-compassion in buffering against academic stress and depression, while fostering psychological flexibility and motivation (Kotera et al., 2022b, 2022d). These insights reinforce the value of compassion-based interventions during transitional life stages where emotional regulation is still forming.

For older adults and individuals with disabilities, CFT provides tools for self-acceptance and managing emotional responses linked to ageing, loss, or social isolation (Clapton et al., 2018). Though research in this area remains limited, emerging work suggests promising applications for promoting healthy ageing through emotional resilience and self-kindness.

To maximise its reach and effectiveness, expanding CFT across diverse populations will require flexible, inclusive, and culturally sensitive delivery models, ensuring that interventions meet the unique developmental and situational needs of each group.

Mechanisms of Change and Neurobiological Underpinnings

Understanding the mechanisms underlying CFT is essential for enhancing its theoretical foundation and clinical application. CFT aims to regulate affect by stimulating the parasympathetic nervous system, and insights into its neurobiological and psychological processes can help clinicians tailor interventions more precisely.

Research has highlighted the importance of integrating physiological and psychological data in compassion research (Gilbert, 2020). An interdisciplinary approach that combines subjective wellbeing metrics with biological indicators, such as heart rate variability (HRV), has been employed to explore how self-compassion training influences stress reactivity, emotion regulation, and resilience (Di Bello et al., 2020). HRV, a marker of vagal tone and parasympathetic activation, has been associated with the efficacy of compassion training. For instance, a study comparing Forest Bathing and Compassionate Mind Training found that both interventions led to improvements in self-reported wellbeing and HRV (Clarke et al., 2021), suggesting that compassion-based interventions can positively impact physiological markers of health.

Furthermore, compassion is considered a motivational system rooted in evolutionary and attachment-based frameworks. Activating the "soothing system" not only counters threat-focused responses associated with anxiety and depression but also fosters neuroplastic changes in brain regions responsible for emotion regulation and social affiliation (Calderone et al., 2024). This aligns with broader neuroscience literature indicating that compassion training increases activity in the medial prefrontal cortex, anterior cingulate cortex, and ventral striatum—areas linked to empathy, reward, and emotional control.

Advocates have emphasised the necessity of conducting randomised controlled trials (RCTs) with longitudinal follow-ups and biological assessments to demonstrate the sustained impact of CFT and establish causal relationships between compassion practices and health outcomes. Integrating biological evidence with psychological models strengthens the empirical base of CFT, facilitating its acceptance among stakeholders in clinical, academic, and policy domains.

Advancing research into these mechanisms lays the foundation for a more scientifically robust and integrative model of CFT—one that validates both the experiential aspects of compassion and its physiological correlates.

Addressing Resistance and Fear of Compassion

Despite its numerous benefits, CFT is not always easily accepted by clients. One of the most significant barriers is the fear of compassion—either receiving compassion from others, offering it to others, or being self-compassionate (Gilbert et al., 2011). These fears are often rooted in early attachment wounds, cultural beliefs, or negative experiences with vulnerability. Understanding and addressing these fears is crucial for CFT practitioners to foster a therapeutic environment that is safe, non-judgemental, and effective.

Empirical research has shown that fear of compassion is strongly linked to psychological distress. For instance, individuals with high levels of fear of self-compassion tend to report increased symptoms of depression, anxiety, and stress (Melsom et al., 2023; Merritt & Purdon, 2020). This suggests that when people struggle to treat themselves with kindness, they may become more susceptible to emotional dysregulation and maladaptive coping strategies (Asano et al., 2017). In such cases, psychoeducation becomes a foundational step in CFT, helping clients understand the evolutionary and social basis of compassion and normalising the discomfort that may arise when they begin engaging with self-compassion practices (Goldin & Jazaieri, 2020; Varley et al., 2024).

Cultural influences also play a pivotal role in shaping attitudes towards compassion. In some collectivist societies, values such as humility, self-sacrifice, and endurance are emphasised, which may lead to misconceptions about self-compassion being selfish or indulgent (Kotera et al., 2022e). Research has shown that when compassion is reframed as a pathway to resilience, social harmony, or collective wellbeing, clients in these contexts are more likely to accept and benefit from the therapy (Kotera et al., 2021a; Seppala et al., 2013). This underscores the importance of culturally sensitive adaptations that respect the client's value systems while gently challenging internalised resistance.

In clinical practice, a gradual and respectful introduction of compassion-based techniques is recommended. Starting with external compassion (e.g., towards others) and moving slowly towards internal self-kindness can reduce defensiveness and build trust. Structured interventions—such as compassionate imagery, reflective writing, and values-based discussion—have been shown to reduce fears of compassion and facilitate emotional healing. Importantly, therapists are encouraged to validate resistance rather than pathologising it, allowing clients to feel understood and supported as they navigate this transformative but sometimes challenging therapeutic terrain.

Training the Next Generation of CFT Practitioners

As the demand for CFT grows globally, there is an urgent need to train a new generation of practitioners equipped with the theoretical knowledge, practical skills, and reflective capacities necessary to deliver compassion-based interventions effectively. Training must extend beyond technical competence to include the cultivation of therapists' own self-compassion, resilience, and emotional awareness.

Recent research has highlighted the importance of self-compassion in therapist development. Trainees and professionals who cultivate self-kindness and emotional regulation report greater levels of motivation, engagement, and resilience—key qualities in sustaining clinical work, especially with distressed or traumatised clients

(Kotera et al., 2021d; Liu et al., 2025). Training programmes that incorporate self-compassion practices such as mindfulness, guided imagery, and journaling are associated with improved wellbeing and a reduced risk of burnout. These benefits underscore the dual function of CFT training: supporting both professional competence and personal mental health.

Effective CFT training also requires cultural flexibility. As CFT continues to be adopted in diverse global contexts, it is crucial that training models are responsive to local cultural values and norms. Culturally adapted teaching methods—including the use of regionally relevant case studies, metaphors, and rituals—can foster greater acceptance and applicability (Sanger, 2020). Furthermore, embedding cultural humility and awareness into the curriculum prepares therapists to work with clients from varied backgrounds with sensitivity and respect (Shilko & Shaigerova, 2021).

Experiential learning has emerged as a particularly impactful approach in CFT training. Activities such as compassion-focused chair work, peer reflection groups, and emotionally focused case discussions help trainees deepen their understanding of core concepts while building relational and emotional skills. These methods also encourage practitioners to explore their own resistance to compassion and to develop strategies for maintaining self-care in demanding therapeutic contexts.

Future directions in CFT education should include ongoing supervision, interdisciplinary collaboration, and the integration of compassion into broader professional development frameworks. Training must be seen not as a one-time event, but as a continuous process of growth that nurtures both the therapist and the therapeutic work.

Policy, Funding, and Institutional Support

For CFT to be sustainably embedded in healthcare, education, and workplace systems, strong institutional backing and progressive policy frameworks are essential. Although CFT has demonstrated effectiveness in addressing mental health challenges across varied settings, its broader implementation depends on systemic factors such as funding mechanisms, accreditation standards, and organisational readiness. Policymakers and institutional leaders play a crucial role in legitimising CFT by integrating it into national mental health strategies, clinical guidelines, and educational curricula.

Recent evidence highlights a shift in how institutions approach mental health—moving from reactive crisis management to preventative and holistic wellbeing models (Patel et al., 2023). In this context, compassion-based approaches like CFT are increasingly recognised not only for their therapeutic efficacy but also for their capacity to support staff wellbeing, reduce burnout, and cultivate compassionate organisational cultures (Kotera et al., 2019, 2021c, 2024a). When compassion is formally endorsed and resourced by institutions, it promotes a culture of psychological safety, thereby enhancing both service delivery and practitioner resilience.

From a funding perspective, CFT offers promising cost-effectiveness (Carvalho et al., 2021; Trindade et al., 2025). By reducing psychological distress and enhancing emotional resilience, CFT can decrease reliance on acute mental health services, improve employee productivity, and contribute to a more engaged and healthier workforce. Integrating compassion-focused programmes into staff development or student support services can also deliver long-term economic benefits by mitigating absenteeism, presenteeism, and turnover (Kotera et al., 2021f, 2022a).

Institutionalising CFT requires embedding its principles into professional development, licensure, and continuing education. Accrediting bodies and training institutions can foster widespread adoption by including compassion-based competencies within practitioner standards and supervisory models. Compassion-focused supervision, for instance, not only enhances clinical outcomes but also supports practitioners in managing their own emotional responses to challenging therapeutic work.

To drive these changes, interdisciplinary collaboration is key. Partnerships between researchers, clinicians, educators, service users, and policymakers can inform robust, context-sensitive policy initiatives that support the sustainable integration of CFT. Moving forward, a coordinated strategy—grounded in compassion and guided by evidence—will be essential for embedding CFT into the structural fabric of global mental health systems.

Recommendations and Future Research Directions

As CFT continues to gain global traction, several key areas for development have emerged to guide future research, training, and implementation. These recommendations aim to strengthen the scientific foundation of CFT while promoting culturally inclusive, accessible, and sustainable practices.

First, there is a growing call for longitudinal and cross-cultural research that examines how compassion-based interventions function across diverse populations. Studies suggest that self-compassion and emotional regulation are shaped by cultural norms and social expectations, which can influence both therapeutic engagement and outcomes. Comparative research that explores these differences—across occupational, demographic, and national contexts—will help tailor CFT to be more responsive and relevant to local needs.

Second, future research should integrate psychophysiological measures such as heart rate variability and neuroimaging alongside traditional self-report tools. This multimodal approach can enhance the rigour of CFT studies and provide insight into the biological mechanisms that underlie therapeutic change. In addition, advanced methodologies such as component network meta-analyses should be employed to isolate and compare the effectiveness of specific CFT components (e.g., soothing breathing, imagery, psychoeducation). Other rigorous approaches, such as dismantling studies, mediation and moderation analysis, and machine learning techniques for predictive modelling, can further refine understanding of how CFT works, for whom, and under which conditions. These methodologies will contribute to a more nuanced, data-driven evolution of compassion-based interventions.

Third, training programmes should prioritise experiential learning, reflective practice, and cultural competence. Evidence indicates that therapists who engage in compassion-based training not only develop greater emotional resilience and motivation but also report stronger therapeutic alliances and reduced burnout. Embedding self-practice and cultural awareness into training standards can improve the preparedness and wellbeing of future practitioners.

Fourth, digital and blended delivery formats represent a critical area for expansion. Online CFT interventions have demonstrated early success in improving access to care, especially among remote, marginalised, or time-constrained groups. Ongoing evaluation is needed to ensure the ethical, personalised, and effective application of these technologies, including attention to engagement and therapeutic presence in digital environments. Innovations such as app-based interventions, virtual reality tools, and AI-supported therapy platforms should also be explored to extend CFT's reach and adaptability.

Finally, institutional and policy-level actions are essential for scaling CFT sustainably. These include integrating compassion-focused principles into mental health guidelines, professional accreditation, and funding frameworks. Cross-sector partnerships between researchers, clinicians, educators, and policymakers can facilitate the development of compassionate systems that support both client and practitioner wellbeing.

Taken together, these recommendations outline a roadmap for advancing CFT as a dynamic, evidence-informed, and globally relevant approach to mental health and human flourishing.

Conclusion

As CFT enters a new era of global relevance, its continued evolution will depend on its capacity to broaden access, deepen theoretical and empirical foundations, and enhance cultural responsiveness. This chapter has outlined a comprehensive vision for advancing CFT that integrates innovations in digital health, rigorous scientific methodologies, and culturally attuned practice.

Progress in the field will require concerted efforts across research, clinical practice, training, and policy domains. Robust, interdisciplinary studies—employing both qualitative insights and quantitative precision—are essential to identify mechanisms of change and ensure that compassion-focused interventions remain both effective and adaptable. Training for practitioners must go beyond technical competence to nurture self-awareness, emotional resilience, and cultural sensitivity. Likewise, institutions and organisations must actively embed compassion into their systems through policy reform, sustainable funding, and inclusive implementation strategies.

By fostering a global community of compassion-focused researchers, educators, and clinicians, CFT has the potential to address complex mental health challenges with nuance and empathy. As a therapeutic model, CFT not only alleviates psychological suffering but also contributes to building more compassionate societies. The future of CFT lies in its ability to remain flexible and integrative—drawing from neuroscience, cultural studies, digital innovation, and grassroots practice—to meet the needs of a diverse and ever-changing world.

Ultimately, it is compassion itself—a commitment to alleviate and prevent suffering—that must remain at the heart of this work. In doing so, CFT can fulfil its promise to transform mental health care into a space where humanity, connection, and healing are not only possible but expected.

Author Contributions Conceptualisation: YK; Investigation: YK, JB, RC, AR, KA; Resources: YK; Writing—original draft: YK; Writing—review & editing: YK, JB, RC, AR, KA; Project administration: YK.

References

Asano, K., Tsuchiya, M., Ishimura, I., Lin, S., Matsumoto, Y., Miyata, H., Kotera, Y., Shimizu, E., & Gilbert, P. (2017). The development of fears of compassion scale Japanese version. *PLOS ONE, 12*(10). https://doi.org/10.1371/journal.pone.0185574

Beaumont, E., Bell, T., McAndrew, S., & Fairhurst, H. (2021, March 16). The impact of compassionate mind training on qualified health professionals undertaking a compassion-focused therapy module. *Counselling and Psychotherapy Research.* https://doi.org/10.1002/CAPR.12396

Calderone, A., Latella, D., Impellizzeri, F., de Pasquale, P., Famà, F., Quartarone, A., & Calabrò, R. S. (2024). Neurobiological changes induced by mindfulness and meditation: A systematic review. *Biomedicines, 12*(11).

Carvalho, S., Skvarc, D., Barbosa, R., Tavares, T., Santos, D., & Trindade, I. (2021, July 16). A pilot Randomized Controlled Trial (RCT) of online Acceptance and Commitment Therapy (ACT) versus Compassion Focused Therapy (CFT) for chronic illness. *Clinical Psychology & Psychotherapy.* https://doi.org/10.1002/cpp.2643

Clapton, N. E., Williams, J., Griffith, G. M., & Jones, R. S. (2018, June). 'Finding the person you really are … on the inside': Compassion focused therapy for adults with intellectual disabilities. *Journal of Intellectual Disabilities, 22*(2), 135–153. https://doi.org/10.1177/1744629516688581

Clarke, F. J., Kotera, Y., & McEwan, K. (2021). A qualitative study comparing mindfulness and Shinrin-Yoku (forest bathing): Practitioners' perspectives. *Sustainability, 13*(12), 6761. https://doi.org/10.3390/SU13126761

Craig, C., Hiskey, S., & Spector, A. (2020, March 20). Compassion focused therapy: a systematic review of its effectiveness and acceptability in clinical populations. *Expert Review of Neurotherapeutics, 20*, 385–400. https://doi.org/10.1080/14737175.2020.1746184

Cunha, M., Xavier, A., Salvador, M. C., & Castilho, P. (2024, April 01). The forms of self-criticising & self-reassuring scale—Short form for adolescents: Psychometric properties in clinical and non-clinical portuguese samples. *Child & Youth Care Forum, 53*(2), 505–524. https://doi.org/10.1007/s10566-023-09765-6

de Krijger, E., Bohlmeijer, E. T., Geuze, E., & Kelders, S. M. (2023). Compassion apps for better mental health: Qualitative review. *Bjpsych Open, 9*(5), e141–e141. https://doi.org/10.1192/bjo.2023.537

Di Bello, M., Carnevali, L., Petrocchi, N., Thayer, J., Gilbert, P., & Ottaviani, C. (2020, June 15). The compassionate vagus: A meta-analysis on the connection between compassion and heart rate variability. *Neuroscience & Biobehavioral Reviews, 116*, 21–30. https://doi.org/10.1016/j.neubiorev.2020.06.016

Gilbert, P. (2009). Introducing compassion-focused therapy. *Advances in Psychiatric Treatment, 15*(3), 199–208. https://doi.org/10.1192/apt.bp.107.005264

Gilbert, P. (2010). An introduction to compassion focused therapy in cognitive behavior therapy. *International Journal of Cognitive Therapy, 3*(2), 97–112. https://doi.org/10.1521/IJCT.2010.3.2.97

Gilbert, P. (2014, March 01). The origins and nature of compassion focused therapy. *The British Journal of Clinical Psychology, 53*(1), 6–41. https://doi.org/10.1111/bjc.12043

Gilbert, P. (2020, December 09). Compassion: From its evolution to a psychotherapy [Review]. *Frontiers in Psychology, 11*. https://doi.org/10.3389/fpsyg.2020.586161

Gilbert, P., Bhundia, R., Mitra, R., McEwan, K., Irons, C., & Sanghera, J. (2007). Cultural differences in shame-focused attitudes towards mental health problems in Asian and Non-Asian student women. *Mental Health, Religion & Culture, 10*(2), 127–141. https://doi.org/10.1080/13694670500415124

Gilbert, P., Clarke, M., Hempel, S., Miles, J. N. V., & Irons, C. (2016). *Forms of self-criticizing/attacking and self-reassuring scale*. American Psychological Association (APA). https://doi.org/10.1037/t54209-000

Gilbert, P., McEwan, K., Matos, M., & Rivis, A. (2011, September). Fears of compassion: Development of three self-report measures. *Psychology and Psychotherapy, 84*(3), 239–255. https://doi.org/10.1348/147608310x526511

Goldin, P., & Jazaieri, H. (2020, January 01). Investigating moderators of compassion meditation training in a community sample. *Mindfulness, 11*, 75–85. https://doi.org/10.1007/S12671-017-0857-0

Kirby, J. N., Tellegen, C. L., & Steindl, S. R. (2017). A meta-analysis of compassion-based interventions: Current state of knowledge and future directions. *Behavior Therapy, 48*(6), 778–792. https://doi.org/10.1016/j.beth.2017.06.003

Kishimoto, K., Asano, K., Colman, R., Kameo, Y., Aledeh, M., Barnes, K., & Kotera, Y. (2024). The development of the Japanese version of the Forms of Self-Criticising/Attacking & Self-Reassuring Scale (J-FSCRS): Implications for cross-cultural research on self-criticism and self-reassurance. *Mental Health, Religion & Culture*. https://doi.org/10.1080/13674676.2024.2313462

Kolts, R. L., Hayes, S. C., & Gilbert, P. (2016). *CFT made simple: A clinician's guide to practicing compassion-focused therapy*. New Harbinger Publications.

Kotera, Y., Asano, K., Jones, J., Colman, R., Taylor, E., Aledeh, M., Barnes, K., Golbourn, L.-M., & Kishimoto, K. (2023a). The development of the Japanese version of the full and short form of Attitudes Towards Mental Health Problems Scale (J-(S) ATMHPS). *Mental Health, Religion & Culture*, 1–13. https://doi.org/10.1080/13674676.2023.2230908

Kotera, Y., Asano, K., Kotera, H., Ohshima, R., & Rushforth, A. (2022a). Mental health of Japanese workers: Amotivation mediates self-compassion on mental health problems. *International Journal of Environmental Research and Public Health, 19*(17).

Kotera, Y., Beaumont, J., Edwards, A.-M., Cotterill, M., Kirkman, A., Tofani, A. C., McPhilbin, M., Takhi, S., Barnes, K., Todowede, O., Ingall, B.-R., Asano, K., & Arimitsu, K. (2024a). A narrative review of compassion focused therapy on positive mental health outcomes. *Behavioral Sciences, 14*(8), 643. https://www.mdpi.com/2076-328X/14/8/643

Kotera, Y., Cockerill, V., Chircop, J., Kaluzeviciute, G., & Dyson, S. (2021a). Predicting self-compassion in UK nursing students: Relationships with resilience, engagement, motivation, and mental wellbeing. *Nurse Education in Practice*, 102989. https://doi.org/10.1016/j.nepr.2021.102989

Kotera, Y., Dosedlova, J., & Andrzejewski, D. (2021b). From stress to psychopathology: Relationship with self-reassurance and self-criticism in Czech University students. *International Journal of Mental Health and Addiction*. https://doi.org/10.1007/s11469-021-00516-z

Kotera, Y., Gilbert, P., Asano, K., Ishimura, I., & Sheffield, D. (2018). Self-criticism and self-reassurance as mediators between mental health attitudes and symptoms: Attitudes toward mental health problems in Japanese workers. *Asian Journal of Social Psychology*. https://doi.org/10.1111/ajsp.12355

Kotera, Y., Green, P., & Sheffield, D. (2019). Roles of positive psychology for mental health in UK social work students: Self-compassion as a predictor of better mental health. *The British Journal of Social Work*. https://doi.org/10.1093/bjsw/bcz149

Kotera, Y., Green, P., & Sheffield, D. (2021c). Positive psychology for mental wellbeing of UK therapeutic students: Relationships with engagement, motivation, resilience and self-compassion. *International Journal of Mental Health and Addiction*, 1–16. https://doi.org/10.1007/s11469-020-00466-y

Kotera, Y., Kirkman, A., Beaumont, J., Komorowska, M. A., Such, E., Kaneda, Y., & Rushforth, A. (2023b). Self-compassion during COVID-19 in non-WEIRD countries: A narrative review. *Healthcare, 11*(14).

Kotera, Y., Lieu, J., Kirkman, A., Barnes, K., Liu, G. H. T., Jackson, J., Wilkes, J., & Riswani, R. (2022b). Mental wellbeing of Indonesian students: Mean comparison with UK students and relationships with self-compassion and academic engagement. *Healthcare, 10*(8), 1439. https://www.mdpi.com/2227-9032/10/8/1439

Kotera, Y., Llewellyn-Beardsley, J., Charles, A., & Slade, M. (2022c). Common humanity as an under-acknowledged mechanism for mental health peer support. *International Journal of Mental Health and Addiction, 22*, 1096–1102.

Kotera, Y., Martínez-Rives, N. L., Aledeh, M., Colman, R., Veasey, C., Harrington, T., Komori, N., Ozaki, A., Griner, D., Ali, Y., & Taylor, E. C. (2024b). Cross-cultural psychology and compassion. *Encyclopedia, 4*(4), 1509–1519.

Kotera, Y., Maxwell-Jones, R., Edwards, A. M., & Knutton, N. (2021d). Burnout in professional psychotherapists: Relationships with self-compassion, work–life balance, and telepressure. *International Journal of Environmental Research and Public Health, 18*(10), 5308–5308. https://doi.org/10.3390/ijerph18105308

Kotera, Y., Maybury, S., Liu, G., Colman, R., Lieu, J., & Dosedlová, J. (2022d). Mental wellbeing of Czech University students: Academic motivation, self-compassion, and self-criticism. *Healthcare, 10*(11), 2135. https://www.mdpi.com/2227-9032/10/11/2135

Kotera, Y., Ozaki, A., Miyatake, H., Tsunetoshi, C., Nishikawa, Y., Kosaka, M., & Tanimoto, T. (2022e). Qualitative investigation into the mental health of healthcare workers in Japan during the COVID-19 pandemic. *International Journal of Environmental Research and Public Health, 19*(1), 568. https://doi.org/10.3390/ijerph19010568

Kotera, Y., Ronaldson, A., Takhi, S., Felix, S., Namasaba, M., Lawrence, S., Kellermann, V., Kapka, A., Hayes, D., Dunnett, D., Jebara, T., Murakami, M., Bakolis, I., Repper, J., Meddings, S., Stergiopoulos, V., Brophy, L., De Ruysscher, C., Eplov, L., … Slade, M. (2025). Cultural influences on fidelity components in recovery colleges: A study across 28 countries and territories. *General Psychiatry, 38*(3), Article e102010. https://doi.org/10.1136/gpsych-2024-102010

Kotera, Y., & Sheffield, D. (2020, June). Revisiting the self-compassion scale-short form: Stronger associations with self-inadequacy and resilience. *SN Comprehensive Clinical Medicine, 2*(6), 761–769. https://doi.org/10.1007/s42399-020-00309-w

Kotera, Y., Spink, R., Brooks-Ucheaga, M., Green, P., Rawson, R., Rhodes, C., Chircop, J., Williams, A., Okere, U., & Lyte, G. (2021e). Teaching healthcare professional students in online learning during COVID-19: Reflection of university lecturers. *Journal of Concurrent Disorders*. https://doi.org/10.54127/QLOU9458

Kotera, Y., Taylor, E., Brooks-Ucheaga, M., & Edwards, A. M. (2023c). Need for a tool to inform cultural adaptation in mental health interventions. *ISSBD Bulletin, 1*(83), 2–5. https://issbd.org/wp-content/uploads/2023/06/JBD_47_3S_Combined-pdf.pdf

Kotera, Y., Taylor, E., Fido, D., Williams, D., & Tsuda-Mccaie, F. (2021f). Motivation of UK graduate students in education: Self-compassion moderates pathway from extrinsic motivation to intrinsic motivation. *Current Psychology*. https://doi.org/10.1007/s12144-021-02301-6

Kotera, Y., Taylor, E., Wilkes, J., Veasey, C., Maybury, S., Jackson, J., Lieu, J., & Asano, K. (2022f). Construction and factorial validation of a short version of the Attitudes Towards Mental Health Problems Scale (SATMHPS). *Mental Health, Religion & Culture*. https://doi.org/10.1080/13674676.2022.2114441

Kotera, Y., & Van Gordon, W. (2021, April). Effects of self-compassion training on work-related well-being: A systematic review. *Frontiers in psychology, 12*. https://doi.org/10.3389/fpsyg.2021.630798

Leaviss, J., Uttley, L. (2015, April). Psychotherapeutic benefits of compassion-focused therapy: An early systematic review. *Psychological Medicine, 45*(5), 927–945. https://doi.org/10.1017/S0033291714002141

Liu, X., He, F., Tian, T., Zhang, J., Ji, Y., & Zhong, Y. (2025, January 20). Self-compassion and work engagement among clinical nurses: The mediating role of moral resilience. *Frontiers in Public Health, 13*. https://doi.org/10.3389/fpubh.2025.1507539

Marques, C. C., Palmeira, L., Castilho, P., Rodrigues, D., Mayr, A., Pina, T. S., Pereira, A. T., Castelo-Branco, M., & Goss, K. (2024). Online Compassion Focused Therapy for overeating: Feasibility and acceptability pilot study. *The International Journal of Eating Disorders, 57*(2), 410–422. https://doi.org/10.1002/eat.24118

Melsom, L., Ulvenes, P., Solbakken, O. A., Curran, P., Eielsen, M., & Wampold, B. (2023, May 25). Self-compassion and fear of compassion in the treatment of chronic depression: Mechanisms of change? *Journal of Consulting and Clinical Psychology*. https://doi.org/10.1037/ccp0000822

Merritt, O., & Purdon, C. (2020, May 04). Scared of compassion: Fear of compassion in anxiety, mood, and non-clinical groups. *The British Journal of Clinical Psychology*. https://doi.org/10.1111/bjc.12250

Morales, A., & Burnett-Zeigler, I. (2024, August 02). A scoping review of culturally adapted mindfulness-based interventions for communities of color. *Journal of Integrative and Complementary Medicine*. https://doi.org/10.1089/jicm.2023.0807

Neff, K. (2022, August 12). Self-compassion: Theory, method, research, and intervention. *Annual Review of Psychology*. https://doi.org/10.1146/annurev-psych-032420-031047

Patel, V., Saxena, S., Lund, C., Kohrt, B., Kieling, C., Sunkel, C., Kola, L., Chang, O., Charlson, F., O'Neill, K., & Herrman, H. (2023, August 01). Transforming mental health systems globally: Principles and policy recommendations. *The Lancet, 402*, 656–666. https://doi.org/10.1016/S0140-6736(23)00918-2

Petrocchi, N., Dentale, F., & Gilbert, P. (2019, September 01). Self-reassurance, not self-esteem, serves as a buffer between self-criticism and depressive symptoms. *Psychology and Psychotherapy: Theory, Research and Practice, 92*(3), 394–406. https://doi.org/10.1111/papt.12186

Sanger, C. S. (2020). Inclusive pedagogy and universal design approaches for diverse learning environments. In C. S. Sanger & N. W. Gleason (Eds.), *Diversity and inclusion in global higher education: Lessons from across Asia* (pp. 31–71). Springer. https://doi.org/10.1007/978-981-15-1628-3_2

Seppala, E., Rossomando, T., & Doty, J. (2013, June 01). Social connection and compassion: Important predictors of health and well-being. *Social Research: An International Quarterly, 80*, 411–430. https://doi.org/10.1353/sor.2013.0027

Shilko, R., & Shaigerova, L. (2021, April 01). Cultural competence in modern global world: Applications for mental health. *European Psychiatry, 64*. https://doi.org/10.1192/j.eurpsy.2021.305

Sommers-Spijkerman, M., Trompetter, H., ten Klooster, P., Schreurs, K., Gilbert, P., & Bohlmeijer, E. (2018). Development and validation of the forms of Self-Criticizing/Attacking and Self-Reassuring Scale—Short Form. *Psychological Assessment, 30*(6), 729–743. https://doi.org/10.1037/pas0000514

Stevenson, J. C., & Akram, U. (2022, December 1). Self-critical thinking mediates the relationship between perfectionism and perceived stress in undergraduate students: A longitudinal study. *Journal of Affective Disorders Reports, 10*, 100438. https://doi.org/10.1016/j.jadr.2022.100438

Trindade, I. A., Soares, A., Skvarc, D., Carreiras, D., Pereira, J., Lourenço, Ó., Sampaio, F., de Sousa, B., Martins, T. C., Boaventura, P., Marta-Simões, J., Galhardo, A., Pereira, A., Veloso, B., Palmeira, L., Carvalho, S. A., Ferreira, N., Matos, M., Castilho, P., … Mind Project Team. (2025, January 03). Efficacy and cost-effectiveness of an ACT and compassion-based intervention for women with breast cancer: Study protocol of two randomised controlled trials {1}. *Trials, 26*(1), 5. https://doi.org/10.1186/s13063-024-08626-4

Uneno, Y., Kotera, Y., Kikuchi, K., Yamada, M., Sugitani, M., Terado, S., Maehara, H., Sakamoto, Y., Sugao, S., Tani, H., Shimizu, A., Kubo, Y., Fujisawa, D., & Muto, M. (2024, September 01). Self-compassion-based online group psychotherapy for bereavement-related grief: The COMPACT feasibility trial. *General Hospital Psychiatry, 90*, 116–123. https://doi.org/10.1016/j.genhosppsych.2024.08.009

Varley, D., Sherwell, C., & Kirby, J. (2024, December 12). Compassion focused imagery reduces fears of compassion irrespective of attachment. *Journal of Counseling Psychology*. https://doi.org/10.1037/cou0000770

Index

A
Adverse Childhood Events, 180
Anxiety, 75, 77–80, 82, 84–87, 89–91, 139, 140, 143, 145, 146
Attachment, 1, 3, 6, 8, 10, 57–63, 65–68, 70
Attentional deficit and hyperactivity disorder (ADHD), 55, 56, 60–63, 67, 70

B
Biopsychosocial, 156, 157, 160

C
Clinical applications, 2
Compassion, 15–47, 156, 158, 162, 164–167, 169, 170, 172
Compassion-focused therapy (CFT), 57, 58, 60, 61, 63, 67–70, 75–92, 97, 98, 101–104, 109, 111–114, 121, 134, 139–141, 143–149, 156–160, 162–164, 166, 167, 171, 172, 177–181, 183–188, 193–202
Cultural adaptation, 194, 195
Culturally modified treatment, 59
Cultures, 17, 19, 20, 23, 26, 28, 29, 33–39, 42–44, 46, 47

D
Depression, 139, 140, 143, 145, 146
Digital mental health, 194
Dyslexia, 75–92

E
East Asian Culture, 125–127
Emotional regulation, 193, 196, 198, 200
Emotional well-being, 27, 31, 35, 37, 39, 45, 76, 80, 81, 86, 88–92, 140
Evolutionary, 156, 157, 163

F
Fear of compassion, 197, 198

G
Global mental health, 200
Group, 156–172
Guilt, 139, 142, 143

H
Heart rate variability, 197, 200

I
Inclusive education, 78, 91

L
Latin culture, 139

M
Mechanism, 2, 3, 18, 20, 24, 25, 27, 30, 33, 34, 36, 42, 57, 62, 78, 87, 114, 134, 143, 181, 182, 187, 194, 197, 199–201

Y. Kotera et al. (eds.), *Compassion-Focused Therapy for Mental Health: International Perspectives*, Advances in Mental Health and Addiction,
https://doi.org/10.1007/978-3-032-12438-8

Multicultural, 156, 157, 159, 160, 162–164, 170, 171
Multiculturalism, 155–157, 172
Multifaith society, 17

N
Neurodiversity, 85, 91
Neuroscience, 1, 6, 10
Northern Ireland, 177, 180, 187

P
Perfectionism, 97–108, 110–115
Practical applications, 8
Psychotherapy, 156–164, 167, 171

R
Religions, 19, 36
Republic of Ireland, 177, 180, 187

S
Self-compassion, 2–11, 16, 17, 22, 24, 27, 32, 35, 38, 40, 60–62, 65, 66, 68, 75, 77, 78, 80–84, 87–89, 91, 123–125, 127, 128, 134, 139–148, 158, 166, 171, 179, 183–185, 195–200
Self-criticism, 1–11, 16, 22, 24, 25, 27, 57, 60, 64, 66, 70, 75, 77–88, 97, 98, 101–105, 110, 111, 114, 121–128, 131, 133, 134, 142, 143, 145–149, 171, 177–179, 184–187, 193, 194, 196
Shame, 75, 77–92, 177–179, 181, 184–187, 193–195
Social mentality theory, 158, 165, 172

T
Theoretical underpinning, 2
Therapeutic alliance, 97, 109, 114
Therapist training, 135
Trauma, 177, 180–187

W
Western and Eastern contexts, 76, 91